Bid

Touching Distance

Touching Distance

James Cracknell &
Beverley Turner

C

Century · London

Published by Century 2012

2 4 6 8 10 9 7 5 3 1

First published in Great Britain in 2012 by
Century
Random House, 20 Vauxhall Bridge Road,
London SW1V 2SA

www.randomhouse.co.uk

Addresses for companies within The Random House Group Limited can be found at:
www.randomhouse.co.uk

The Random House Group Limited Reg. No. 954009

A CIP catalogue record for this book
is available from the British Library

ISBN 9781780890937

The Random House Group Limited supports The Forest Stewardship Council
(FSC®), the leading international forest certification organisation. Our books
carrying the FSC label are printed on FSC® certified paper. FSC is the only forest
certification scheme endorsed by the leading environmental organisations,
including Greenpeace. Our paper procurement policy can be found at:
www.randomhouse.co.uk/environment

Typeset by SX Composing DTP, Rayleigh, Essex
Printed and bound by
CPI Group (UK) Ltd, Croydon, CR0 4YY

For Croyde, Kiki, Trixie; all of our amazing family . . . and every person whose life is touched by brain injury.

(And Bev, it's only from reading your words that I truly understand what you've been through. I adore you.)

Prologue

[James]

The wheels turn, my feet circling, trying to apply continuous pressure, shoes clipped on to the pedals so that the bike and I are one. At times, it's hard to sense where my body ends and the carbon frame begins. This is what cycling feels like at its best, the perfect symbiotic relationship: without me, the bike is nothing; without it, I'd be plodding significantly slower down Route 66 than the twenty miles per hour I'm averaging.

It feels great to be out of Death Valley, off my feet and back on the open road. The broken metatarsal that crippled me on foot offers barely a twinge in the comfort of a rigid carbon-soled cycling shoe. The sun is slowly rising but it's already hot, touching twenty-one degrees. It warms my lungs and the back of my throat but the crew have kept me hydrated. I don't even have to worry about the fluid as long as I drink at the required rate and my urine passes their osmolality analysis. And it's an absolute joy – urine testing aside – like being a professional athlete again. All I have to do is get to Lake Erie. I smile, thinking how much fun it will be to row across it with old mate Matt Pinsent.

Then I'll get back on the bike to New York until I finish my journey across the United States with a swim to the Statue of Liberty. What date is it? July twentieth. We're making good progress. I'd dearly love to be the first man to go coast-to-coast on this unique route across this beautiful country in less than twenty days under his own steam.

I remember Bev kissing me and saying that I'm the only athlete in the world who has the skills to do that, though admittedly the rowing part excludes most people. And am pretty sure she was just flattering me. Whatever – I feel like the luckiest man in the world. It's been six years since I retired from full-time rowing. Six years of trying to work out who I am and what I want to do with my life.

I've finally reached a stage where I can see over the horizon and into my future without panicking. The film of this trip should – touch wood – be a success for the Discovery Channel. I'll finally get a good contract that will make my hobby my job. Bev and I have been talking about trying for a third baby. That's something to look forward to! I miss the kids: Croyde with his boundless energy and Kiki with her endless cuddles. I push the pedals a little faster. The quicker I get home, the quicker I can see them.

A car passes, one of the very few I've seen at this hour, but the road is wide, two lanes in each direction, and I'm keeping inside the line of the hard shoulder. I feel perfectly safe.

I lift up and stretch my back, which gives the added benefit of allowing my saddle-sore ass some relief. I assess my body for any aches and pains that my physiotherapist Mark will get to work on later, but aside from those associated with sitting on a bike for over fifteen hours a day, there aren't any. I sit back in the saddle; take a deep breath. I've never felt so alive.

And then . . . there is nothing . . .

1

[James]

I see so much of myself in my mum, Jennie. She was, and is, the most obstinate person you could ever meet – a vastly under-estimated character trait. She has a phenomenal memory for even the smallest detail, which I had too, and it is incredibly useful in arguments – or used to be, when I had a memory. Like me, she wants to win any argument, but – unlike me – she will quickly back down and seethe silently if she senses real conflict. Coming from a working-class background she didn't have the same luxury of pursuing dreams that my parents had given me. She trained as a physiotherapist and went back to work after I was born. In the hospital where she worked I used to hang out at the crèche.

It isn't difficult to see where I get my competitive and stubborn streak and my ability to endure boredom: Mum. One story from her childhood absolutely sums her up. As she wasn't allowed to leave the table until she had cleared her plate, she'd hide something she didn't like in her cheeks like a hamster or under her tongue for up to half an hour and then spit it out when her mother wasn't looking. I'm just annoyed that I didn't know that trick when I was young. I'd have secreted a whole vegetable platter in my cheeks to be allowed to get down from the table and run around.

On the other hand, I failed to inherit some useful traits from my dad, John. Patience and mathematical ability are the two most glaringly obvious omissions. He certainly doesn't look back fondly upon Tuesday and Thursday nights when I had maths homework and, after a long day in the office, he'd have to explain simultaneous equations to me for the tenth week in a row. He commuted into London every day Louise and I were at school – he still did until just three years ago. I remember asking him how many days of his life he'd wasted sitting on a train. In hindsight that probably wasn't the kindest way of thanking him for giving me an incredibly fortunate upbringing. He should have replied: 'At least it wasn't a total waste of time, unlike your maths lessons. Plus I paid for the bloody things.'

His work ethic influenced me, I'm sure, but also his ability to look at the most negative outcome of every situation. It is far too positive to say that he's a 'glass half empty' kind of guy. He is more a 'smashed glass that some bloke is threatening you with down the pub' kind of guy. When I sold my first house, I had a week before the sale was completed on the second so for seven days I was going to be very rich. I remember Dad warning me when I said I was going to put all the money in Barclays Bank . . .

'If it goes bust, you'll only get eighteen per cent of your money back.'

'Don't be stupid,' I told him. 'A bank isn't going to go bust.'

This was before banks went bust.

Another line which might sum up his character was said

in Sydney, when I'd just won the Olympic gold. 'Congratulations,' he said, 'now you can get a proper job.'

Mum and Dad met at a youth club in Wimbledon when they were teenagers. But it could all have been very different. I could have had Nookie Bear as a stepbrother. Roger de Courcey, a guy who went on to win *New Faces* as a ventriloquist, went to the same youth club and Mum and he took a shine to each other. I met him once when I sat next to him at Matt Dawson's testimonial dinner. He was just telling me about the strippers he regularly met while performing a bluer version of his routine at stag nights, after which he handed me one of his cards and said, 'Ask your mum to give me a ring sometime.' As much as I liked Nookie Bear, I thought I probably wouldn't.

There's quite a lot of water lapping about our family tree. On my dad's side, one of my great-grandfathers was a naval engineer who fought in the Battle of Jutland in 1916, and on my mum's side my great-grandma was a lady's maid to the colonel's wife on a troop ship where she met her husband, my great-grandpa Fred. Luckily I never met her, as when we chucked insults around rowing lakes, the one (in fact the only one) I knew in Russian was 'your mother swims out to troop ships!' They didn't seem to like that one much. I'm guessing my great-grandma wouldn't have either. Then there was their son Sidney, my mum's dad, who was such a good swimmer he was schoolboy champion in 1911. I only know that because my mum still has the certificate somewhere.

Of my two grandmothers, I always thought Catherine Davis was the toughest. She didn't dish out praise easily, a trait that Mum, and subsequently I, inherited. We're supportive without thinking that out-loud praise is necessary. It's something I have to temper with Croyde and the girls (that's my girls rather than a west London harem I've developed). As Bev says, 'Twice as many hugs and kisses as tellings off.'

My granddad on my dad's side, George Cracknell, suffered more bad and good luck than is normal in one life. On the rough side, his dad died when he was young, meaning the five kids had to be split up. The two girls stayed with their mum, but the three boys had to go into an orphanage. Apparently, his life ambition was to be a jockey. Instead, he ended up being a fitter for Rolls-Royce and Dad remembers him having long negotiations with Jimmy Savile about the exact details of the seats in his custom-built Rolls.

George's sisters never married, although one of them was engaged to a lad who died in the Second World War, and grew up to be my great maiden aunts, Glad and Vi. I get the impression Dad found his visits to them a bit oppressive when he was a kid. They had a dining table with a very heavy tablecloth on top and if he farted he was made to go and sit under it until the coast was clear again. According to them, this was fairly often. And to be honest, nothing much has changed apart from the fact that we haven't got a heavy tablecloth and his back might not react well to time spent under the table.

But at some stage in the 1950s George's luck changed. He won the pools and was able to buy outright the house he was renting. When I first heard that story I thought he must have won about £50,000, but in fact George's third prize was £1,500. That was enough in those days to buy a house. It changed their lives and hauled them up a class or two. So by the time I came along John and Jennie Cracknell were a middle-class family with a house in Sutton, a sensible car and a cat called William. We moved to Pyrford when I was one. They did regret opting for the 'sensible' car. Mum still holds me accountable for making them sell the Triumph Herald they had in 1972 because it was too small for a baby in the back. I know how they feel. I still hold Bev accountable for making me sell my 1968 Mustang Fastback 390GT that I had shipped back from the States. Especially as the proceeds of the sale went towards our 'exciting' new roof.

My stubborn nature showed through at an early age. I can still picture the dread of my first day at primary school. I was in the classroom doorway causing a one-kid blockade. I wouldn't go in. My arms and legs were spread out like a starfish, clutching on to the door frame. I'm sure I was modelling myself on William the cat when I tried to put him in the bath, spread-eagled and desperate not to get a dunking. I was amazed at the time that his legs were not only *that* long but he could extend them entirely at right angles to his body. I had no idea cats could do that. These things seriously impress a boy of five. Especially one who is determined not to go to school.

Sadly, there was one other determined character in my story and that was Mum. She was mortified by my behaviour, but I was never going to win. She gave me one last shove, I fell through the door and she buggered off.

This is a fairly representative story of a childhood in which my own strong will entered daily battle with outside forces (generally called Mum) that were equally adamant that I would not succeed. Ironically, of course, she was my inspiration. But it took me a few decades to realise that, let alone admit it. She always wanted the best for me; as a five-year-old, I just saw someone who refused to lose.

You couldn't blame her though. I was a very shy, unsociable little boy. I liked to win at everything, even arguments, even when I was wrong, until the people around me reached breaking point and gave in out of sheer exhaustion. It's a quality I've maintained. I loved penknives, tools and bicycles. I hated vegetables that weren't carrots, potatoes or sweet corn. My mum and I would have a battle of will over just six peas which I could spin out to thirty minutes of grief before being forced to admit defeat. I was horrible to my younger sister and an occasional visitor to A&E. My godfather once clean bowled my front teeth instead of the stumps playing cricket in the garden. As they were only my milk teeth, Mum didn't bollock him.

Like most energetic boys, I saw sleep as a waste of time, with the result that I was found at least once face down in a plate of spaghetti bolognaise, fast asleep. Academically, I wasn't the sharpest tool in the box. I didn't set the sporting fields ablaze with lightning pace or dazzling ball skills, nor did I have the ability to accurately read a game. Neither NASA nor Manchester United was beating down my door. You could say my main quality was, and is, mindless enthusiasm – that quality that saw me right a couple of decades later on an Olympic rowing lake. In fact, Mum, who was a physiotherapist at the local hospital, treated one of my old teachers after I'd won the gold medal in Sydney. 'Well,' she said to Mum, genuinely mystified, 'I would *never* have had him down to be an international sports star. I wouldn't have thought he could apply himself to anything for that long.'

*

I'm getting ahead of myself. Before there was rowing and adventures, Beverley and the children, a smash on the head and a new version of me surfacing, there was a perfectly conventional and relatively benign beginning in Pyrford, a leafy commuter suburb of north Surrey where my younger sister Louise and I were raised amid the screeches and thumps of sibling rivalry.

My first memories go back to the black-and-white tiles on our dining-room floor (apparently they were very sophisticated in the 1970s – my mum's still convinced but I think she's the only one), my dad's car, a lovely nut-brown Escort, and his cigars. They weren't a manly Cuban or a Clint Eastwood-style cheroot, but a campish-looking brown cigarette. My mum often tells the story of my disappointment with what I thought was her choice of chocolate fingers, after I'd chomped a few down. I think I remember eating them but it could be that my mum just told me about it. You never really know what's a genuine memory or just family folklore handed down over years that forces its way into your brain.

Like the incident of the leopard-skin underpants. Mum and I remember this in very different ways. I think Mum's rewritten it (as well she might) or I had a sudden change of personality (which wouldn't end up being my last) midway through my career at Pyrford Primary School. It was a fancy dress party and we all had to go into school dressed as a prehistoric man or woman. Clearly it was intended with an educational theme in mind. I certainly learnt a lot. Most of the kids came with some sort of shaggy caveman coat and had filled a pair of tights with rolled-up newspaper to use as a club. Not me. For some weird reason I paraded around in a pair of leopard-skin Y-fronts (which I admit were vaguely prehistoric man-like, if he had been clever enough to catch and skin leopards, making growling noises. Not surprisingly, that episode put me off fancy dress for life, but my mum insists it was I who chose to wear the offending pants. I still don't believe her. In over twenty years of living away from home and being free to buy my own pants, I have yet to venture down the animal print road. I'd never say never but so far there are no signs of a safari theme in my top drawer. So I don't buy Mum's denials. Being painfully shy, I really don't think I would ever have wanted to parade in a pair of leopard-skin Y-fronts *on my own* in a roomful of eight-year-olds waving clubs. I claim it scarred me for life, and, anyway, it begs the question: why did I have leopard-skin pants in the first place, to which Mum has an unconvincing mumbling answer. Convenient for the woman who owns several leopard-print umbrellas, handbags and pairs of shoes.

Maybe it was a subconscious revenge for the sheer amount of shame and embarrassment I brought down upon her over the years.

I was less than two years old when I fell down the stairs and broke my collarbone. Not long afterwards Mum received a visit from the health visitor to ask her one or two questions. It was a while later that Mum realised they were checking up on her to make sure I was being properly treated, which gave her an early bout of mortification.

One of the worst things I did to her happened when I was about four years old and due for my 'developmental' check. This was a routine investigation to see how well a child was progressing through a variety of minor tests and a chat. Maybe that format should have alerted Mum in advance. Being extremely shy, 'chats with strangers' would not be an area in which I'd excel if there was such a thing as a set of Top Trumps on International Rowers. Mum had taken the day off work, loaded Louise in the pram and faced a twenty-five-minute walk to the clinic, with me meandering alongside like a wayward dog (hopefully without the constant urination, although I can't guarantee that). When we got there, I refused to cooperate in any way whatsoever. I wouldn't say a word. Not one word, nothing. Mum was becoming increasingly desperate and embarrassed and I came away with an apparent IQ of zero. And probably a sense of triumph. Mum was furious and bollocked me all the way home.

I suspect this would have been one of those occasions when Dad also got involved. Being an accountant, he wasn't around during weekdays: he went to work before 7 a.m. and didn't come home until around 9 p.m. By then I would have spent hours winding Mum up and he'd come back to find her in a state. Of course, this was long before parenting books and Supernanny taught us all about 'positive parenting'. He'd smack the stairs with his hands, pretending he was running up to get me. This was one of his tricks that I soon became wise to, but the end result was the same. I remember his face, when he rolled his tongue back under his teeth – a definite sign of impending doom – and I'd think, 'Whoa, I'm in trouble now.' But I never remember feeling contrite and saying to myself: 'I'll never do that again.' Not even when Mum graduated from whacking me with a wooden spoon to a more effective spiky spaghetti one. I tried squirrelling the offending spoon under my bed and only discovered, when being spanked by another one, that Mum was well stocked in the utensil department.

Mum says I was unbribable – and strangely that's something I take great pride in hearing. But I suspect Mum just wasn't prepared to go all out and up the value of the bribe. Or to come up with some creative offers. Everyone has their price. And boy, I am no exception.

Louise arrived when I was two years old.

Mum says that when she came home from the hospital with Lou in her Moses basket, the first thing I did was take a swing at her. At that age it clearly wasn't a conscious decision. But it highlighted the insecurities and flat-out jealousy I was feeling.

As we grew older, it was glaringly obvious that Lou was smarter than I was, more musical, more popular, more sociable, better at sport and, annoyingly, even more talented at my specialist subject – arguing. She could also dish out a phenomenally effective dead leg. These skills translated into a far more stellar school career than I had. Her lowest grade at school was higher than my best. She never received less than an A grade at anything until her GCSE results came back as 9 As and a B. Needless to say, I made full use of my mockery skills regarding the errant B. But the school put an end to my gloating. They insisted she would never have got a grade as lowly as a B, sent the paper back to be re-marked and sure enough it was returned with an A.

She's a grade eight performer in music theory, piano and flute – demonstrating the same tenacious determination to stick at something that seems to run in the family – and at sport she was county sprint champion, in all the school sports teams and better than me at swimming. So my relentless piss-taking at her failure to pass her cycling proficiency test didn't really cut it.

Grade As at A level followed, but rather than choose Oxbridge (much to the annoyance of my parents, neither of whom had been to university) she went to Manchester and came home four years later with a good knowledge of music, clubbing and a first in Biology and German.

And I was a shy, awkward, unsociable little boy who had to be brought home from parties early because I was miserable and who, if forced, would just read *The Twelve Labours of Hercules* over and over again.

Lou was told off way less than me, which I resented, but even then I probably understood why. One of the incidents she remembers is me waiting for her to finish an essay in fountain pen and then squirting it with my water pistol. And even running wet, it would have been a better essay than mine. I got us both stuck up an oak tree in the garden that I'd made her climb and Dad had to fetch us down with a ladder. When she was very young, I'd tottered across a plank while carrying her over the foundations of the extension to the house we were having built. The builder, watching helplessly nearby, almost had heart failure as we both toppled into the pit, narrowly escaping being impaled by the spikes in the bottom. At least I didn't just drop her, I selflessly threw myself into the pit as well.

We were constantly bickering, which, I'm ashamed to say, sometimes crossed over into bullying on my part. Lou says if you think Bart and Lisa Simpson you won't be far from the truth. To be fair, that's giving me too much credit. Bart's better on a skateboard, and more funny. Although I'm pretty sure I've got him covered in the classroom. From Lou's perspective she never started an argument and when I got frustrated by the fact she was winning the row she hadn't wanted to have in the first place, I lamped her.

When Dad graduated from his Escort to a Cortina, she

remembers us both on the backseat – a shiny black vinyl number that would absorb heat and burn so hot in the sun we both had to sit on a towel – with me claiming two-thirds of the space for myself and guarding the demarcation line like a warrior. I don't believe this. My mum, who had a well-developed sense of fairness (as I do now), would never have allowed even a 49:51 split.

Like most older siblings, I had firm views on what Lou wasn't allowed to do. She couldn't like Adam Ant, for a start, because I did. Luckily, a-ha came along to distract her and I wanted nothing to do with them. I liked John McEnroe so she was only allowed to support Bjorn Borg. My favourite number was eight, and so she had to have another one.

The worst of it though was that I never let up. I was relentless. It was a trait that later may have helped me extract the best from myself in a sporting context but it didn't make for the best brother. Looking back, I can see why although Lou always loved me, she really didn't always like me. I was horrible. And then I had the audacity, because I was so shy, to use her like an envoy when we went away on holiday. We'd be camping in France and there'd be this big congregation of kids and I'd say: 'Right, you go over and make friends with them.' She was my own Kofi Annan.

She would obligingly go over to the kids, quite unabashed, and I'd hear her say: 'Hello, my name's Louise . . .' and get the whole process going. Then I'd saunter along and join in, probably saying something mean about her in an attempt to make the group laugh. My ingratitude was breath-taking. It is quite painful to look back on it and write it down as I regret how my insecurities and frustrations would come out in a way that made Lou's childhood less fun than it should have been.

I was the only one who was allowed to be like that though. If anyone else messed with her, I would defend her instantly. There were a couple of bigger boys on one of our holidays getting a bit rough in the swimming pool and apparently I saw them off in heroic fashion.

In my (admittedly) slim defence, she was brilliant at niggling, winding me up, and definitely did not suffer in silence. She was always screeching to Mum, but our parents, who were both only children, had absolutely no idea what to do with us. They operated on the basis of the time-honoured ostrich theory: 'Ignore it/him. It/he will go away.' I didn't. If ever a child was not going to go away because he was ignored, it was me.

I was right about primary school, by the way. It was rotten. They made you sit down and the milk came in tiny little bottles. Then, thanks to Margaret Thatcher, it stopped altogether. I was disgusted.

Outside school, I was happier. My most treasured possession was probably my penknife collection but I also enjoyed cycling. It was my first taste of freedom. I remember asking my parents for a drop-handled bike for my birthday one year and waking up hugely excited only to find a new shiny green bike . . . *with straight handlebars.* Not one to abandon my principles, I decided to make it a drop-handled bike. This was easy. I just held the brake levers, which were below the straight bars. Which obviously meant I couldn't stop. I rammed a parked car, fell off and smashed the teeth on either side of the teeth that had been clean bowled before.

I'm not too contrite about these incidents. There can't be

many people who haven't fallen off bikes. Or been bitten on the arse by a German shepherd guard dog while running illegally through a windsurfing site on their way back from cleaning their teeth on a camp site in France. Maybe those in the latter category are slightly less numerous. I had to go to hospital to have the wound examined, and perhaps even more insultingly the dog had to be checked out too. I expect they took its temperature the same way they did mine, with a thermometer up the bum, which was worse in every way than being bitten by the dog. I was not impressed. Perhaps Nelson was on to something when he said: 'Hate the French like you hate the devil.'

I'll always remember my mum's reaction. She was – and still is – baffled by the fact that that while the teeth marks in my backside were only too clearly visible, my shorts had survived entirely intact. How did that happen, she wanted to know? It seemed to be the entire focus of her concern. But then I suppose she was used to my adventures by then.

My phenomenal ability at school to gaze out of the window for hours at a time had convinced my parents that they needed to do something fairly drastic to stop me bumping along the bottom of educational attainment, since I didn't seem particularly talented in any other direction (apart from relent-less goading of my sister). So they targeted Kingston Grammar School, a fee-paying school but not an extortionate one, and set about trying to get me in at the age of ten. The slight issue was the entrance exam – the first exam I would ever take in my life.

When my primary school headmistress was told of the plan, she said my parents were wasting their time. She obviously had no great faith in my skillset, which was fair enough, as it mainly involved saying nothing, not setting the playing fields alight and daydreaming.

But on the day of the entrance exam, I got a taste of Granddad Cracknell's good luck. I sat next to a very bright boy who was left handed and had miraculously clear handwriting. Hence my brilliant interpretation of the English comprehension, which made no sense at all to me. It was all about some pig called Snowball bossing a horse around. It was ridiculous. It also turned out to be from George Orwell's *Animal Farm*, but that one had not made it on to my reading list alongside *Five On A Treasure Island* and the recurring *The Twelve Labours of Hercules*.

I know I got the last question wrong because he finished before me and turned his paper over. I screamed 'No' silently to myself and wrote gibberish. But it seems I had done enough. I was accepted at Kingston Grammar School, no doubt to the reeling shock of my former headmistress. So began a regular shuttle run by lift, train, bus to get to a school where I knew nobody and where I feared that the regulation uniform (red and silver striped blazers) would get me chased and smacked about by the kids from the local school, the school I would have attended had it not been for my sneaky plagiarism.

Looking back, that was a turning point of my childhood.

Mum had taken me on a trial run of how to get to school and back before my first day in 1982. It involved a twenty-five-minute walk or a lift to West Byfleet station, a journey by train and then the No. 65 or 71 bus to the school gates, then cunningly reversing the process on the way home. She says she did wonder whether I would make the obstacle course intact on my first lone attempt. Of course I couldn't. It was all Jez

Cartwright's fault. We sat next to each other on the first day – seating being arranged in alphabetical order – and it was his firm view that the 281 bus was essential, the 65 or the 71 weren't. He was wrong. It meant that I missed my train and was horribly late, driving my mum frantic with worry. I have always been susceptible to someone who appears confident. Jez Cartwright was only the first.

Once a few of the older lads at school stole detonators from the guard's carriage on our train and then lifted gunpowder from the CCF – Combined Cadet Force – hut at school, with the intelligent idea of causing an explosion in the neighbouring park. It was never going to end well – especially as detonation was so close to school – but of course I went along to watch the bang. I remember quite a few people being suspended for that but I was deemed too young to know what I was doing. One of the older boys involved was eventually expelled for knifing someone's bag. He was a nice guy. I liked him, if not his knife skills.

Something I remember most clearly about school – and it came back to me with consoling clarity during my Atlantic row with Ben Fogle – was the words that a teacher called Mr Bond had written on our white board. It just said: 'All Things Must Pass'. It might have been an important philosophy for our benefit, or perhaps just his way of getting though the day. It certainly stuck with me. No matter how bad things get, they will be over in time.

I was right about my school uniform. It did get me beaten up. It was absolutely horrible. I looked like a deckchair. It wasn't a posh school, but it not only made me look like a deckchair but a blazer-loving spectator on the riverbank at the Henley Regatta. At that age, in that outfit, I was fair game, and chased regularly until I learnt to wear my blazer inside out and carry my hockey stick like an offensive weapon. It's amazing how resourceful you can be when you're threatened with a good kicking.

So Mum and Dad's best-laid plan had worked – to a point. I was in a good school, I'd learnt which bus to take, how to avoid a beating, I hadn't been expelled and I knew not to detonate a bomb in close proximity to school. But the crucial issue – raising myself to academically average – was still pending.

I remember being in class in my second year when a teacher was reading out our average percentage for the end of year exams. My name was read out third. I was thinking that was pretty good when it dawned on me that the names of all the clever people were being left right to the end. They were reading them out in reverse order. 'Fuck me,' I thought, 'I'm not very clever. I'm not even average. I'm a bottom feeder.' That realisation, at the age of twelve, was a low point.

I didn't make up for it in sport. I wasn't exactly talented at football as I was not blessed with great coordination for ball games. Hockey wasn't too bad as whatever your ability you still got to smack a ball really hard. We actually had some good coaches. In fact, an old boy of the school was Richard Dodds, who would become famous six years later as captain of the 1988 Olympic gold medal-winning GB hockey team in Seoul. (Steve Redgrave was in the crowd watching that match, having already won his own gold in the rowing. At least I'd ditched hockey by that point and had started mucking about in a boat.)

Arguably the biggest benefit to our performance as a school hockey team was our 'luck' in having an all-weather pitch. This meant we could train and play matches regardless of the weather, even when it was pissing down with rain or freezing cold. Then the all-weather pitch was replaced with the latest in climate-ignoring torture known as 'AstroTurf'. The head of PE repeatedly told us that we were unbelievably 'lucky' to have at our disposal the first generation of this new all-weather fake grass.

'Luck' and 'ground-breaking technology' were not the first words that sprang to our minds when we played. The turf was 'lubricated' with sand, which took the skin off your hands, arms and legs if you took a tumble. It was nothing like the surfaces used by today's American footballers in the NFL which has been refined by millions of dollars' worth of research and actually resembles grass. Ours resembled sandpaper.

Cricket, likewise, had its problems but even I'd struggle to blame the wicket. We once played Tiffin, the school opposite, in an under-12 match. We got them all out for 12. Brilliant! Then they got us all out for 10. I was second-highest scorer on 1. I thought: 'This is no fun' and then got another bollocking from my mum. She'd dropped me off for the game at 9 a.m. and wasn't due to come back and pick me up until after lunch. Suddenly, she's getting this phone call at 9.45 a.m.

'Game's over. Can you come and pick me up?'

'I've only just got home!'

'Yeah, but it's all over. It was close though. We only lost by two runs.'

'What did you get?'

'Ten.'

'No, what did the team get?'

'That was the team's score.'

Also, the kids' cricket I played had ridiculous rules. When I played for Pyrford the idea was that everyone had a turn at batting, whether they were out or not. A great idea although not a particularly good lesson in sport. I was just walking from the boundary rope to the crease when it was my turn to bat, when the batsman from my team hit a ball in the air towards me. I thought: 'Brilliant! I'll catch that.' But, apparently, I wasn't supposed to. I was sent off the field before I even got to the wicket. 'This is just rubbish,' I said to Dad.

It was clear that I wasn't going to be the next George Best or Ian Botham, so I gave Martin Johnson a go. They didn't play rugby at my school but there was a local junior club so I played for them instead. It was fine at the beginning. We played touch rugby for kids where grievous bodily harm wasn't part of the tactics. Then I got put up an age group because I was tall and that's when it went to full contact. I was twelve. And I was getting beaten up every Saturday morning.

Thankfully my dad was in charge of my rugby career. If it had been my mum, I'd still be playing now. She wouldn't let you give up anything unless you had a valid excuse such as full cardiac arrest. No mere muscular-skeletal reason (like getting beaten up) would have been remotely good enough. But Dad was no great fan of getting soaking wet and bored every winter weekend and, between us, we just quietly allowed my rugby career to slip away.

Around that time I made an interesting discovery. Kingston Grammar's playing fields were down by the Thames near Hampton Court. One afternoon, just hanging round the outfield of the cricket pitch (allegedly fielding), I happened to notice a rowing boat go by. It struck me that everyone was doing something. Not necessarily at the same time, but still. No one was standing around like a numpty.

And that's how I got into rowing. It turned out rowing is a sport where you take out what you put in. My physical attributes, which you could describe as being big and long-limbed, combined with my relentless persistence, were better suited to endurance sports, rather than being coordinated or a punching bag on a Saturday morning. In rowing, skill will get you to a certain point but then it's just a case of committing and knuckling down to it. I was a natural knuckle-downer. It suited my personality, where a relentless will and ability to persevere were key attibutes. At last, I had found something I could be good at.

I remember my first lesson clearly. We were all in singles (a rowing boat for one) and most of us fell in almost immediately. I wasn't one of them. I made it at least ten metres but the coach flipped me in anyway. I didn't mind. It's a bit like skiing. You need to fall to realise that nothing too bad is going to happen and so gain the confidence to get really stuck in. The weird thing was they held the swimming test only after tipping us in the river the week before. Even then I thought that was a funny order to do things. One of the boys couldn't swim and I had to help him out of the water and back on to the landing stage where he was told that he needed to learn to swim but was still allowed to go rowing. Of all the arse-backwards arrangements. I'm sure Health and Safety have tightened up that loophole now.

So I took up rowing because it meant I could 'do' something. Ironically, Steve Redgrave took up rowing to *stop* him having to do something: namely, spend the afternoon in school. Dossing on the river seemed infinitely preferable to him. The fact he turned out to be amazingly good at it was just a pure stroke of luck.

Neither of us became rowers because it was our childhood dream. Yet the sport would change our lives.

I began to obsessively divide my time between rowing and school. Annoyingly they were at the same place so I had to attend the latter to do the former. I'm not sure when but it became a matter of principle to go to school every day, whether I felt ill or not. In my entire time at Kingston Grammar I never missed a single day, even when I had an operation to have my appendix out. Although this is another of those occasions where my mum's account and my own deviate considerably.

What I remember is feeling rubbish in the morning, even complaining before school of stomach ache and suggesting that I blemish my attendance record by staying at home and watching TV. By the end of the day I was doubled over in pain and passing out in chemistry. I got a detention for not concentrating – not my first. When I got home, Mum took me to the doctor who sent me straight to A&E where they stuck a finger up my bum and then took my appendix out that evening. None of that is in dispute. But I reckon she insisted I went to school the following Monday morning and gave me a walking stick because my class was going on a biology field trip. And she reckons I was the one who insisted on going to school because I didn't want her to win. What I can believe of both of us is that the unbroken record of attendance wasn't far from the front of our minds. It was a challenge. Neither of us had much time for quitting. If you ask her now, she says: 'I didn't want him to go. I felt like a terrible mother.' But she has the same competitive streak that I do. Dad and I have often shared a smile when Mum is homing in on a Trivial Pursuit victory, even if it means beating the children. And she definitely doesn't take kindly to giving them unearned points. As I've said before, she has a deep sense of fairness. My instinct is to agree with her and let the little ones learn that you can't always win. But I try to hang on to the idea that you should also build their confidence – something that her generation didn't take as seriously.

Luckily, no great post-operative harm was done following the removal of my appendix. Nature intervened. It was the weekend of Michael Fish's hurricane and so the school was closed anyway, so I convalesced at home and my record survived intact.

I definitely didn't rush to school to keep up with a string of girlfriends. There weren't any. I was useless with girls. Shyness was and still is a factor but a lack of stimulating conversation might also have played a part. I did ask out one girl. Her name was Rachel Stovell. I didn't even ask her directly. I asked her friend to ask her. Three times. She said no. Every time. It wasn't entirely my fault. Girls had only been introduced to the school in the last decade so there was a pretty wild imbalance between the numbers (70:30 when I was there). So the girls, no matter what they looked like, were much more in demand than the boys. As a result of market forces, a bloke who didn't speak much and spent all his time on a river or sweating it out on a rowing machine was hardly seen as a catch.

Later, my hair was a problem too. I was having a love affair with Sun-In, a hair lightener. My head looked like an orange pineapple. This was partly due to my unbounded admiration for the US basketball star, Denis Rodman. He was an exhibitionist, who bleached his hair and covered himself in tattoos and piercings. He was the pioneer of tattoo-covered sportsmen. I thought he was amazing. It turned out that he was a shy and introverted kid growing up, so attached to his mother that he refused to go to nursery school. Ring any bells? Admittedly his upbringing wasn't in a leafy suburban commuter town. I liked him because he was different. I felt different too.

I still do. I try not to get obsessive about the same things as other people. It took me ages to get an iPad and I still haven't got an iPhone simply because everyone tells me they're really good. I hear Bev call Kiki a 'contrary Mary' and silently think, 'I wonder where she got that from . . .'

It was because of Rodman that I got my first tattoo, lying to the guy in the shop about my age. I was seventeen and the proud new owner of a skull with a Mohawk on my ankle. I was so pleased with my act of rebellion, but I wasn't going to let my mum know so I covered it up with my sock. I don't think like that any more. If you're going to have a tattoo, draw or choose one with a reason, ask mates who'll give you an honest answer and get it out there. When I designed and drew my next tattoo – the sun (ironic for a British rower who had spent half his life getting rained on) – I stuck it where everyone could see it on my shoulder.

But while I was still underage and under my parents' jurisdiction, my rebelliousness was distinctly middle class. I still had a fear of the law (aka Mum). They objected to my hair but couldn't really do anything about it. My mum used to get a hairdresser to come to the house, but I refused to let her cut my hair. I think she must have resorted to desperate measures. My sister remembers our neighbour, Howard, leaning over the fence one day whilst trimming his hedge and cutting off the top of my pineapple with a pair of shears. This sounds incredible to me, but on the other hand, I think Howard would have been too scared of my mum not to comply if she'd suggested it, plus he'd have loved doing it. I imagine Mum took it as a significant tactical victory – which is probably why I've blocked it out of my memory!

And yet despite my rebellion stage, I was furious that Kingston Grammar never did make me a prefect. When I went on to represent Britain in the World Junior rowing championships, I was the only person in my year who had won international honours at sport, but they still didn't make me a prefect. I couldn't understand it. All right, in my role as captain of the boat club, I'd decked a crewmate for going out the night before a race. But Shep, our teacher/coach, didn't even tell me off so I reckon he agreed with me. It was a big race and a friend of ours was playing in a band the night before. I wanted to go, but knew I shouldn't. So I didn't. We were relying on one another. In rowing you need to have absolute trust in each other and if one person has a bad day, then you'll lose. I had my suspicions about this other guy, so on the morning of the race I casually had a word with him.

'Were they good last night?'

'Yeah, yeah. Great,' he said.

That's when I hit him.

I've always had, thanks to my mum, a deep hatred of things I perceive as unjust. In my view, it wasn't fair on anyone else who'd looked after themselves the previous night. It was a belief I would fail to temper leading up to the Sydney Olympics when I completely stopped talking to crewmate Tim Foster for putting his hand through a window at a party. Injury was one thing, but what I considered to be a self-inflicted injury was something else.

If I'm honest, they also didn't make me a prefect for a few other reasons. I was still shy and would have been pretty bad at showing prospective parents around the school; I was never there at lunchtime as we always had to do some training and this was when prefect duty was obligatory; if they could see into the future, they'd know I wore cowboy boots under my suit when I collected a prize at speech day for somehow passing my A levels and winning international honours in the same year and I would turn up to school for my A levels with a perfectly shaven double mohawk. The school took such exception to this they made me go into the examination hall with my blazer over my head and sit at the back because they said I would disturb the other pupils. I thought that a guy coming into the hall with a blazer over his head would be much more disturbing, but knew when it was best to keep certain thoughts to myself.

So strangely they never made me a prefect and I'm still slightly annoyed about it now.

You do, though, as you get older see things in a new light. My relationship with Louise, for instance. Having wound her up when we were young, I wish I could go back now and change things. Could I have been nicer? Yes, way nicer. I was jealous, although I didn't see it as jealousy at the time. I worry that I undermined her in some way despite her being so clever, attractive, sociable, sporty, musical and popular. Many years later I said 'Sorry for being such a shit' to Louise. Typical of our family, she brushed it aside and said it didn't matter. I guess it was some consolation that she knew I'd be there in her corner when she needed me. Perhaps it did matter though. And perhaps I should have made more effort to make it up to her. But at the time I found it difficult to feel sympathy for the golden child.

I think my dad (who failed his A levels first time round) considers she wasted her first class honours degree at university because she didn't want to become a doctor or a lawyer. That's the Holy Grail when you grow up in a middle-class area and it definitely wasn't going to be my destiny. So my parents put their faith in Louise, who could have walked into any career she wanted.

Instead, she went for what I think was a more fun option. We lived at home together for a short time after she had been to university. I was in the British rowing team and she was trying out for the British partying team – and would have aced selection. We used to pass each other in the morning. I was heading out to training and she was coming in from a night out. After that, she went travelling for four years. At one point my dad was getting so desperate, he was planning to go halfway round the world to drag her home.

But Lou and I have always been there for each other and always will be there for each other. She proved that love when I really wanted to buy my first motorbike (without Mum and Dad's knowledge). She cleaned out her bank account for me, despite thinking the opposite of what I thought – that it was neither a cool nor a sensible thing to do. Unless of course she figured I might get knocked off it.

The moment that brought Louise and me close remains the worst moment and week of my life. It was when her first daughter Eva was born and I arrived home to discover that her labour hadn't gone well. I didn't know how badly until I saw her face in hospital. Eva was a beautiful baby, weighing over ten pounds, but suffered brain damage from a lack of oxygen due to birth asphyxiation when the umbilical cord became wrapped round her neck during the last minutes of labour. The specialist team at Queen Charlotte's Hospital Neonatal Unit cooled the baby's body to 5–6 degrees in an effort to reverse the injury to the brain. It works in some cases but it didn't work for Eva. She lived for just seven days.

I was so upset at the time for Louise that when the chaplain at the Neonatal Unit said something like: 'Whatever happens is God's will', I told him to fuck off. But at home I just sat on the kitchen floor crying for Louise and her husband Jon. I'd never known such devastation.

When Louise left hospital, she and Jon came round to our house. They couldn't face going straight back home with all the baby things there. As I opened the door, she just fell into my arms.

I think Dad changed a bit afterwards. On the fourth anniversary of Eva's life and death, I asked him if that was the worst week of his life as it was mine. He said either then or my first few days in hospital in Arizona.

Eva is still very much part of our family. I made SPARKS – Sport Aiding Medical Research for Kids – the charity to benefit from the South Pole Race I did in 2008–2009 as they fund the primary research in the field of birth asphyxiation. I took a photo of Eva on the sled with me, which I buried at the South Pole. It was a very emotional moment. Louise now has two other children, Jossie and Reuben, who are often round at our house or vice versa as we live practically in the same street. How she and Jon have coped with such a tragedy has been inspirational.

Understandably, Louise didn't want to go straight back to work at the Natural History Museum (where she managed the development of the museum exhibitions) after Eva had died. She decided to take a year off and did a part-time course in horticulture to give her something to focus on. It was a national course with exams and, as usual, she got the highest mark of the year. Out of 100, Lou got 98. In true Mum style, her first question was: 'Which two did you get wrong?' It was not meant nastily. She's really bright and would have been genuinely interested. And perhaps her competitive streak would have wanted to know if she could answer them herself.

Bev tries to remind me that lying can be 'a necessary social lubricant'. But I'm really obsessed about telling the truth. This can be inconvenient to say the least. I have an abiding memory of Mum bollocking not just me – but her mum too – for being unacceptably tactless on one of my birthdays. I'd had a calculator as a present – probably Dad trying to steer me into becoming an accountant. How doomed that was. Just to experiment with my new toy, I was adding up people's ages. 'Me six, Louise four, Nana seventy, Mum twenty-one . . .'

Nana said: 'Mum's not twenty-one. She's thirty-one.' It's funny, but I still remember how angry Mum was – with Nana for busting the secret and me for broadcasting the fact. Although I'm assuming Dad already knew that she wasn't twenty-one. If he didn't then he'd have been annoyed to find out he didn't have a twenty-one-year-old wife, but slightly pleased he hadn't married a fifteen-year-old.

As a family, we never had huge, on-going, grudge-bearing rows. Both Mum and Dad dealt with conflict by relying on 'time being a great healer'. I think that meant we never got to the root cause of any issue but it doesn't alter the fact that I admire Mum and love her so much. She's always thinking of other people but at the same time, she's incredibly demanding of them. As am I. And probably even more so since my accident.

*

Rowing as a 'career' hadn't crossed my mind, especially as I wasn't a world beater, which is hard aged sixteen. Plus there was no money in it whatsoever, so the accountancy gene must have been kicking in at some level. Lottery funding hadn't been invented and to me it was just a sport that I enjoyed. Meanwhile, Jez Cartwright was doing the Potential Officers' Course for the Royal Marines after our GCSEs. That seemed like a plan of sorts. I thought I'd have a go too. I'd been six foot tall since the age of 13, so at least I'd match their height requirements and training for it gave me a goal.

I passed the endurance test round the assault course at Lympstone and the long run through the surrounding countryside, attacking it with the mind-set and determination of an endurance sportsman. I kept going, despite them deliberately offering us the opportunity to bail out into a warm Land Rover at any stage. No amount of cold, wet mud would make me do that.

Despite that, I failed because they said that I didn't yet have the necessary mental maturity, but they invited me to come back and try again. I never did. I regretted not becoming a Marine for a long time. Mates in the regiment were getting a huge amount from it in terms of life experience, confidence, ladies on leave, a shared bond and sense of sacrifice which inevitably led to strong life-long friendships. Only the Sydney Olympics in 2000 made up for the feeling that I'd wasted an opportunity to truly test myself.

My parents must have wondered what I was going to do when I left school. So did I. I wanted to study sports science at Loughborough but Dad didn't think it was a proper subject. So I turned down the offer and went to Reading instead to do geography (a proper subject), with very few hours of lectures a week and a useful proximity to the club Steve Redgrave rowed at. If you want to be good at something, why not match yourself against the best, was my reasoning. If I could beat him one day every month, then one day a week, then every day, I might have a chance at making it. At least that was my reasoning.

I came out three years later with a geography degree. What now? You could say I fell into teaching – very literally – and it wasn't an altogether stress-free arrangement. My first school was a comprehensive in Hounslow. Geography, my chosen subject, was not on the core curriculum, so I tried to make it feel like a surprisingly interesting subject for the kids when the time came for them to choose.

I certainly surprised them in my first lesson. The classroom was at the bottom of a set of stairs and I was running down towards it with a pile of hand-outs to give to a class of thirty-five. My teaching assessor was waiting, as was most of the class, outside the locked classroom. The ten that weren't were walking down the last few stairs in front of me. My fatal mistake was looking down to check my lesson plan. The bell goes, I trip over . . . and I take them out. All ten of them. I landed right on top of them. The hand-outs I'm holding sail down the corridor just like a croupier's cards. They fly, speeding past twenty-five aghast eleven-year-olds while the other ten are crying underneath the six foot four teacher who's just crashed on top of them. The assessor looked at me for some time, then silently gave me a thumbs-up sign. I think he was being sarcastic.

But I was quite glad the kids were there because I could properly have hurt myself otherwise. You could argue it was a ten-kid wipe out. On the other hand, it was a useful ten-kid cushion too.

Worryingly, I still see some of my ex-pupils sometimes. They come up to me and say, with a slight smile: 'You used to teach me.'

'Sorry,' I always say. 'What are you doing now?'

'*Not* geography!'

At least I helped them make a decision.

So I guess you could say that teaching wasn't really my vocation. What I really enjoyed was walking to the back of the class during lessons, releasing a silent fart and then watching them blame each other. It amused me for a whole year. Amazingly, they never caught on.

And the Royal Marines had the audacity to think I was immature.

2

'I've never seen any athlete who can push themselves into the black like James.'

Jurgen Grobler, GB rowing coach

[Bev – post-accident]

*The neuro-rehabilitation ward is a depressing place. Even the Arizona
sunshine can't brighten the communal area in which old ladies paint
tiny stained-glass windows and young men with shaved, scarred heads
play with Lego. I've told the therapists that James has a reputation for
'mindless' (I wince at the word) enthusiasm for repetitive tasks. They
put a board of tiny black-and-white pegs before him and start the
clock as he attempts to transfer the colours to the opposite side. 'Well
done, James,' praises the occupational therapist, 'that was forty-five
seconds. Let's try and do it faster.'*

*James leans back in his chair, kicks at the pillowcase stuffed with
his things at his feet and looks around the room. He can't be bothered.
He couldn't care less about the time. He stands to go. 'James, sit
down. Let's do that again. Swap the whites and the blacks.' He sighs,
leans on an elbow and waits a second even after the stopwatch is re-
started. He doesn't listen to hear if he's improved but walks away and*

34

falls asleep on a physio bench.

The occupational therapist notices the confusion and worry written across my face. 'Frontal lobe patients struggle with motivation,' she says kindly. 'Let's try something more physical.'

The unit has a 'hand bike', a low seat behind two handles that can be turned around in a circular motion. It's a safe way to exercise for people who may struggle to balance. James looks contemptuously at the piece of kit. 'What's the point of that?'

'A bit of exercise, darling.' I think of the hours he used to spend in the gym. 'It might make you feel better.'

The physio sets him a goal: two minutes of gentle arm turning. He manages thirty seconds, walks away, bored. He has to be reminded of his two-minute aim. There is a woman with a stopwatch setting him a physical goal and he can't be arsed. I'm shocked. I watch him give up on every activity they encourage him to complete. Motivation, determination and an unwillingness to quit are the very essence of James. Where has my husband gone?

[James]

It's the 1999 World Championships in Canada. A year before the Sydney Olympics. We're winning. The GB coxless four, i.e., four men in a rowing boat, are four seconds up on our rivals, ahead of world record pace, with 500 metres to go. I want one huge assault on that finish line. This is our moment. We will lay down our marker to the world, I want to let our opposition know that they will be racing for silver come Sydney 'Go! Go!' I yell excitedly.

'No!' Steve Redgrave shouts back.

What?! Steve, not yet Sir Steve, but still the dominant rower Steve, one of the greatest British Olympians of all time Steve, is refusing to get stuck in. 'Go!' I shout again, more urgently this time. We have the power to crush the opposition. We have the ability to break our rivals a year before we race them in Sydney for Steve's fifth Olympic gold medal. But he's backing off? What's the matter with him?

'Go! Go! Go!' I shout.

'No,' overrules Redgrave finally. That's a 'no' then. We win by less than a second against the rest of the field including Australia and Italy, the record remains unbroken, and I am utterly pissed off with him. 'What the fuck were you doing out there?' I yell, still livid as we step off the podium clutching our gold medals.

Calmly he asks me a question. 'Do you want them to go away and think they've got to improve by five seconds to beat us or think they've only got to improve by half a second to beat us?' That rushing sound is the wind leaving my sails. Rather than being lazy, the wily old bastard, is thinking of nothing but Sydney.

That night I went out, drank too much and got arrested.

The evening began with all of us out for a drink. Some of us were sensible about this and some (one) of us weren't. Steve and our crewmates Matt Pinsent and Ed Coode came out for a little while, celebrated the win and then went back to the hotel. I, on the other hand, stayed drinking with a lot of new friends I'd suddenly made. It could have been my round of tequila shots that made me so popular. Soon strippers arrived on the dance floor, and I decided that it was a fine line of business to be in and joined them. This didn't go down very well with the management.

I got my revenge for being thrown out by relieving myself by the outside wall of the nightclub. Unfortunately, that's when I heard 'Put it away, son', and thought, 'Ahhh, a bouncer!' So I instinctively put my hand out in a manner intended to ask this gentleman to back off. But as my arm reached the point of no return, I noticed it was not a bouncer at all. It was a policeman. With a little more force than I meant, I palmed him in the face and he fell over.

At this point another policeman swept my legs from under me with his nightstick and suddenly I was on the floor having my hands cuffed behind my back before being loaded into a police car. I couldn't miss this opportunity: I tried to get out of the handcuffs Houdini-style until the brakes of the car were slammed on and I flew forwards, attractively flattening my face against the Perspex that separated us villains in the back from the good guys in the front. 'Sit back,' came the instruction. I sat back. With both my handcuffed wrists and my tail firmly between my legs.

At the police station they demanded my shoelaces and belt. 'I'm not going to commit suicide.' I said incredulously. 'I've had a good day. I won the World Championships.' They looked dubious.

'All right,' one said. 'Show us your medal and you can go.' I reached into my pocket and – of course – I'd lost my medal while making so many new friends in the nightclub. They slung me in a cell.

It would be good to say that the Great British cavalry came riding to the rescue. But the truth is much worse than that. It was a bloody Australian. The only person who came along to vouch for me was a guy called Mick McKay, a double Olympic gold medallist and one of our rivals from the so-called Oarsome Foursome. He looked at me knowingly. 'I've been in a few of these!' he commented. No more needed to be said.

The next morning Jurgen said I was an embarrassment to British rowing. But actually (or rather worryingly) I think my stock went up in global rowing circles. I'd raced, I'd won and I'd been arrested all in one day. My middle-class rebellion had reached new heights. But it had to stop. I knew that Jurgen would try and drop me from the four if I gave him the slightest opportunity between now and the Games. So my aim from that moment onwards was to make myself undroppable.

Getting to the Olympics wasn't exactly a smooth path. My 'rowing career' is a tale taking in the inevitable dunkings, poverty, petulance, injustice, a dead body, illness, injury, heartbreak, fights, tears and holding on to an electrified fence in Austria with my teeth. If someone made a film, it wouldn't have the soundtrack to *Chariots of Fire*, *Rocky* or *Gladiator*. Worryingly the theme to *Benny Hill* would probably work better.

My knowledge of the Games began with the LA Olympics in 1984. I was a twelve-year-old boy mesmerised by the jetpacks in the Opening Ceremony. I then watched Daley Thompson delivering personal best after personal best going head-to-head for the gold medal with Jurgen Hingsen over two days in the decathlon and then whistling his way through the National Anthem. This is what sport is all about, I thought. Daley came to Kingston Borough Sports Day in 1985 and I got to hold his medal. I remember thinking how great it would be to have one of those but I knew it wouldn't come from track and field. In the 110 metre hurdles (which is what I was doing that day), it would be a close race between me and a glacier.

Seb Coe and Steve Ovett made an impression on me too. Coe for his fluid, graceful and powerful running style as he won the 1,500 metres. Ovett for what I saw as bravery in running the final of the 1,500 metres with respiratory problems. He'd already collapsed in the 800 metres semi-final and both friends and doctors advised him not to compete in the 1,500 metres, but he ignored them. He battled for three laps, dropped out and was taken away on a stretcher. At least he can look back on LA knowing he'd found his limit.

Even as a twelve-year-old boy, watching those three athletes I understood the elation, pain, effort, desperation and importance of the Olympics. And I wanted it. Well, in truth, I wanted the medal.

A year later I took up rowing and, to be honest, the connection between it, me and the Olympics had yet to be made. I was picked for the school's under fourteen eight, which began inauspiciously when leading the National Schools Regatta (the biggest race of the year) I caught a crab, which means that I didn't get my oar out of the water in time, the oar handle goes over your head and gets stuck parallel to the boat, acting as a handbrake. So we finished last. I don't entirely blame myself for this. As novice schoolboys, our boat was a bit like a drunken spider with everyone doing something different, but I was the one who was in control of my oar. No one would sit next to me on the bus going home and our coach may not have helped on this front by calling me a 'piss artist' as I exited the boat, which aided 'my mates' determine exactly where the blame lay. If I'm honest, if I wasn't the one who caught the crab, I'd have been the same. On a positive note, it was the last I crab ever caught.

The following season was a bit better and the season after that was better still. I was now a bigger fish in what if I'm honest was a smaller pond. I'd gained strength and fitness over the summer from training hard for the Marines' Potential Officers' Course. By 1989 I had qualified for the World Juniors and, significantly, I had met the man who I had seen rowing to a gold medal at the Seoul Olympics. His name was Steve Redgrave.

Steve lived in Marlow and coached my junior rowing partner at the time, Nick Clarry, who also lived and rowed in Marlow, and so we ended up being coached by Steve on a Saturday afternoon. I figured this wasn't the time to tell him that I had won two goldfish at a fair that summer and named them Steve and Andy after him and his partner (the late Andy Holmes) at the Olympics. It turned out to be a wise choice. I didn't want to give him another reason to remember the first time he coached me. He pushed Nick and me off and we fell straight in. I bet he didn't think that in less than ten years' time, he'd be trusting this dozy kid to help him earn a fifth gold medal on a rowing lake in Sydney.

Pretty soon he went from mythical status to just a grumpy coach to us. That's what happens to hero worship when you actually meet people. You find out that the people you look up to are just human. But boy, was he an awesome athlete. In 1990 he was at his peak, a phenomenal performer, both in his strength and his feel for a boat. Our first year in the coxless four together was the only one where he wasn't fighting two serious medical problems as well as the rest of the world and a brutal training regime. For that year he was only battling colitis. Three weeks after the 1997 World Championships, he was diagnosed with type 1 diabetes. From this point he became more and more impressive to me, not only because he kept going, kept fighting. But the fact he never, ever moaned or gave up or used it as an excuse for underperforming.

We shared that trait – if not the haul of Olympic bullion – of not wanting to give up. I'd carried on with rowing through all the less glamorous bits, even the day when our under-14s eight suddenly felt really heavy on the way back to the boat-house. We couldn't work out why but we were going so slow. When we finally got back we realised that there was something caught on our fin. It turned out to be a dead body. We were as helpful as we could be before the police arrived. We moored him up by his arm and, being schoolboys, gave him a good prod to investigate what a dead body felt like.

In 1989 I had thirty-five seat races (an individual race for your place in a boat) for the Junior World Championships and I didn't lose any of them. I'd fought my way up the squad day after day following a shocking race in the long-distance time trial at the start of the week. After which I thought I'd be on the first coach home. I was selected for the coxed pair – neither the most glamorous nor the fastest boat. It was the first time in twenty years anyone at our school had earned international rowing honours. I'd never been on a plane before. Plus the event was in Hungary and aside from a holiday in Spain when I was one I'd only ever been on camping holidays to France.

We were shit. Our boat came nowhere at the Champion-ships. Even though we were the bottom ranked boat in the team with minimal expectations of us, I was gutted. But, there was a real sense of satisfaction and inspiration in being there, seeing it, and boy did the whole experience give me the moti-vation to not only come back next year but to win. And that's what happened. In a four that included a schoolboy called Greg Searle, we became World Junior Under-18 Champions.

That was the first of a number of significant events for my rowing career. The next was the fall of the Berlin Wall and the ripping down of the Iron Curtain, which gave a man called Jurgen Grobler the freedom to travel. Another was that I began to feel I was good enough to go to the Barcelona Olympics.

The thing about rowing is that you can't do it with a trampled shoulder. This I discovered six months before Barcelona. Our coach Jurgen discovered this fact too (although I suspect he already knew). A word about Jurgen. He is the most successful rowing coach in the world. He arrived at the Leander Club in Henley-on-Thames three weeks after I did. Fresh from the toppled wall and the drug-fuelled East German regime that dominated rowing in the 1980s. In his new-found freedom he emigrated to Britain with his wife and bribed his young son with a rabbit to ease the settling-in process.

He might have been seen as a controversial appointment because of rumours of drug use in his previous teams. I more than anyone can't abide drugs in sport and believe that if there is a lifetime ban from the Olympics for testing positive then that punishment should stand. What East Germany did to its athletes was despicable but the reality is that, drug-fuelled or not, the East German rowers under Jurgen trained full-time rather than trying to juggle employment and training at the same time.

Jurgen was a smart operator. He spotted that, as a group, rowers were mindlessly enthusiastic, competitive and easy to trick (especially me, which was annoying as I still fell for it even though I could see it was a trap). He therefore decided that the best way to get a dynamic training session out of us after a hard session on the water was to organise a game of touch rugby. It worked. We'd happily spend all day out there accidentally getting fitter.

But the plan went wrong a few days before Christmas in 1991 – the winter before Barcelona – when Steve took matters into his own hands. He and Matt organised a game but there was no 'touch' about it. It was a 15-a-side match against Marlow Rugby Club. Being oarsmen, we weren't exactly used to contact unless someone didn't look round when they were rowing. The scrum was not our best weapon and neither was lightning speed. What we had in our favour was fitness, effort, relentless enthusiasm and the fact our coach wasn't around that weekend to bust us.

There were quite a few spectators, mainly the old boys from the rowing club who had come to see what these young idiots were like as sportsmen when a boat wasn't involved. Not very good, as it turned out. I discovered this after less than twenty minutes when I was lying full stretch on the ground with my shoulder erupting in pain. Eighteen stone of Matt Pinsent had just stamped on me.

I couldn't carry on but I couldn't drive myself to hospital either. My incessant whimpering combined with the fact that I was in the Olympic squad eventually forced one of the old guys to take me to A&E where it did not take long to realise that sporting injuries rank as self-inflicted so you're some-where in the queue only slightly ahead of a burglar who's fallen on railings while trying to climb through a second-storey window. The crescendo of throbbing pain in my shoulder was drowned out as a doctor told me I'd destroyed my acromio-clavicular joint. In layman's terms, this meant that I'd separated my shoulder. I had also destroyed my chance of going to Barcelona.

I regained some form and in the end I was offered the role of 'spare man' or water boy as it's otherwise known. I turned it down. It would kill me to be there and not race, especially when I knew (or believed) that I was a better rower than many of the guys on the team. When I told the selectors I wouldn't do it, their reaction was: 'You'll never row for Britain again and you've lost all your funding.'

The funding wasn't the big issue. I was already in debt, plus Sports Aid grants were awarded according to your world ranking. In 1991, I'd come seventh, and being water boy at the '92 Games would have left me without one at all. So my response to their threat of not rowing for GB again was a petulant: 'It's a boring sport and I don't want to do it anyway.'

The Barcelona Olympics survived without me. While Steve won his third gold medal – his first with Matt Pinsent – I was on a rugby tour in Canada with Reading University. That might seem a strange decision given that rugby was the reason I was missing the Olympics. Come to think of it, it was a strange decision. I guess that's why there aren't too many world leaders or Nobel Prize-winners aged nineteen. The decision-making ability in teenagers seems to be slightly skewed and impulsive.

Despite trying to close my mind to what was happening in Spain, I found myself at 4 a.m. one morning, beer in hand, watching the final of the men's coxed pair which was won by Great Britain's Searle brothers in a fantastic race. I was genuinely delighted for them but a part of me felt frustrated. In 1990 I'd raced and won with Greg Searle in the Junior World Championships and here he was just two years later picking up an Olympic gold. It frustrated me horribly, not just because I was jealous, but because I knew I had the talent to be in that position but I'd let myself down.

Despite my current branding as a 'trouble-maker' in British

rowing I decided to come back and have another go at it. An awkward conversation was had, beginning with me saying: 'You know I said that it was a boring sport . . .' They took me back but I'd lost my funding. In my last year of university I made it back into the national team, coming sixth in the eight at the World Championships. Then I made the decision to take a year out after university for the 1993–1994 season and give rowing everything. I lived in Kingston with mates, trained at Molesey Boat Club alongside the Searle brothers and worked in a pub for cash in hand.

To be fair, my parents had given me the choice of living at home for free or living away and making my own ends meet. I didn't want to live at home. It was important to me to be independent. My parents also took the view that I should stop being seen as a rebel. They hadn't been very happy when they'd bought tickets for the Barcelona Olympics only for me to tell rowing to sod off.

But I wasn't a deliberate rebel. I just thought – frequently – that the people who ran rowing were wrong. In 1994 I was rejected from the four and put in the eight, despite winning a lot of trial races. I had a massive sense of injustice and no faith in the selectors. So after the World Championships I decided to concentrate on sculling and try to qualify for the double for the Olympics, arrogantly figuring that it was better to be one of the two best people in a double (two-man boat) than an eight. A sound theory apart from I'd never raced a sculling boat internationally and we'd never qualified one for an Olympics before. I figured though that whether it ended in success or failure, at least my fate would be in my own hands.

Sculling on your own or in a two-man crew can be a hard

and lonely business, but I was determined to keep going, and a year before the Atlanta Olympics in 1996, I'd qualified a boat – a double – with a partner, Bobby Thatcher. Ironically, our training partners were Steve Redgrave and Matt Pinsent, for entirely technical reasons. It was not an equal arrangement, as a double scull (two oars each) is faster than a coxless pair (one oar each). So basically, we were cannon fodder to help them go faster – there's a reason why Jurgen is the most successful coach ever. If the best chance of me picking up a gong in Atlanta was as cannon fodder, then fodder gladly reported for duty. Steve and Matt were lucky that Bobby and I were so desperate to gain any insight we could. We were like grateful dogs taking scraps from their owner's table.

Nevertheless, when Steve and Matt boarded the plane for Atlanta, as the spearhead of the entire GB team and gold medal favourites, Bobby and I were also USA-bound as members of the Olympic squad. I'd made it. My parents had bought tickets again, and this time they would see me race.

How wrong I turned out to be.

Atlanta 1996. It wasn't the best run of events. For a start there was a terrible hold-up getting our athletes' accreditation. I know that because I was the hold-up. We'd already filled out countless forms and been warned that getting our accreditation would be harder than getting past security at MI5. In reality the process was quicker than I thought, even managing to avoid any inner cavity searches.

But then there was the hand scan. I was intrigued and totally baffled by how it worked. Instead of just taking my plastic accreditation and moving on, I started to ask the guy behind the counter a set of ever more complicated questions. His explanations weren't good enough for me, although they were for the snaking queue of multi-national athletes that was forming behind me. One of them shouted: 'Are you going for the fucking accreditation gold medal? Stop asking questions and get fucking moving!' I swiftly jumped on the bus to the Olympic Village.

Calling it a 'Village' does the place a disservice. It's a kingdom. The Athletes' Village at any Olympics basically fulfils four crucial roles: it houses, feeds, entertains and acts as a transport hub for 12,000 athletes. No media are allowed in and it is situated right next to the Olympic Park, including the Olympic Stadium, Aquatics Centre, and Velodrome.

Athletes from every nation were grouped together, although swimmers and the track guys were kept apart since the former finish their events before the latter have started, making for potential disturbances. The rowing team were sharing flats in the Village, with several bedrooms off a communal kitchen and lounge. We weren't much fun. We went to bed at 9 p.m. and got up at 4 a.m. every day. It wasn't very exciting but if you wanted to be on fire at 10 a.m., which is race time, you had to trick the body into thinking it was much later in the day.

The plan for rest and preparation seemed to work very well until Cuba moved into the block of flats next door. They seemed to be able to survive on virtually no sleep and actively participated in singing and drumming every waking hour. But in fairness to them, they weren't the only distraction. The main item on that agenda was the food hall. 'Hall' was an understatement. It was a football pitch sized palace filled with food. And it was free.

It's great when you've finished competing as there are kebabs, curries, Chinese, full English breakfasts and even a

McDonald's available twenty-four hours a day. But although I have good discipline when it comes to training, I'm less blessed in the self-control department around food. I wasn't the only one. I met a mate of mine – Monster, an Aussie – in there at 4 a.m. sometime during the second week. I'd some-how over-estimated the number of Big Macs I needed and so I offered him one of mine. 'Nah, I'm good, mate,' he said. 'I've had seven already.'

But for us, the biggest problem was the distance to the rowing lake. It's most frustrating that all the major cities in the world have neglected to build a 2,000-metre lake right in the middle of town. So the rowing venue in Atlanta (Lake Lanier) was an hour away on the bus. Unlike the potential medal-winners on our squad I hadn't seen the course. I was shaking with adrenalin and anticipation when we turned the corner for the first time to see the water lying out in front of us. I leapt off the bus and just stared. The water was warm (which would make for fast times) and we had exclusive access, unlike our training lakes in Europe that we shared with water-skiers, who make not only waves but force us to think we could have chosen a more fun sport.

But the stress of that hour-long journey on a cramped bus in forty-degree heat and humidity was getting to us. Even though racing was a still a few days away, a number of rowers from other nations seemed to have their 'race pits' (adrenalin-fuelled, BO-reeking armpits) up to speed already. Not pleasant to endure on a hot bus for two hours a day.

Meanwhile, my partner Bobby and I were under a good deal of self-imposed stress, trying to improve fast and learn from our mistakes after a season interrupted by, largely, Bobby's back injury. The result was a vicious circle where our tension made our rowing deteriorate, and that only increased the tension.

A combination of the frustration and the stress of a clock continuously counting down intensified every emotion and reaction. So much so that after one outing Bobby and I squared up to each other on the landing stage and had to be pulled apart. This would have been bad enough in private but was far worse in front of the whole Olympic regatta, including our opposition.

After we'd put the boat on the rack and mumbled an apology like two Premier League footballers who have been forced to do so by the referee, we had to have our crew photo taken. Surprisingly enough there weren't many smiles. We didn't look like we wanted to be in the same country, let alone the same boat. But at least we were able to vent our residual seething anger on somebody else. That somebody was the poor guy in charge of the buses back to the Olympic Village. No buses had arrived to pick us up from the lake for an hour and there were hundreds of hot, frustrated, angry and hungry rowers in the queue. And by queue I mean mob and we were about to cause a riot.

It was a transport cock-up, one of many in Atlanta, and was not swiftly sorted either. Eventually a convoy of buses was sent to get us, and I'll always remember the shocked face of the first driver to arrive when he was greeted like the Second Coming.

But that's not the bus story that wrecked my Olympics. That happened two days later. It was the day of the Opening Ceremony. Bobby and I, now reconciled, were undecided about whether to go or not as we were racing less than thirty-six hours later. Attending the Opening Ceremony meant a late night and wearing a Parade Uniform (complete with panama hat) that looked better suited to 1896, not a century later.

But there were two reasons why we wanted to go. Unless Bobby or I found an ability to knock out sub-10 seconds 100 metres in the next week, it was going to be the only time we walked into a packed Olympic Stadium and felt we were part of something very special. The inspiration it would give us could be the secret ingredient in raising our performance. We also wanted to support our sport and Steve, who would be leading out the British team and carrying the flag (using just one arm, the show-off).

So as we set off for Lake Lanier that morning we still didn't know exactly what we were going to do. It started well, we left the Village on time. But from there it went downhill, specifically the slip road on to the freeway. Something was definitely amiss down the sharp end of the bus. The driver started screaming and shouting while the AOCOG (Atlanta Organizing Committee of the Olympic Games) volunteer tried to calm him down. The bus was going at least fifty per cent slower than all the other traffic, eventually reaching one hundred per cent as we stopped on the hard shoulder, amid a torrent of raging abuse in a Babel of foreign languages from the massed ranks of us rowers.

Eventually the volunteer tapped the microphone and said through the tannoy: 'The driver would like to say a few words.' We waited, amid a sarcastic slow handclap, to find out what the hell was happening. 'Sorry for the delay folks,' he said. 'I'm not comfortable on this route. I've never driven on a freeway before.' This admission was followed by a wave of silence. Now what?

I discovered something. 'Bus minutes', as I like to call them, are about five times longer than regular earth minutes. We were told we'd be cooped up in this hot, sweaty prison for two hours. It felt like ten. The seats weren't made for guys ranging from six foot three to six ten (none ever are – but that's a different rant) and on top of that was the potentially lethal combination of thwarted energy and anger as we absorbed the fact that we were missing our last training session before a race due to a ridiculous, unforgivable and utterly avoidable administrative mistake. It made for a bus full of hot, angry, uncomfortable and very nasty-smelling sardines.

The air conditioning was fighting a losing battle and so the tension, anger and pathological hatred of bus drivers weren't the only things being passed from athlete to athlete. We were eventually rescued two and a half hours later by our 'experienced' driver and driven back to the Village, which was like finding a pound but losing a tenner. We'd achieved nothing and ended up back where we started.

Bobby went straight to the food hall but I wanted the British team doctor to give me a quick once over because I didn't feel right. Unusually for me (at that time), I had a headache and felt rubbish from the shoulders up. I was hoping it was just psychosomatic after our ordeal on the bus and sharing germs with fifty other athletes. My race was in thirty-six hours' time.

The GB team doctor was Richard Budgett, who also had the distinction of rowing with Steve Redgrave in 1984 in LA. As a gold medal oarsman himself, he would surely understand my feelings and give me the reassurance I needed. He felt around my neck and ears, then looked inside my ears before doing the same in my mouth. 'Say ahhh,' he instructed. I did.

'I'm afraid there's no easy way to tell you this,' he said gently. 'But you've got tonsillitis. It's in the very early stages but will get worse before it gets better.'

I felt I was in that scene in Star Wars where Luke Skywalker, C3PO, Hans Solo et al are trapped in a water-filled rubbish dump with the walls closing in. My Olympic ambitions were just about to be crushed to death. Richard didn't have to guess how I was feeling. Fat tears were running down my face. 'I'll go and get Ann [Steve's wife and the rowing team's doctor] and we'll work out the best way forward.' He stood up and went out, closing the door behind him and leaving me in my own private world of pain.

It was a slumped, blubbing, self-pitying mess that greeted Ann and Richard on their return and I hadn't even yet moved on to think about the people who were going to be affected by me not being able to race. Namely, Bobby, our coach and my friends, who were at last to see the reason why I'd been such a crap mate over the last couple of years. But I was thinking most of all of my parents. It was the second Olympics they'd bought tickets for and yet again they weren't going to see me make it to the start line.

Ann rubbed my shoulders sympathetically. She was an Olympic athlete herself. She understood what it was like for someone who had put everything into representing their country only to be withdrawn at the last minute. But she also possessed the ability to make definitive, tough and what could be called 'ruthless' decisions. She nodded. 'Early stage tonsillitis, which is going to get worse over the next forty-eight hours.' I wondered who of the two would break the news to me that my Olympic dream was over.

Richard had a duty of care to Team GB as a whole. Ann

obviously shared that concern but her primary thought had to be for the rowing team and she would have had to be beyond human if one person did not stand out above all others: Steve.

There was a huge amount of pressure on him and Matt. They were favourites, defending Olympic champions, world champions and Steve was going for his fourth successive gold medal. Despite having been unbeaten since 1992, victory was not a certainty. Their chances were not improved by a contagious sick-note in the same apartment. Would that influence the decision or the action that was taken?

It was Richard who spoke. 'We can't let you train tomorrow or race in the heat. It's going to get worse and you won't do yourself or Bobby any favours.' He addressed the next part of his speech to the floor. 'It's better to let him train with Guy Pooley tomorrow, give them half a chance.' At least I think that's what he said. The words were coming to me as though we were all under water. A change in the voice momentarily dragged me up from the bottom of the pool. 'Your Olympics aren't over,' Ann said. 'The heat is on Sunday and the next race will be Tuesday at the earliest. You could be OK again by then.'

That seemed to me a bit like a French revolutionary telling a member of the bourgeoisie not to worry, they'd sharpened the blade of the guillotine and so it wouldn't hurt as much. I was still going to miss the heat.

So I didn't have to worry about attending the Olympic Opening Ceremony after all. I watched it on television instead in a tiny quarantine room, the size of a broom cupboard, near the Olympic swimming pool with one equally tiny window through which I would hear – over and over again – the national anthems of America and Australia as they won race after race.

At some stage in my incarceration I was allowed back briefly to the apartment to get my things. I had been told the coast was clear and everyone else was out at training. Not true. While I was in there, Steve Redgrave arrived and I thought he was going to rip my fucking head from my shoulders. I'd never seen him so angry. He and Matt were moving themselves to a hotel by the rowing lake and I always wondered whether my illness was the excuse for them to escape the Village and all its transport problems without being accused of getting special treatment. Although in my opinion they deserved the right to that special treatment anyway.

I couldn't watch Bobby and Guy's race – it wasn't on television – but I quickly heard that they (not surprisingly) hadn't done very well.

I never did get to tell Mum and Dad before the race that I wouldn't be in the boat. These were pre-mobile days and although I called their hotel and left a message, they didn't receive it in time. The first thing they knew about it was a boat paddling towards them that didn't contain their son. They are incredibly stoic people, but it was horrible, especially as this wasn't the first time it had happened.

The only other time I was sprung from my cell was to have lunch with Princess Anne. As an athlete with nothing to do, I was 'selected' for a chat round the lunch table. Even by my poor standards, I don't think I was the best company that day. I chose not to bring up this meeting four years later when she was handing me my gold medal in Sydney.

By the time I was allowed out of quarantine and back into

the Village, Bobby and Guy had been knocked out. I could come back for what they call the C/D semi-final but I still didn't feel a hundred per cent. I raced but after a minute I was blowing out my ass. I deliberately never did find out where we finished until researching for this book – seventeenth. I still hadn't spoken to my parents. I did eventually, of course. They were upset but I got the sense that they felt that this was just 'typical' of me. Looking back, they didn't really understand the sacrifices I was making on a daily basis. They thought I was wasting my time – and my education.

My Olympics were over, so it was time to hit the beers. That was some salvation. Lining up shots, joining Bobby in being sick (I blame the tonsillitis) in the back of a cab, we were finally a team. We weren't the only ones. During the second week when a lot of the athletes had finished competing I found a couple shagging in a lift when I called it to go to my floor – in fact, I think they got married and are still together. So I took the stairs and went through the laundry room where another couple were shagging over a washing machine. I'm not so sure how their future worked out.

But no one in the British team had performed thus far. It was all down to Steve and Matt. The night before their race a bomb went off in a park and they knew nothing about it until they woke at 4 a.m. Even then they were unsure whether their event would be on that day. Steve was really feeling the pressure. He'd even, I found out later, suffered a panic attack during a press conference that he'd managed to cover up.

But they won. They won in an Olympic record time that stood for sixteen years until it was broken during London 2012. In the moment of victory and relief, Steve told the world to shoot him if he ever went near another rowing boat again. Little did he know that not only would he compete in one more Olympics but he'd be putting his career, his life, his unblemished record into new (and at this stage almost wildly unpromising) hands. Mine.

I had a huge decision to make after Atlanta. Would I carry on and risk wasting (according to my parents) another four years of my life? I was a twenty-four-year-old student, studying for a part-time MSc (Masters) in sports science, with my career as a geography teacher behind me. I didn't own a house and I was claiming income support. I was amassing debts and staring down the barrel of a miserable winter. National Lottery funding would come in the following spring, but with no international ranking I did not qualify for assistance.

Then I heard that Redgrave and Pinsent were intending to switch to a coxless four for the next season. As I was beating them in tests and trials on a daily and weekly basis, I could see no reason why I couldn't get in that boat. If they remained a coxless four until Sydney 2000 it would be a big deal: not that Steve Redgrave was going for an unprecedented fifth gold medal but that I'd have the chance of getting one. I couldn't and wouldn't miss this opportunity.

I stopped training with the other rowers at Molesey. I went back to my old school coach, Shep, and trained in Kingston out of sight of everyone else. I buried myself in tough winter sessions on the river and beat myself up in the gym. Determined to make it impossible for Jurgen to leave me out. Five months later I won the singles trials and came second in the pairs trials.

'Congratulations,' said Jurgen. 'You're in. For now.'

Obviously Steve knew me quite well by then and would have trusted Jurgen's judgement. Even so, he may have remembered me as a loose cannon when I was younger. The teeth incident, for instance. We were in Austria, over 2,000m up a mountain on an altitude camp with nothing to do except train. I had a bet with Gary Herbert (the cox in the Searle brothers' boat that won gold in Barcelona) that I wouldn't bite the electric fence. We crossed the fence daily on our way down the mountain to the rowing lake and I'd already tested out the current with my hand. It wasn't too bad, plus I had no fillings. With no metal in my mouth, I figured I'd win. Steve thought I was insane and refused to take part.

I won, and I held on the longest but I refused to take the money because it didn't really hurt enough. I need to feel I've earned it. In the end I relented as I needed some cash to pay my share of the Sky card we'd bought along with a satellite dish to get some TV up the mountain. As I said, everyone has their price. MTV and a bit of news was mine.

Some people said Tim Foster and I had been given a poisoned chalice by making up the four. If we won in Sydney it would be Steve's success, if we lost it would our fault. That's not how I saw it. Matt and Steve were putting their Olympic records in our hands. There was no reason for them to trust us, but I was prepared to row myself into virtual uncon- sciousness – what Jurgen called 'rowing into the black' – to make the boat go faster.

Despite their experience, Steve and Matt never pulled rank. In all the interviews they did they always stressed that it wasn't the pair with two other people strapped on the end. They always stood with Tim and me in the centre of photos so that we couldn't be cropped out. They trusted us with their careers. That meant a lot. But athletes are very selfish people. They didn't want to row with me because they wanted to help me; they wanted to row with me because Jurgen thought we were the best four people in the British team and together had the best chance of winning. That was it. Very simple.

I think Steve and I are more alike than he cares to admit, although I think he's fuelled by negative energy rather than positive and I'm a lot more extreme. The only person I've ever met who's more extreme is Jonny Wilkinson. On an advert shoot, I got the opportunity to ask him: 'What's the best moment of your career?' I thought he'd say the dropped goal in 2003 to win England the Rugby World Cup. Instead he said, 'Oh, I was training at Middlesbrough . . .'

Apparently, he would only allow himself to stop training when he had landed five kicks on the 'T' of the rugby posts from the halfway line. He'd stay out there all day if he had to, but on this particular day he had just arrived on the pitch where Middlesbrough FC were training down the other end. With his first five kicks he hit the target (the crossbar of a football goal) every time. The footballers just stopped training and applauded.

For us, applause was not our most familiar soundtrack. Grunting, chewing and the thud of large bodies falling off the rowing machines were more common, not to mention the occasional burst of argument.

All of us had our bad times leading up to the Olympics, with the exception of Rip Van Pinsent, who finds that the best way is to sleep a confrontation away. Tim had put his hand through a window during a party, so he had his injuries, window-related and otherwise; Steve was battling to get his diabetes and colitis under control and I split up with my Danish girlfriend, Emilie. Typically self-absorbed, I thought I was a very nice boyfriend; I just happened to be doing a lot of rowing in 2000. For her it was all too much. She'd been ground down by my selfishness. She told me it was all over five months before the Olympics. It came completely out of the blue to me. If I'd paid more attention to her, it would have been less of a surprise.

It might seem incredible to remember it now but there were some rumblings, mainly in the media, that perhaps Steve shouldn't be in the four at all, based on the fact that at thirty-eight he was too old, too ill with diabetes and colitis, and his body had taken too much of a beating after twenty years on the water. In our final ergo test, which Matt won, beating me by a couple of seconds, Steve fell off the machine completely shattered forty seconds behind us. I was worried about him. I had faith in him. I also had faith in Jurgen making a tough decision. Jurgen wasn't afraid to be unpopular; he was more afraid of losing.

We were nearly there. There was only time for one more argument – I was convinced we could be using a better boat, backed up by losing our last World Cup race in Lucerne – and then we'd be on our way to Australia, along with a new boat, costing £30,000 in air freight.

I'd been to the Olympics before and not made it to the start line, so even though it was great to be there in the Village in Sydney, I knew it could all go wrong.

The countdown clock ticked down. Would this be third time lucky for my mum and dad? My sister arrived for the semi-final and I still hadn't injured myself horribly or contracted a contagious disease.

The day of the final was a strange one. Matt was nervous and couldn't eat. Steve was checking his sugar levels. Ann gave us a lift to the lake in a van and we were on the water training in the dark. People had already turned up. It was an amazing moment, rowing into the dawn with a crowd yelling good luck to us. Matt's not the most emotional guy but he was crying as we pulled the boat out of the water.

As time went on, I was very nervous. Before putting our boat on the water, I was crying myself, I was so wound up. Our race would last six minutes. Six minutes to determine whether the last four years had been a waste of time. We watched the pair race before us. Ed Coode and Greg Searle. They were winning by four seconds at the halfway stage and came fourth. Not even a medal. That reminded us how fragile it all was. It reminded me forcefully that there is no such thing as a certainty at the Olympics.

Our turn now. We climbed into our boat and Steve sellotaped a bag of sugar near my feet. It was his insurance policy, just in case he fell into a glycaemic coma from the exertion. Despite that, I remember sitting at the start in the bow seat thinking I wouldn't have anyone else in the world in this boat other than the guys in front of me.

Then we went.

It wasn't how I'd envisaged it. It was an average performance. But we'd trained so hard trying to raise our level that our average was better than everyone else's best and the scoreboard hailed us Olympic champions: 1. Great Britain; 2. Italy; 3. Australia. Slowly it dawned on me. We hadn't lost, I hadn't been the one to ruin Steve's record. Relief was my biggest emotion.

'Well, that wasn't very good,' was the first thing Jurgen said to us.

3

[Bev – post-accident]

James doesn't want to get in the ambulance outside our house. He wants to unpack his bags from America, check his emails on the home computer and get back to real life. But the paramedics and the doctor who accompanied us on the flight back to England are waiting for him. 'This is bullshit!' He stomps upstairs into our bedroom and forgets why he went in there. I think I'm going to cry as I put some clean T-shirts and shorts into a bag. He snaps that he doesn't like those ones and gets out some others, exactly the same.

Having been empty for a month, the house feels cold and unwelcoming. I'd expected to feel better being home, but reality has suddenly hit: this wasn't a nightmare that would end when we left America. This is now our life. And this angry, unkind and aggressive man is my new husband.

I follow the ambulance in my car, consciously remembering to drive on the left again. London's September warmth is a blessed relief after the Phoenix heat. My heart aches for James as he's led out of the ambulance – refusing the wheelchair – and taken to his room.

I spend the day wanting to see the kids – who are in Henley-on-Thames with my parents – and hoping that James will feel settled at the hospital. I fill in form after form as James doesn't know the answers to questions about his injuries and recovery so far. Every time they ask him the date of his accident, he looks at me, blinking, knowing he needs my help but embarrassed at having to ask for and accept it. We meet physios, occupational therapists, speech and language therapists, psychologists and neurologists who I must tell over and over about the care James has had so far.

Between meetings, I grab half an hour of deep pregnant-jet-lagged sleep. By 6 p.m., I'm starving and offer to nip out to bring us back something to eat. James snaps, 'Don't you have anything better to do? Just get out. Why are you hanging around here?'

Perhaps a better wife would take a deep breath, accept that it's the injury talking and smile sweetly. But I can't. My patience has temporarily run dry. 'Yes! I've had better things to do for the last month that I've spent looking after you!' I storm out and drive home, crying all the way. As I pull up to the house, the phone rings. It's James, cheerful, as though nothing has happened. 'Hi, beautiful, when you come tomorrow, can you bring my laptop? Thanks.'

[James]

Women don't throw themselves at rowers. Not this rower anyway. Sad, but true. And despite me making exceptional efforts on the hair front.

They might throw *things* at rowers, our sweat-ridden spandex, for example, which is artistically draped over the radiators, chairs, sofas, lamps, and bicycles in their living space. But themselves, no. They either have more sense or, in my case, failed to see the advantages offered by my social awkwardness.

I entirely accept that I have not been the ideal boyfriend to almost all the women in my life, unless they happened to rank 'monosyllabic', 'awkward', and 'making them look brilliant on the dance floor' as standout qualities. 'All' is a slight exaggeration too. I met a beautiful and really lovely girl in Atlanta in Emilie – Em – and then I met Bev, who was and is amazing. Apart from that I was bloody rowing all the time.

I wouldn't say rowing made me selfish. I think full-time sportsmen and women have to be single-minded to the point of selfishness. It's not that I just thought of myself, it's that I didn't think of anyone – including myself, if that makes it any better. Admittedly it's not much of a defence, m'lord.

So things began poorly for me on the romantic front when Rachel Stovell turned me down three times in the third form at school. But at least I managed to lose my virginity in the least troubling way possible. A girl I'd been out with a few times, who wasn't at my school, decided I was in need of a jump start. I should have felt used and abused. But I didn't. It felt great.

Eventually, in the sixth form I went out with a girl called Siobhan and we were together long enough for her to come over and see me in Atlanta years later. We had a close relationship but one strangely better suited to being a decade or so older. I couldn't do what most twenty-year-old guys would do to show a girl a good time. By the Atlanta Olympics we were only 'together' in the loose sense. We hadn't seen each other for a year because she had been travelling round the world and I had been busy mucking around in a boat. I clearly wasn't my usual self in Atlanta and I didn't show her the most romantic time. We'd always been able to talk but now I couldn't even do that. Somehow Siobhan faded from the picture. Flying home in disgust. That left me free to drown my sorrows at the post-rowing party at the venue where the only music I or non-residents of the Southern US states could recognise was the Macarena song. Perhaps you could say we danced to it; at least it had set moves, handy as rowers are not normally blessed with rhythm. So there was a lot of hanging around the dance floor.

The most sought-after females were the lightweight crews (weighing under fifty-seven kilograms as opposed to in excess of ninety), but the problem at the Olympics is that there is only one double scull event for them, plus one reserve, so there are not nearly enough of them to go around – three per nation compared to thirty-plus blokes.

I'd had two days on the beer at that stage, so I was busy leaning on the bar, successfully avoiding the dancing. I got talking to Emilie, a lovely Danish reserve, who was very attractive. I hadn't seen her around but that was mostly because I'd been in quarantine. If I hadn't, I (like all the other rowers) would have noticed her.

I impressed her sufficiently with my Macarena moves (beer helped and the number of times the song was played enabled me to get a vague grasp of the routine) to be allowed to follow her back to where the Danish team were staying. A hotel rather than the Village. I'm sure nothing happened, mainly because I woke up in the hotel corridor. The Danish team had all gone. I was there on my own. The cheeky cow had left with not so much as a goodbye. I picked up a couple of other strays and we did the Walk – followed by a Bus Ride – of Shame back to the Village.

But the human spirit has a powerful ability to recuperate. In the second week of the Olympics, my mental state substantially shifted from being an Olympic-standard manic-depressive to an Olympic-standard drinker. I'm not a huge fan of official ceremonies but even I'm surprised I can't remember the Closing Ceremony at all. Perhaps because I shut it all out when it dawned on me what a failure it had all been. I saw Emilie once more in the Village but that was it, no number swapping. I'd like to rationalise that now by saying that I didn't own a mobile or have a place to live when I got back, so she wouldn't have been able to reach me at any number I gave her. In the unlikely event of her actually calling.

But months later I got her number from a Danish rower working in London who said Emilie had asked after me. Despite it being four months after Atlanta, I made her a tape of music and sent it to her. That's how backward and socially inept I was (never mind being trapped in the 80s). At least I made the compilation from CDs rather than recording songs like a cheapskate off the radio.

My taste in music must have done the trick because Emilie came to live with me in Henley while I was training for Sydney. I loved sharing a home together. Our different approaches to life were refreshing, although this ultimately ended up as something we couldn't overcome. I vegged out most of the time when I wasn't on the water – sorry, I mean rested, refuelled, recuperated and recovered – and it was great to not only have some company but her company. We didn't go out much and I'm afraid my practical side was much better developed than my romantic one. Sleep and food were my main highlights. It was not a terribly exciting world for a partner, especially one who had to diet for their sport while I was obliged to eat 6,000 calories a day. The wound was already there, and I was rubbing salt in it. I was so focused on rowing, I hardly noticed the strain Emilie felt.

Emilie was still trying out for selection herself in a Danish boat for the Sydney Olympics, but it was incredibly difficult when she lived away from home. Plus she was taking a graphic design course at university. It was hard trying to split her life in two different directions and then be there for me. In the end, I think it all became too difficult for her.

It all came to a head at the pairs trials in the spring of 2000, less than five months before the Olympics themselves. For a full month I just devoted every waking hour to the prospect of Tim and me beating Steve and Matt in the trials. It was going to be the last time the great men ever raced in a pair together. It was the last chance for anyone to beat them and if that was going to happen, I wanted Tim and I to be the ones to do it. I was overtaken by pure competitive drive. It dominated my every thought. It was my focus and motivation. When we succeeded I came back to Em feeling more relaxed and happy and thinking: 'Hooray, everything's wonderful.'

She didn't agree. 'I'm leaving,' she said.

There went the rug from under my feet. I was in shock. I shouldn't have been, I should have seen it coming, but typically I was looking in a different direction. I felt terrible. I was visibly, miserably upset. And right in the middle of it all I had been booked to go on a TV show (agents – you've got to love them) called *Game Girls* to talk about our gold medal prospects in Sydney. One of the show's hosts was a stunning girl called Beverley Turner.

We had a chat after the show. Masking my feelings was not one of my main assets and I mentioned that my now ex-girlfriend was moving out that day. She seemed concerned but we didn't overanalyse it. And I didn't fail to notice that she was good-looking, open, intelligent and, because she and her brother had been competitive swimmers, she seemed to understand the psychotic behaviour of sportsmen.

The day afterwards I had to drive up to Leeds for treatment on a sore hip. I called the programme's researcher and managed to persuade him to give me Bev's number. Surely fortune favours the brave, so I called and left a message. As it was the first time I'd ever made the first move with a girl, the least I deserved was for her to phone. I drove all the way up. And I drove all the way back from Leeds. There was no reply.

Nothing new there then. I wouldn't say I was comfortable in the presence of women. The shyness I had when I was younger was still there. I was never capable of charming them into bed in the first five minutes of conversation.

Here's a classic example. I was at a New Year's Eve party in Wales and solely due to the fact that I arrived late, driving down the M4 from London, I was in with a chance. All the Welsh guys were pissed by 10 p.m., at which point I'd just arrived. Some of the young ladies were in far better shape so it was a target-rich environment for a bloke who could actually stand up and string a sentence together. We were in a pub, a lock-in, on a farm and there were some cracking barns and outhouses. I managed to persuade a lovely young Welsh lady to accompany me outside as her 'date' hadn't even resurrected himself to see in the New Year and had left her very disappointed.

The barn was packed handily with hay so wasn't freezing cold (despite it now being 2 a.m. on 1 January 1993). Mind you, it wasn't the most waterproof and being vaguely gentlemanly in an attempt to get into the young lady's undergarments I volunteered her my coat and a blanket I'd found. They worked. Although not as I had imagined. She thought I was a nice guy and felt sufficiently comfortable in my company to fall soundly asleep.

[Bev]

It's early 2000, and the dawn of an exciting new concept called digital television. As crazy as it now sounds, ITV did not yet have its many cousins: ITV1, 2, 3, 4, +1 and so on. I was into my second year presenting the UK coverage of the NBA for good old-fashioned ITV. The head of sport, Brian Barwick, had secured the rights for the National Basketball Association of America – a gig that I'd won primarily on the back of the likes of Gabby Logan and Kirsty Gallacher. Female sports presenters were suddenly all the rage and I happened to be in the right place at the right time.

I'd been interviewing Dwight Yorke for a magazine called *Total Sport* and it was his agent who suggested me to Barwick. I was a freelance journalist, a former competitive swimmer and an ex-model who wasn't afraid to prat about in front of a camera so I can see how all the pieces fitted together. But I was no basketball expert and spent many hours trying (and often failing) to com-prehend the difference between the Eastern and Western Conferences; the LA Lakers and the New York Nicks; free throws and three-pointers.

The first series in 1999 was headed up by me and former Olympic runner Derek Redmond. We'd spend Friday afternoons in a white Soho dungeon delivering links about games we hadn't seen and trying not to descend into deeply unprofessional fits of giggles when Derek tried to get his tongue round names like 'Michael Olowokandi'. I adored working with Derek; we had lots of common acquaintances including his ex-wife, swimmer Sharron Davies. But after one series of the Saturday afternoon show, Derek decided life was too short to blag his way through the NBA – despite the fun of spending one weekend a month in America – and went off to run his many successful businesses. He also hated door-stepping the players with a microphone as they emerged from the showers wearing only a towel. Strangely, I never really minded that bit.

Brian Barwick was a loyal ally and mentor, keeping me busy with various gigs including ice hockey, British basketball and a brand-new show for his spanking new channel: ITV2. I was introduced to Trish Adudu, who was making a name for herself as a bubbly sports reporter on the new Channel 5 news bulletins. Trish had ambitions to produce TV (she is now an award-winning documentary maker) and had an idea to make a female-orientated sports chat show.

We shot a pilot called *Sports Shack*, with highlights that included Dwight Yorke in the studio doing the ironing. This morphed into *Game Girls* – a weekly chat show in which we basically interrogated and just fell short of sexually harassing unsuspecting male sports stars including boxer Audley Harrison, high-jumper Ben Challenger and a rower named James Cracknell.

I'd met this James guy once before. We had our photograph taken together at the end of 1999 alongside Dermot O'Leary in a women's magazine feature on 'Faces of 2000'. James had struck me as handsome but shy and oddly intense. And as I was madly in love with my boyfriend at the time, we shared little more than a brief chat about mutual friends (that swimming connection again).

By the time we met on the set of *Game Girls*, I was newly single and in no way looking for a fella. As always, the team had drinks afterwards in the Green Room and I found myself in the corner talking to James, who confessed to being in the midst of a break-up himself. He struck me as sweet and sort of wounded with a huge neon sign across his forehead that read 'Not-Over-Ex-Girlfriend. Keep Clear'. When I got to know him better, I could look back on that day and realise that he was just being James –

wearing his heart on his sleeve as his girlfriend was literally moving her stuff out of his house while we chatted. A few days later he called and left a message asking me to call him. Rarely in life have I had such an instinctive belief that the time was not right. I didn't ring. But I kept his number.

[James]

When Bev first met me on her TV show I'd been a miserable would-be Olympian with a failed romance on my way to Sydney as sidekick to the great Steve Redgrave. When we met again, at the airport, on our way to film a 'celebrity special' TV show called *Desert Forges* in Jordan, I was a happier Olympic gold medallist, now reunited with Emilie while repressing the knowledge that the relationship wouldn't last.

When I came home and Emilie came back from Denmark to try again as a couple, I did attempt really hard to include her in everything, all the post-Olympic celebrations. It was difficult though, because unless you were Steve Redgrave, with a knighthood pending, the invites weren't always plus one. It wasn't working out, our relationship. I suppose I knew that deep down but I was trying to solve the shallow problems first. I was making an effort to include her in things, which was one thing, but didn't ask myself the fundamental question: are we still right together?

She wasn't jealous of my success, but I suppose she was understandably resentful. She had, after all, been a rower herself. It made it doubly hard for her that her dad had won the gold medal in Tokyo 1964 in the coxless four – the same boat as us – so I was the would-be 'golden son-in-law'.

Still, in the spirit of trying to include her, when *Desert Forges* came up in Jordan we'd decided that I'd waive the fee but take her with me for a romantic break in the Middle East. This goes to show my inability to understand what most females mean by 'romantic break' and my ignorance of world politics. It all kicked off between Israel and Palestine, so Em and I decided it might not be best for her to come. That's when I met Bev again.

Emilie knew of Beverley because she had a friend who had been at Manchester University at the same time as Bev. As a former model and a very outgoing and highly intelligent girl on her way to a first class honours degree in English, Bev had been – in Emilie's friend's estimation – intolerable. When I came back, Em just assumed I'd slept with Bev, which I hadn't. I wouldn't have done that to her.

But the damage had been done. It provoked the final argument. And Emilie and I broke up for the second, and last, time.

[Bev]

I'd flown out of Sydney as everyone else was arriving for the Olympic Opening Ceremony. I'd had a blissful fortnight visiting two old friends that I had lived with in Australia for nine months two years previously. I was glad of the break as life was busy: I was presenting a late-night music show, *Videotech*, on ITV; continuing with the NBA; popping up on shows like *This Morning*, *Never Mind the Buzzcocks* and all of those cheap 'talking head' documentaries that were so popular in the early new millennium. I was writing for a few magazines and newspapers while still harbouring ambitions to write books one day, and dating a lovely, funny journalist who I'd met when he was interviewing me for an article. I was still living with my sister Cal and old friend Lauren in a rented house in Chiswick, spending the weekends in dressing gowns, drinking tea and watching TV, nursing hangovers and reliving various late-night shenanigans. Our lengthy conversations would be regularly interrupted by one of us dashing from the room after being on the verge of wetting our pants with laughter.

Our parents would often come down from Manchester and I'd get home as much as I could. Mum absolutely loved the fact that I was on the television. She'd never brag, but I imagine she set the hairdresser's alight, getting her blow-dry and talking about Our Bev in London! While Mum sometimes couldn't hide her disappointment if we swam badly at a gala, our parents have always been brilliant at giving praise. They are two very different characters, which my brother Adrian summed up perfectly when we gave an interview to the *Sunday Times'* 'Relative Values' section: 'If Mum was the waves pushing us on, Dad was the rock to cling to. If we'd had two mums, we'd have gone mad and with two dads we'd never have got out of bed.'

As always, I rang Mum when I was offered a little job for Channel 5 – a new game show called *Desert Forges*. 'Like *Fort Boyard* in the desert,' my agent said. 'You'll be on the celebrity special. I don't know who the other people are. You'll have to ride camels and stuff.'

I arrived at the airport looking forward to a few nights in the Jordanian desert, feeling incredibly lucky to be getting these bizarre but fun opportunities. An assistant producer introduced me to Kate Charman, presenter of *Guinness World Records*, and Darren Campbell, Olympic runner. 'And this is your teammate . . .'

James looked completely different. The hair was the same – blond-ish and messy – and he was tanned from the Australian sunshine, but it was his demeanour, the eye contact that had changed. He stood taller and held out his hand. The old shyness was still there, but he was a different man. 'Hi, Beverley, er, we've met before.'

'James!' I was genuinely pleased to see a friendly face. Especially one at a height of six foot four with wide shoulders and sparkly eyes.

Kate Charman has since become a great friend and is one of the funniest women I know. She now has three young children in the Wiltshire countryside and runs a stupidly beautiful home while her husband Jason Durr acts his way between London and Hollywood. But for one weekend in October 2000, she was the outrageous potty-mouthed TV presenter who made us all drink too much vodka and end up at a karaoke bar singing Jennifer Rush's 'The Power of Love' with two Olympic champions. Actually, it was Kate and Darren who sang, James and I were both far too shy to do that and were frankly too busy enjoying one another's conversation. But I'd also like to blame Kate for the fact that the whole production crew ended up skinny-dipping in the sea outside the hotel at 3 a.m., despite the fact that Darren Campbell can't swim and had to be dragged naked and spluttering onto a floating pontoon as the Jordanian moonlight reflected off his backside.

Earlier that day James and I had proved to be pretty much useless at the game show's physical tasks. Covering short distances put Campbell at a considerable advantage and Kate somehow managed to win every event while looking glamorous and offering pithy remarks to the cameras. I recall ending up defeated, face down with a mouthful of sand.

By 'End of Part One', Team Turner–Cracknell was out, leaving Campbell–Charman to go for the gold ingots that they would need at the final 'Forge' stage. In keeping with the show's theme, James and I were chained together for two hours in a Bedouin tent where we could watch our adversaries on a monitor being generally brilliant and entertaining during each subsequent challenge.

There was nothing else to do but talk. James confessed that even though he had got back together with Emilie, the girlfriend that he had broken up with when we last met, things were tricky after the Olympics. I could sympathise – with her as much as with him! I'd known several swimmers who struggled to make the adjustment after an Olympics and some who had retired from sport without ever really finding a new identity that made them happy. I felt for the girl. I bet this good-looking bloke could be really hard work . . .

But he was very calm. He reminded me of a surfer: laidback and contemplative; tanned and healthy but with the soul of a searcher – I could see it, even then. This was a man who would probably find it hard to be happy and satisfied with his achievements. I had to push him to talk about his win in Sydney – he put it down to just being in a boat with Redgrave and Pinsent.

On the plane back home, he reached across the seat and his hand gently brushed the back of my neck. It sounds ridiculous but that was when I knew that this man was my future husband. At the airport, we didn't want to say goodbye. We both knew that if we could feel so attracted to another person, our current relationships were probably living on borrowed time.

A day after arriving home, and after a couple of texts, James turned up on my doorstep. We walked to a pub on the Thames and he stayed the night, sharing my bed but sleeping in his trousers. It was a mild October night and we awoke sweltering at 3 a.m.. 'Bloody hell, James, you can take off your trousers – I won't accost you!' Emilie had still not moved out of their home. 'No,' he insisted. 'It's not right.'

'In that case, can you not wear jumbo cords next time? I'm baking here.'

But it was sweet and honourable and gentlemanly. He was the perfect antidote to the risk-taking, showbizzy types I was used to meeting. His clean-living morality was refreshing and reassuring. He was trustworthy and devoted to his sport. Despite staying up until after midnight, sober but chatting and snogging in the way that only new lovers do, he still left at 6 a.m. to drive to training at Henley. I listened to his car leaving, full of respect for such commitment. And went back to sleep for three hours.

A few weeks later we attended a charity event in London. The next day the papers ran headlines such as 'Slam Dunk! NBA Bev bags rower' and 'Basketball Bev Dates Oarsome Cracknell'. It wasn't the first time I'd been linked with blokes in the press, but it was the first time that it didn't cause even a ripple of difficulty. We laughed at the number of basketball-related quips that could be fitted in a paragraph and the fact that in the accompanying photos James appeared to have a bouffant.

I knew that James would never be photographed falling out of a nightclub at 2 a.m. into the arms of a Page 3 girl. He was definitely naive (or simply inexperienced) when it came to newspapers, but I had no anxiety about his ability to keep his trousers on. He'd already proven that in a bed with me!

I soon took James home to meet my parents and brother, knowing that as two families who endured the travails of minority sports, they'd get along well. We drove up north in my convertible Saab and chatted about our families. I warned James that our house was small but our welcome was big, and if we stayed together my mum would treat him as one of her own. This would mean lots of love, loyalty and support, but also the odd bollocking if she felt he was out of line.

We went to Nutters Restaurant in Lancashire, a fabulous place owned by accomplished chef Andrew Nutter, a friend from primary school. Mum didn't look convinced about this rowing chap, until I announced that he used to be a geography teacher and she visibly relaxed: one day he could get a proper job!

On the motorway journey back to London, James asked what I liked about him. I didn't hesitate. 'You're safe, stable and secure.' I'd meant it as a compliment.

'Oh great!' he replied, laughing. 'Not sexy, dangerous and adventurous then?'

'In my experience, such qualities are highly over-rated.' If only I'd known.

[James]

Things moved quickly between Bev and me, which is how, one year after we'd been teammates in Jordan, I found myself about to propose to the woman I loved. I'd planned this with military precision. What could possibly go wrong? While we were on holiday in Croyde Bay, North Devon, I decided to surprise Beverley with the question. I didn't want just to drift into an engagement. So, with the collusion of her sister, I designed a ring for Bev and planned to ask her to marry me at sunset on the beach. I wanted it to be as romantic as possible.

And didn't I cock it up. Not in the sense that I asked the wrong person. It was just the aesthetics weren't quite as I'd expected.

We'd been out for our evening meal but somehow, a harmless discussion about work had fallen into bickering and I'd missed my moment. It was October, dark and cold, but I reckoned we could manage a moonlit saunter along the beach.

'Let's go for a walk,' I said as we left Billy Budd's, the pub we were staying in.

'No,' she said. 'It's freezing. I'm tired.'

'What, not even a short stroll on the beach?' I cajoled.

'No, our room is literally here.' I'd forgotten to account for Bev's strong opinion on most matters.

So, like the Marines, I had to 'change and adapt'.

'Er, OK.' I took a deep breath. 'I thought I'd show you the campsite I used to stay at.' She looked at me as though I was mad. So I started the prepared material there and then. 'Because you're the most amazing woman I've ever . . . I thought you might . . . marry me.'

'No!' she howled. 'Not in front of the fudge shop!'

So we went round the corner and in my confusion I went down on two knees rather than one to finish the deed and give her the ring. Gratifyingly, she cried.

Driving up to Manchester the next day, I found her staring at the ring. Not in an 'aaaah' way, more in an 'Oh God, I'm stuck with this for the rest of my life' way.

'What's wrong?' I asked, my sixth sense skills clearly working better than my ring designing ones had.

'No, it's all right,' she said in the sort of tone women use when it's not all right.

Outcome: the ring was melted down and we started again, ending up with a ring that she was delighted with. But the overall result was the same. I was engaged to Beverley Turner. And I was the happiest man alive.

There followed, as is the way in life, a stag night, a wedding and a honeymoon which were all memorable in their own way – not that I remember the end of at least two of them! The stag night was a little weird because I had to train right up to the wedding in order to have three weeks off for the honeymoon afterwards. It coincided with a set of international sprint races on the Serpentine in which I was competing in a pair. So there was no question of the lads and I embarking on a trip to Prague or Ibiza or wherever blokes normally choose to go to lose an eyebrow and chain themselves naked to the local lamp post/stripper.

We only had one night and we needed everything in one place (especially because of our uncanny ability to lose each other if we are not within a five-metre radius). Meal, bar, club. So we found somewhere off Leicester Square. Me, my mates, some rowing guys, Matt Dawson and my dad. Dawson was a wise addition. He turned out to be terrific at making sure my dad got steaming drunk. This worked on two levels – Dawson's attention was focused on someone else, and my dad's inappropriate comments became incomprehensible.

At one point my dad, always an accountant at heart, went to the bar and asked for 'Twenty tequila vodka Red Bulls, please.'

The lady behind the bar said: 'That's two hundred and fifty pounds.'

He was stunned. 'That's a family holiday!' he spluttered. I thought he was going to get thrown out.

He phoned my mum in the morning from his office's over-night accommodation and told her: 'It was all very good except I appear to have lost my trousers.' He spent hours looking for them before eventually discovering that when he rolled in at 4 a.m. he had put them neatly in the Corby trouser press.

He sobered up enough in time to send me a letter on the eve of the wedding. It read: 'James, well, here we are, the happiest day of your life. You don't need us to tell you how lucky you are to be marrying Beverley – she is a fantastic girl. Mum and I wish you every happiness. As for me, I shall watch you both with pride and be thinking back to all those times I said "Don't do that". Don't resign from the school boat club. Do you really want to buy 141 Reading Road? I wouldn't go on after Sydney. You were right. I was wrong. I guess you will always be an independent spirit, and rightly so. You now have the perfect mate (in every sense of the word) to go on with through life. Look after her. All our love, Mum and Dad.'

[Bev]

By the eve of our wedding, James and I had barely seen each other for ten weeks. I'd had an amazing time reporting on the Tour de France for ITV, driving across spectacular scenery, staying in a different hotel every night for two weeks, eating brie and baguettes and interviewing men-machines such as Lance Armstrong on the top of Alpe d'Huez. Before and after that trip, I'd been away most weekends at the F1 Grand Prix – feeling like an outsider as everyone around me grew excited at traction control, obscenely expensive yachts and the ability to flout rules about cigarette advertising to developing nations. It was not my natural habitat. James was hanging around various European waterways getting stressed about rowing in a pair with Matt Pinsent and being generally rubbish on the phone every time we managed to speak.

As with every other bride I've ever met, wedding organisation was a purely female pursuit and one wall of our office at home was completely covered in Post-it notes. I oscillated between resenting the responsibility of single-handedly organising an event for 150 people and feeling terrified that anything left to James would be at worst, forgotten and at best, half-arsed.

At midday on 10 October 2002, I said my vows, having absolutely no doubt that I was marrying the right man. He wasn't perfect: he could be grumpy and anti-social when rowing wasn't going well; he could do better in the romance department and was the messiest man I'd ever met, but this struck me as a relatively short 'to-do' list to carry down the aisle.

Clearwell Castle in the Forest of Dean was the perfect venue for us: grand but not ostentatious; ceremonial but secular; pretty and rural but convenient for guests. Plus it had a great dungeon with stags' antlers on the wall where we could dance till 1 a.m., after which our mates would stumble down the hill to the B&Bs in the village. My eighty-year-old aunty Nora made a beautiful white wedding cake and the chef from the Leander Club created an elaborate chocolate castle, which was served up at the disco and mopped up by the edge of my dress along with spilt beer and red wine.

At 11 p.m. it was scheduled that we would all assemble on the castle ramparts to watch fireworks across the Forest of Dean. At 9 p.m. the venue manager came and asked if I'd heard from the fireworks people. I located James and got him to focus through his drunken haze. 'Baby, you know you had one job? The fireworks? Remember the fax?'

'Yeah, yeah, I did it . . .' He was dragged back onto the dance floor by Pat and Cath, my mum's oldest friends and fellow darts players. But by 10 p.m., when there was still no sign of the fireworks people, I asked him again. This time, he looked off into the distance, as a foggy memory came into focus. 'Ah . . . I was meant to fax them the confirmation wasn't I?'

We put the fireworks budget behind the bar, and at the pub the next day, everyone agreed it was a good thing – who wouldn't have preferred a vodka Red Bull to a Catherine wheel?

It was simply a brilliant day. My dress had a stupidly big bustle (I had to sit back to front on the toilet) but I felt fabulous; fortunate and full of optimism for our future.

[James]

Our wedding day was fantastic. One standout moment was Bev's dad's speech where he made mention of my glittering career. 'James makes a boat go faster backwards,' he said, 'which, I suppose, is a good thing.' I thought that just about summed it up.

And so we were ready for the honeymoon, to which I had given some thought. Give me credit. I wanted it to be a romance-packed, unforgettable road trip and so I'd decided to splash out on the 'top of the range' – such as it is with Cruise America – thirty-five-foot, seven-berth campervan. We flew into Boston, where I spent a few days pretending to be interested in Harvard University and a couple of museums around the place, before picking up our van.

It was impressive. It had a double bedroom at the back, separate shower, toilet, kitchen, and lounge. Ahead of us was the open road to America. Our rough plan was to set off through Salem and then see the Niagara Falls. I was a geography teacher once, after all, and the desire to show Bev a geographical feature, even if slightly clichéd, was irresistible.

[Bev]

The campervan trip was James's idea. But harbouring wonderful memories of childhood caravan holidays and having had my fair share of stuffy hotel rooms over the past year, I could picture the beauty of the open road: American diners at dawn; no deadlines to meet; impromptu roadside stops and a bed as a permanent companion!

James was adamant that we opt for the biggest motorhome we could afford, so with the words 'I'm going to spoil you baby!' ringing in my ears, we collected our Recreational Vehicle. Weirdly, the Sade track, 'By Your Side' – which accompanied my walk down the aisle – came on the local radio as we pulled out onto the highway. We exchanged 'Aah' looks as we dismounted the kerb and with an almighty clatter, plates, cups and a surprise step ladder leapt from their hiding places and rained down upon us.

We set off towards Salem, Massachusetts, circled the town five times and discovered that the visitors' centre was closed. We had no 'campground directory' and would need to find four empty parking meter spaces if we were ever to stop our thirty-five-foot beast. We did a sixty-three-point turn in a supermarket car park and headed for the coastal town of Gloucester, stumbling across the Cape Ann Campsite and beginning a trend of arriving at every location in the dark.

It had started to sleet and the campsite owner looked bemused as she took our fee for a one-night stay and gestured in the general direction of a very large field before heading back to her warm sofa in front of the TV.

Neither of us had ever been very good at reading instruction manuals, but how hard could it be to plug a twenty-first-century RV into an electricity supply? After twenty minutes on the phone to the Cruise America helpline, we concluded that the campsite's plug socket must be faulty, so we executed another sixty-three-point turn and snuggled the love bus into another berth. No joy. I called the campsite owner in my best polite English-idiot voice, and she trudged reluctantly up the hill with her hood pulled tightly around her head. She glanced at the socket and flicked the 'on' switch. I cowered, mortified, beneath the window. James offered cookies to her hunched shoulders but she didn't look back. 'We,' announced James with an element of triumph, 'are not only the most stupid people in America, we are the most stupid people on a *trailer park* in America.'

I ate dinner of pasta with a tea towel tucked in my collar, conscious that I'd have to keep the same clothes clean for three weeks. The Pinsents were currently honeymooning on a private island in Fiji. James looked at me cursing as I got pasta sauce on my sleeve and started the catchphrase of the holiday, 'Who needs Fiji, eh, baby?' We went to bed laughing at our stupidity and realised we were still only twenty minutes outside of Boston.

We woke up utterly frozen. We could actually see our breath. James had got up at some point in the night to put on furry long johns. 'At three o'clock I tried to see if you were still breathing,' he said romantically, 'but I couldn't move my head as it was frozen to the pillow.'

Once the heating was turned on, tea made and breakfast poured we attempted to plan our journey with only a map of America on such a grand scale that our current town didn't even feature. And things were about to get worse.

The RV had two water tanks – one for fresh water and one for waste. Emptying and refilling these tanks is the bane of the RV user's life, but the ten-foot hose attached to the van means the procedure should be quick and clean. Unless your hose snaps the first time you use it.

Perhaps James was showing off his manly strength as I captured the intricacies of sewage disposal on the video camera, but with one swift pull, the ten-foot hose became a nine-foot hose dangling from his hand with just one foot still attached to the van.

Positioning that over the small circular grids at campgrounds was going to take some nifty parking.

Cruise America suggested buying another hose. James suggested nicking one off someone else's van during the night – the words of a man already nearing his limit.

Only the scenery on the way to Vermont was keeping us calm. We swept north through New Hampshire, finding the Goodwood Lodge Campsite in the dark. That night I slept in trousers, two jumpers, a woolly hat and gloves. But it wasn't totally unromantic. We did zip the sleeping bags together. Unfortunately, James's broad shoulders acted like a three-foot tent pole when he lay on his side and the cold wind blew in, down my back. He thought I was being romantic as I snuggled into him, but I was actually using him as a windbreak.

In the morning we discovered we were parked in a field of yellow diggers. It was freezing cold, raining hard and blowing a gale, just in time for the red light to come on warning us to empty the sewage tank. I watched my new husband crouched over a tiny hole with one foot of pipe, hoping that he wouldn't notice the sneaky poo I'd had when it was too cold to go outside.

Ten hours of ceaseless rain later, and realising that every campground closed for the end of season on 15 October (the previous day), we made a decision: it was time for a hotel (with a large car park). The Lang House's warm hallway was all shiny creaking floors, floral prints and the smell of baking bread. There was a choice of pillows, a TV and a shower that could be used without first turning on a pump.

As the capital of Vermont, Burlington is a sophisticated little town of cosy candle-lit restaurants and intimate bars. We got dressed up and headed out in a cab only to be stopped at a door for not having our passports. 'I'm *very* flattered,' I beseeched the boy-bouncer, 'but do you really think I'm younger than twenty-one?'

'Sorry, ma'am, it's the law.'

James ran the fifteen-minute journey back to the hotel in the rain. I think he had some aggression to get rid of.

We woke with hangovers but at least we weren't dressed for hiking. It was a bright and breezy one-hour ferry trip to Lake Placid in New York State. We drank hot tea on the deck, relieved to be finally out of a raincoat, and then drove through the Adirondack mountains as Eva Cassidy's 'Fields of Gold' played as another apt soundtrack to the spectacular autumnal vista. I'd catch glimpses of James, looking ahead, driving carefully through wet, winding roads, and be overwhelmed with love for him: strong and capable – or maybe it was just the sight of a man in charge of his rig, the Yorkie effect.

But the contentment didn't last long. We arrived at the Winter Olympics venue too late for a tour; got lost trying to find Lake Placid itself and passed the same restaurant three times looking for our campsite. By the time we did find it – in the dark – James took pity on me and sent me to bed with a book to 'relax and warm up'. He performed a comedy routine in the rain as I watched from my sleeping bag and he pretended to be blown about by the gale as he hooked up our water and electricity. We had nothing for dinner except instant pancake mix, one blueberry bagel and a tube of (disgusting) squeezy cheese. Not even milk for tea. But none of that mattered. We were stupidly in love.

[James]

I got my revenge for Bev flouting the no crapping in the trailer policy: my trailer trash diet. She came in and found me crunching a Dorito while sucking on a can of squeezy cheese and then eating a cracker. A glorious routine I repeated until one or the other had run out. Cheese and biscuits, a la trailer park. Bev was not loving my choice of food, including – perhaps especially – my addition of pancake mix to go with the squeezy cheese. Not to mention squeezy chocolate and squeezy strawberry sauce. But any further culinary adventures were curtailed by the discovery that our battery was flat. I obviously blamed the bears for coming in and listening to the radio, so we had to get a neighbour to give us a jump start. 'It's all part of the joys of camping,' he laughed. I think Bev wanted to punch him in the face.

It wasn't all bad. It had stopped raining and here was our romantic liaison in the car park at Walmart (the advantage of an RV) en route to Niagara Falls, followed by the novelty of shopping in a store where you can buy shotguns and cuddly toys in adjacent aisles under the same roof.

Our diet significantly improved when we went on a tour of the Ben and Jerry's ice cream factory, where they stressed the local, sustainable and community aspects of their business. Unable to resist when the guide asked if there were any questions, I enquired as to why they'd just sold out to Proctor & Gamble. This did not push us to the front of their free sample line.

[Bev]
In Niagara we had a revelation: we could keep the heating on at night without flattening the battery! I woke in celebratory mood – not even caring that I'd reached the end of my clean knickers – and took a hot shower. Sadly, I didn't realise that the tank needed emptying until I saw my wedding pedicure in three inches of water that wasn't draining away. We couldn't drive to the disposal area

as the water would have splashed all over the floor of the van. All we could do was empty the shower tray with a cup into a pan and then empty the pan outside. James wasn't amused, especially when I tried to be helpful by doing the washing up. 'What are you doing?' he yelled, crouched on the floor. 'A plughole is a plughole! A tank is a tank!'

The next morning was my birthday and exactly two years since we shared our first kiss. James woke early and sneaked out, returning with a birthday cake fashioned from marshmallows, ablaze with twenty-nine candles. 'Oh wow!' I effused. 'You said you were going for a poo, you old romantic.' But his efforts didn't stop there. While I went for a swim in the campsite's indoor pool, he made breakfast and cleared up! That's really all I've ever wanted in life.

The residents of our next stop would have been proud of him: Seneca Falls – the birthplace of the Women's Rights Movement in 1848. We wandered around the thought-provoking feminist exhibition but unfortunately none of the electrical displays were working. James sidled up behind me and whispered – a little too loudly – 'They wanna get a man in here . . .'

[James]

The visit to Niagara Falls concerned me slightly. I wanted to take Bev across to the more impressive Canadian side, but that meant going through the US–Canadian border and I wasn't sure whether my previous arrest for 'being intoxicated in a public place' would have me black-flagged on their computer. I decided to be the most polite Englishman in the world. 'Oh hello, officer. Lovely day. Of course, by all means, do have my passport. Cracker? Squeezy cheese? My wife and I . . .'

It kind of worked, marred only by hysterics from Bev at my bizarre behaviour.

There were other memorable moments in our trailer. We went flash one day and decided to have a takeaway pizza delivered, and there was the time that a neighbour popped his head in the window to find Bev over my knee being (jokily) reprimanded. But, in general, we decided that the time had come to trade the beast in for something a little more practical, like a 4x4. A double win for Bev as it meant we got to stay in hotels for the second half of the journey, unless I could convince her to kip in the back of the wagon. If I could, it would be concrete evidence that I'd married the right girl.

In anticipation of this great event, we hadn't thought about food. We'd assumed we'd eat at a local bar where we dropped off the trailer, but in the event Bev didn't like the look of it. So we ended up having to dig a day-old pizza out of a bin. Impressively, this was Bev's idea not mine. It was that ability to adapt to any situation that made me love her so much. There is certainly no doubting that we had fully embraced the spirit of the trailer lifestyle.

[Bev]

With typical ineptitude we arrived at the Grand Canyon in the dark. We knew it was out there. We just couldn't see it. And we were busy avoiding large wildlife in the headlights of our new silver 4x4. But the next morning, with the constant moving wearing me down, we checked into our hotel to be greeted by an adorable Estonian boy who asked if we'd like a room 'overlooking the forest or the parking lot'. We laughed in disbelief, opting for the forest after a few seconds' mock consideration.

James had to ask. 'Has anyone ever said parking lot?'

'In three months,' the receptionist said in his wonderfully strong Eastern European accent, 'not one person has said parking lot. I have three weeks left. I want just one person to say that before I leave.'

That day was my honeymoon highlight: a six-mile hike down the Grand Canyon. I set about collecting a few provisions from the local store as James shook his head. 'It's a half day, Bev, we're not scaling the north face of the Eiger.' But I was genuinely nervous that he would expect me to perform on the same level as an international athlete. And besides, alongside the warnings of dehydration, hypothermia and falling, the brochure recommended that hikers 'Eat twice your normal daily calories.' I need not have worried.

Despite insisting we take many warm layers in case the weather turned, I was soon baking in the sunshine and resorted to walking in my bra while James trudged behind carrying drink, food, cameras, sunscreen and many spare jumpers. Occasionally, one of us would look up and utter the erudite observation, 'It's bloody massive.' James checked his watch the second we stepped out of the canyon. 'Excellent. Three and a half hours – the brochure said that would take six.'

The vulgarity of Las Vegas came as a shock after the beauty of the Grand Canyon. We checked into a suite at the Venetian with floor-to-ceiling windows looking out onto the main strip. In Vegas we watched Cirque du Soleil; partook of some timid gambling; dined well; bought some new clothes and missed the campervan not one jot. But we knew it was time to leave when the indoor gondolas and fake clouds on the ceiling started to look quite classy.

[James]
An exciting 'just-like-the-movies' moment occurred while driving out of the desert towards Los Angeles. I saw a highway

Left: me aged 4. The last time I wore collars wider than my shoulders. Right: me, aged 11, and Louise, aged 8. I'm clearly unhappy that she has more swimming badges and longer shorts than me.

Above: mum (Jennie), Louise, Me (21) and Dad (John) at my parents' silver wedding anniversary party in 1993. My freebie T-shirt supports the Manchester 2000 Olympic bid (I clearly dressed up for the occasion).

Below: Kingston-upon-Thames Grammar School's First Eight, 1989, Head of the River Race. Those desperate expressions suggest we've still got 10 minutes to go.

Moments after the 5th Olympic Gold for the Big Fella (Sir Steve Redgrave).
I'm not letting go of those coattails.

Bellies in, chests out, adopt camp hip stance (Sydney 2000).

If 5 gold medals means you get a sweaty hug from Matt Pinsent, I'm glad I've only got 2 (Sydney 2000).

My favourite photo of all time just out of the boat before we had seen or spoken to anyone else (Sydney 2000).

10th October 2002: the wedding of James Cracknell and Beverley (claw-hand) Turner in the Forest of Dean.

Hot tea on the open deck. Our 'luxury' 8 berth honeymoon motorhome, crossing from Burlington, Vermont to Lake Placid.

The start of the honeymoon, windswept on Wingaersheek Beach, Boston, Massachusetts. What could possibly go wrong?

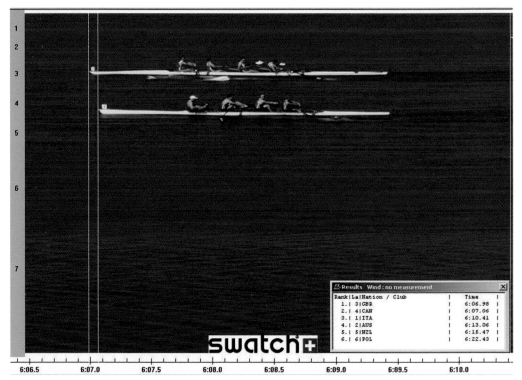

Rank	La	Nation / Club	Time
1.	3	GBR	6:06.98
2.	4	CAN	6:07.06
3.	1	ITA	6:10.41
4.	2	AUS	6:13.06
5.	5	NZL	6:15.47
6.	6	POL	6:22.43

Photofinish in Athens Olympic final. The most important 6 inches of my life.

40°C in Athens, 2004: fans showing the same spirit that made London 2012 so special (you can bet there's always a big banana).

I like to think I'm shouting, "Thanks for the race! Three cheers for Canada!"

I knew all that training was going to pay off, not just the Olympic gold but a kiss from a beautiful lady and I hadn't even ditched the sweaty lycra.

James holding 11-month-old Croyde on the podium at the Athens Olympics, before passing him back with the words, 'You gotta earn it, little man'.

patrol car sitting on a ridge as we sped by and then admired its wheel spin in a cloud of dust as it set off in pursuit of some speeding idiot. It took me a little while to realise that *I* was that idiot and it was chasing *us* down. Much to Bev's amusement, I once again became the most polite, posh English bloke in America as the police stopped us and searched the car. 'Oh, good afternoon, officer, can I tempt you with some squeezy cheese . . .?'

In LA we stayed near Venice Beach, in the Hotel California, 1670 Ocean Avenue, Santa Monica. Bev was initially impressed that the hotel had been built in 1670, which would indeed have been impressive given that the *Mayflower* only arrived in Massachusetts in 1620. I had to sadly disillusion her. 'It's the address, baby.'

We hired bicycles to cycle along Venice Beach and gaze at all the weirdos – sorry, 'flamboyant individuals' – on the beach, and went to an LA Lakers game at the Staples Center. I'm a massive admirer of the ballers' skills but my admiration was lower than Bev's, who, worryingly for me, had seen most of them in the locker room when she was covering the sport for ITV. The crowd aren't anywhere near as spontaneous as football crowds in Britain. They basically shout what is on the screen above the court and manage to eat their bodyweight in snacks during the game. There weren't any away fans so it was a chance to catch up with friends whilst Kobe Bryant and his mates did their thing in the background.

From about halfway through the honeymoon, I'd tried to ensure I went running every day. Admittedly not the most romantic of gestures but I wanted to make sure that when I pitched up for training again, my body didn't go into total shock. It did its job. At least I coped better than Bev on our return who had a few jetlag issues. I went training on the first day at 8 a.m. and when I came home again at 2 p.m., I found her still in bed. I was impressed that she could actually lie in that long without getting bedsores.

Bev and I learnt a lot about each other in our time away. She learnt that I could drive non-stop for nine hours if given a finish line, enough cookies and a can of squeezy cheese. I'd learnt never to trust her map-reading skills. And thanks to that RV, we'd discovered that despite the situation, we could make each other laugh.

'Who needs Fiji, eh, baby?'

4

[James]

Sometimes you have to remind yourself just how bad things are. After Sydney I decided to keep a diary of the next four years so that the golden glow of winning didn't lull me into forgetting what the emotional and physical ups and downs of four years' hard training for an Olympics was really like. I wanted to document the shit time, hard work and emotional turmoil that gets lost and forgotten among the chaotic, elated aftermath of a gold medal followed by the relentless passion in chasing the one you haven't got. I wanted to remind myself how high the highs were but also how much I struggled when I felt I not only had to motivate myself but Matt as well.

I still have some of the diaries, pages of closely written words describing family, a newborn son, friends, broken ribs, geekily accurate training logs, boat speed, as well as a spillage of the frustrations and spectacular rows I had with both crew mates and Beverley. It wasn't all repetitive. I noted when I learnt a new word: 'fractious'. It was supposed to explain our new son's irrationally grumpy behaviour – but was swiftly commandeered by Bev and her mates to use it to describe their husbands.

But I am pleased to see, looking back, that sometimes my romantic side blasted through.

'Friday 10 October 2003 (First Wedding Anniversary): Bought Bev a plant and some red roses that matched our wedding flowers. That appears to have been the masterstroke as Jenny the midwife was round and they were saying husbands would never think of doing something as cool as getting wedding coloured flowers . . .'

On the other hand: as Tuesday 8 July 2003 describes it, Bev was 'chucking plates and smashing jugs'. I'm assuming this wasn't the final flourish of a Greek-themed dinner, more that I was going out to a rowing event that evening. We must have patched things up because an entry further on mentions 'great sex'. But the fact I'd been motivated to write it down as an occasion shows that the row had had an effect on me.

It may sound trivial, but much of my frustration at home stemmed from the fact I'd swapped sides in the new pair I had formed with Matt Pinsent. Without going into boring technical detail, it means that usually your oar sticks out of one side of the boat but now you swap hands and it sticks out of the other side. People very rarely swap sides, for the good reason that it's bloody difficult. It's like a tennis player suddenly changing from a single-handed groundstroke to a double-handed version or a golfer dismantling and rebuilding their swing. It's not impossible, but it won't feel as natural for a long time, if ever, and therefore you're not as consistent. My frustrations at home also came from the fact that I, unlike Matthew or Steve, wasn't good at leaving rowing and its associated problems at training. I carted them around in my head until I got back on the water the next day. I can't have been fun to live with.

There was a good reason that it was me who had to change sides and not Matt. As Sir Edmund says in *Blackadder Goes Forth*: 'The likelihood of the Western Front moving is the same as a Frenchman who lives next door to a brothel.' For 'Western Front' read 'Matt Pinsent'. I am not suggesting, by the way, that he does or ever did live in proximity to a house of ill repute (if he does it'll at least be a high-class one as he's got a nice gaff in West London); it's just that he's large and immovable. Even more so than I am. Which is saying something. So when one of us had to switch sides, it was pretty evident who that one would be. There was also a nice aside that only one athlete had claimed Olympic gold rowing on different sides of the boat. Yep, you've guessed it – Stevie boy!

This was a long-term added pressure that I could have done without, especially as it was internal. Some athletes win their Olympic gold medal and relax, feeling as though they have succeeded. But I'm not one of them. Mind you, I didn't have the best of role models. Matt went on to win four gold medals, Steve five and Jurgen had been winning them since the 1970s come to that. It must be something within the people who get attracted to the repetitive and masochistic 'pleasure' of rowing. We seem to go on and on. According to Bev, it's the same in almost every area of my life.

So after all the agonies of training for Sydney, I settled down for more, including trying to win again in Athens, marriage, fatherhood, taking on a law degree, suffering a broken rib and posing naked for Elton John's charity.

Obviously, something had to give. Slightly worryingly, I chose the law degree and still posed for Elton's charity! I'm guessing it's not a great loss to the Bar that I chose rowing over wearing a wig and defending villains. I like to think I'd have ended up putting my repetitive endurance to good use by arguing in a courthouse but the reality was as a trainee solicitor it would probably have been spent by the photocopying machine.

[Bev]

After the honeymoon we returned to normality with the small matter of the Athens Olympics on the horizon. Even though it was still 18 months away, our lives inevitably had to revolve around everything that was necessary to get James to that start line in the best possible shape. That date, 14 August 2004, was set in stone and non-negotiable.

I've always looked at the wives of sportsmen who follow their over-achieving beaux around the world with fascination and perhaps a little jealousy. It would be so much easier to check in and out of hotels, pausing only to buy expensive shoes in front of the paparazzi and to ensure your husband's room service is waiting for him, than to pursue your own ambitions – no matter how small. But if I was to adopt that role, I would quickly become a resentful, frustrated, irritating, hollow, alcoholic wreck (albeit with *much* better shoes).

I'd earned my own money since I started dabbling in the world of fashion modelling at fifteen. At Manchester University, I lived in a typically grim student house with mates, but enjoyed being able to buy an extra round of drinks, pay my own rent and treat myself to the occasional killer handbag. Those older models – nearing the ancient age of thirty! – who were searching for a wealthy husband were a portent of a future I was desperate to avoid. I was an old-fashioned feminist – albeit with a fondness for good moisturiser and regular waxing. I never longed for massive wealth, but took great comfort in financial independence. I can never quite shake off the realisation that women died so that my generation could have their own bank accounts. I knew that James was the man for me during a discussion of feminist linguistics and the reasons why I wouldn't take his name. 'Why should she?' he shrugged. 'There are no circumstances under which I'd change my name.' It wasn't quite the cultural analysis I was reaching for, but he succinctly summed up the disparity.

In January 2003, I was about to start another year working for ITV as one of the presenters on their coverage of F1. I was miserable. On day one the director took me to one side and said that they'd been told by ITV to bring 'a pretty female presenter on board'. Now, as I approach forty, I might accept such a statement with a certain coy glee. But as a proud twenty-nine-year-old looking to develop my journalism skills and to be taken 'seriously', I was floored. His attitude pretty much set the tone for the duration of my stay. I'd spend four days at a Grand Prix working on short videos to be used in the build-up to the race that might be dropped at the last minute. The other presenters would go silent when I walked into a room. It was a bizarrely competitive world of TV types who were constantly looking over their shoulders. I knew that my pieces would be inherently 'fluffy' as I looked wowed by the fireworks at the Monaco Ball or shopped 'excitedly' with the drivers' wives. I became rather good at acting thrilled to step out of a helicopter in high heels beside a driver who might grunt something trite at my awful questions. I was at best underwhelmed and at worst, embarrassed.

I'd return to James at our home in Henley feeling lost and demoralised. I had a good contract and my own mortgage to pay.

As a jobbing presenter, I was incredibly lucky. Millions of people would swap jobs with me. But that knowledge merely added to the guilt I was already feeling. So, during a good moan over a glass of wine to a friend who had just landed a job at a successful publishing house, the idea of *The Pits* was born: a warts-and-all analysis of F1 from the inside: the invidious ways in which the sport swerved tobacco-advertising restrictions; the psychology of the drivers; the friction of business versus sport and the challenges of being a woman in that testosterone-filled world. It would be tough – I'd get a small advance and need to write 90,000 words by December 2003 while also working at the Grand Prix. But I was driven by the need to do something that I could be proud of.

And then I got pregnant.

[James]
Having decided to carry on rowing, anything other than winning gold would mean I'd wasted four years. On the plus side, I had already proved I could do it and having a guy with eight-and-a-half-litre lungs hanging around in your boat isn't the worst situation to be in. However, we only had one day off every seven weeks and if Jurgen had been allowed his way it would have been just one day and on a fixed date – yep, 29 February. So family life and rowing didn't blend well.

At first, at least from the outside, it seemed as though we were adjusting well to life in a new boat, especially if the annual World Championships were any guide. Matt and I raced two events – the coxed and the coxless pairs – at Lucerne 2001. With the Olympics still three years away, it was a challenge that appealed to us. It also appealed to Jurgen as no pair had ever won both events at a world championships or Olympics. In fact, Steve Redgrave and Andy Holmes had come the closest, winning gold and silver in 1987 and following that up with gold and bronze at the 1988 Seoul Olympics a year later. Jurgen fancied being the first guy to coach a crew to achieve the double. I'd be lying if I said the appeal of winning two gold medals in different boats, especially now the events were held within two hours of each other rather than on consecutive days, didn't at least partially fill the motivational difference I felt in preparing for a World Championships rather than an Olympics. Plus I had Matt's motivation to consider.

In 1998 he'd shocked me two weeks out from the World Championships when he said in a crew meeting that he was bored and struggling to get himself up and going. I couldn't relate to that. Admittedly, at the time, I'd won a single World Championships and no Olympics whereas Matt had five Worlds and two Olympics in the bag. But that comment had stuck with me and I was aware that with ten global titles on the mantelpiece he might find this year tough without an extra challenge.

What made it even more difficult was that unlike previous years the finals were now scheduled just two hours apart. So it meant we'd have to warm up, race, wind down, cool down, recover, warm up and be ready on the start line two hours after we'd sat on it the first time. In reality, that meant we'd only get around thirty minutes on dry land. With our premier event and the one with the tougher competition – the coxless pair – on second, we'd be tired from the first one and the opposition would be even more motivated to beat us. The Redgrave effect was still in play: never mind what we'd won over the last four years alongside Steve (over a decade for Matt), to our opposition we'd just been in the right place at the right time to be pulled along by him. I'm not going to argue with my good fortune to have ridden his coat tails for four years but they didn't know what went on in our boat and you underestimate – and wind up – Matt at your peril.

We won the coxed race by as small a margin as possible, less than 0.4 seconds, to conserve energy (Matt's mantra for life), warmed down, warmed up and got ourselves back on the water for the second race. We'd lied to each other throughout the warm-up – or at least I lied to Matt – about how fresh we felt. But by halfway in the second race there was no hiding the fact that we weren't exactly fresh, passing the 1,000m mark in fourth, five seconds behind a crew we'd beaten in the semi-final. I knew what the other crews would be thinking as I'd have thought the same: 'We've got those fuckers now! Arrogant bastards!' With 800 metres left I called our sprint for the line that we'd normally do with just 300 metres to go. We picked off third, then second and finally caught the leaders Serbia on the line, winning on a photo finish by one 100th of a second. It was the only time we were ahead in the whole race.

If I could find my diary entry for the next day I would be complaining about a stinking hangover. My last recollection of the night was Bev dancing on a table in front of a couple of hundred frustrated Balkan oarsmen who'd been training up a mountain for the last couple of months. She said the next day that it was a walk in the park compared to the Haçienda in Manchester in the late 1980s.

Afterwards, Bev and I went on a romantic holiday to a luxury resort in Mauritius. I spent most of it in bed, sadly not with the beautiful woman in question but with a serious infection helpfully diagnosed by Bev as man flu. Whatever I had caused 15–20 nosebleeds a day, sickness and even more worryingly complete lack of appetite, despite the free buffet. Which shows just how bad I was feeling.

Despite achieving something special at those World Championships it still didn't feel natural and right for me to rowing on the other side. So 2002 – although a year where I was lucky enough to marry the woman I loved and respected so much – was a shit one in so many ways. That is how much sport can affect a sportsman's life and mental state. Bev's recurring nightmare was that we would lose the World Championships – honestly it was Bev's not mine, or at least not just mine – because she knew I'd be so wretched it could ruin our wedding in October. She was right: I would have been miserable, and it probably would have, but luckily we never had to cross that bridge.

After 400 metres of the final we were already in the lead and I told Matt to move over, as he had the rudder, and give the Aussies in the lane next to us some wash, i.e. the 'bounce' from the stern wave coming off the back of our boat. It would make it choppy and uncomfortable and slow them down. Matt, however, is more honourable than me; he shook his head and refused.

But that didn't stop me lying to him down the track in the final. At the halfway stage, I checked our time and it was 3.05. 'Fuck me, five seconds ahead of the world record!' So I told Matt it was 3.10. If I'd told him the truth he may have worked out that we might have (in fact had) gone off too hard then backed off in case we needed some extra gas later on. I figured kill them now and we won't need any gas at all; after three-quarters' distance they'll be racing for second. We won in a world record time that stood until it was broken at the London

2012 Games by a Kiwi pair who thoroughly deserved it after an unbeaten Olympiad. We were named the best crew of all the world champions, the best of the best. Effectively, we were the Top Guns of rowing – if not quite as cool or attractive to the opposite sex.

[Bev]

I've never been any good at maths and on the night before James left for a three-week training camp in Austria, my inability to calculate the intricacies of the female cycle resulted in a farewell to my new husband that was to have long-lasting consequences in the form of our first-born son. It hadn't been part of my plan. I would have to miss the last few Grand Prix and getting the book finished with a new baby due three months before submission would require some focus. But I had always wanted children and James was keen that he would not be an 'old dad'. I knew that my mum would offer unconditional babysitting help and I imagined writing *The Pits* while the baby napped. James was predominantly training in the mornings and spending time at home in the afternoon so he would share the childcare. He'd often said that if we had kids, I could return to my career and he wouldn't mind being a stay-at-home dad. I would be a woman of the twenty-first century: one of those who could 'have it all'. We had absolutely no idea what we were talking about.

I wanted to give myself the best possible shot at a natural birth because I believed that as I was fit and well, there was no reason to make matters more complicated, and also because I needed to bounce back and finish the book. I'd heard about the Birth Centre in London that – although private – cost little more than a holiday and provided ten months of one-on-one care. I set about learning hypnobirthing: a form of deep relaxation used as a natural form of pain relief, and the practitioner agreed to come round to our house as James and I were never in the country at the same time to attend the group classes. Hypnobirthing places lots of emphasis on the partner's role during the birth. That appealed to me – surely if it all went wrong it would be James's fault!

We'd both lie on the floor of our flat as she talked us into trance and within ninety seconds James would be snoring loudly. This wasn't exactly the 'bonding' process I was looking for but when James was then taught to 'hypnotise' me we did find common ground – in our inability to be grown up enough to learn the technique without descending into hysterics. Frequently I had to go outside and walk around the garden, doubled over with laughter so hard that I almost went into labour. I totally believed in the principle: fear causes tension; tension causes pain. Perfecting the techniques, however, was another matter.

[James]

After the wedding and our honeymoon, I was on a training camp in Greece at the start of the new 2002–2003 season where Jurgen, Matt and I were having, ironically, our end-of-the-season review. I said I didn't want to row in the pair any more. I wanted to try rowing in a four. I felt a bigger boat would allow me to perfect my technique and extra personnel would freshen up what I thought was becoming more of a business-style partnership than a try-anything, risk-taking racing team. We'd proved ourselves to be the fastest pair ever in the season before so we wouldn't be swapping boat classes after being given a hiding and I felt the partnership dynamic was needed to give us the best chance at the 2004 Olympics. Jurgen and Matt thought I was crazy. We had just won the World Championships, broken the world record and been arguably hailed the best of the best by scooping FISA's Crew of the Year prize. Yet here I was saying we weren't good enough. Funnily enough Jurgen said no.

As we entered 2003 I was still unsettled. Normally spring is an enjoyable time of year for an international rower. The clocks have gone forward and the days are getting longer and you are emerging – or at least should be – from the winter days where ice forms everywhere, including up your nose, and you wonder why footballers can wear gloves without looking like prats, but not supposedly better-educated rowers. Perhaps earning over £100k a week makes you worry less about what people think of your glove-wearing habits. Something I'll happily report back on if that situation ever happens.

For international rowers spring marks the shift from months of single sculling where you are assessed individually into pairs where that assessment carries on in a boat of two. For me it wasn't just the physical change of swapping from a one-man boat to a two-man boat or changing from operating two oars to one; it signalled the first time since the World Championships that Matt and I would have a consistent run in the pair. So the issues I'd been told I had to put to bed (my technique on bowside and our need to challenge each other in every aspect of rowing in order to move forwards), which had been made easier when I was sculling and not in the same boat as Matt, suddenly wasn't possible. And funnily enough, rather than time being a great healer, nearly four months of sculling hadn't made my rowing technique improve for the pair. Put it this way, neither of us skipped down to training the first morning looking forward to hitting the water again together in earnest. It probably didn't help that I'd referred to this day as the 'return of the remedial rowers' and somehow Matt thought I was being negative. Looking back I can understand that for someone who motivates themselves on positive energy it must have been extremely difficult to have someone who not only comes from the other end of the spectrum but is vociferous about it as well. Especially as the last time we were on the water together we'd won the World Championships and broken the world record. To me though that was part of the problem: yes, we'd done tough individual training in singles but our opposition would have spent those four months rowing together, covering 4,000–5,000 kilometres and honing their technique to beat us. We were already the strongest and arguably the fittest, but it was our technique – OK, mine really – that needed the work, and although the single was good for fitness, it wasn't helping my rowing.

This was around the time of the Eights Head of the River Race, held over the Boat Race course, with 500 boats racing against the clock on the same day – an occasion that marked the switch from the long winter time trials (the Head races) to the summer regatta season. So it traditionally is marked with an informal post-race celebration. Coincidentally (or not), Jurgen somehow always managed to schedule our 2,000-metre ergo tests forty-eight hours later. It was my least favourite six minutes in sport. For me, it's all the bad bits of rowing without any of the good. You're racing a machine, in a gym where the paint is peeling, there are weights and bars, no boat alongside you to race and your senses are deprived even of the riverbank passing by. Your power, speed and predicted time are rammed down your throat every stroke. While the machine is attacking your legs, heart and lungs, simultaneously the feedback on the screen is attacking your mental strength.

It's no surprise that twenty per cent of the squad used to come down with a cold or man flu on that day and another ten to twenty per cent would stop during the test. I never did, not because I didn't want to but I knew that I'd have to do it again anyway, if you stopped once it would be easier to stop another time and your crewmates would lose respect for you. In fact I'd have lost my self-respect and the machine would have won.

I'm sure there are worse things to do in sport. I've never spent two rounds in the ring being clubbed by one of the Klitschko brothers – let's face it, I wouldn't last one punch, let alone two rounds – but at least (in my mind) I could run away or the referee would stop the fight or at least count to ten. But on an ergo, the machine is always going to win and it's guaranteed to hurt. The good news is that we only did it twice a year.

This preamble probably explains the following diary entry:

'Sunday 30 March 2003: Thought I'd go out for a few beers. Didn't want to drink with ergo test in a couple of days. Turns out that my willpower is weaker than my thirst for a beer or at least need for a night out. Came home and much to neighbours' delight me and the boys sang karaoke into the early hours. Despite thinking I was Anthony Kiedis it wasn't big or clever especially with what's coming this week. Night out won't make erg test better in any way but letting off steam with mates will dull the mental pain and frustration I know is coming when we get back in the pair.'

Jurgen was most definitely a rock to me throughout my rowing career. As infuriating as we'd find him, we also knew without doubt he was the third leg to our stool, and yes, I would have made changes to the training, but I also knew he'd get us to be in the best shape on that one crucial day every four years. Plus, if a hard decision had to be made along the way, he'd make it. That didn't mean I agreed with him but the respect, trust and care I had for him was genuine.

I also felt this way towards our support team, which is why a situation we had on the way back from a training camp frightened and affected me so much. We were just emerging from Heathrow and had been waiting for a couple of minutes when one of the support team's trolleys rolled into my calf and ran down my Achilles. I was about to fire off a sarcastic tirade when I saw the reason why the trolley had rolled away from him. He was falling backwards, frothing at the mouth and making a horrendous gargling noise. I'd never seen anyone having a fit before and, at the time, didn't even realise what it was. Coping under pressure in a situation you're trained for is one thing, but coping under pressure in a completely new one is a whole different ball game. Especially watching someone you care about enduring something horrendous without a clue what to do or how to help.

I caught his shoulders and head as he fell, letting him collapse on top of me. As we tumbled back I protected his head from making contact with the kerb. I could see blood starting to seep from his mouth. His jaw had locked tight and my instant fear was that he had bitten his tongue, so I forced my finger through his ferociously grinding jaw and whipped it round the inside of his mouth, while shouting at an open-mouthed bystander to call an ambulance.

Thankfully the chilling gargling noise he had been making stopped but I could feel his heart pounding away as I cradled him in my arms. I'd just laid him out on top of a trolley and made sure something was under his head so that his wife wasn't greeted with the sight of me cradling him, but nevertheless the scene that greeted her as she rounded the corner at Departures is something no spouse should ever have to witness. I'll never forget the distraught look of panic, concern and unconditional love that washed over her face. At least he was calmer now and although there was blood on the side of his face, he'd stopped foaming at the mouth and his breathing rate had slowed. An ambulance came and the relief of being among experts who knew what they were doing was palpable.

At that stage it hadn't even crossed my mind that in less than twenty hours I was due to be on a coach (it's not all luxury glamour in the rowing world but at least we got to have a fry-up on the ferry) heading for Belgium for the most important race since the previous year's World Championships – the national selection trials, where Matt and I were expected to win and ratify our place in the coxless pair.

Writing this a decade later is horrible on a number of counts: the clarity with which I remember the scene, the feeling of helplessness, and watching the suffering of someone for whom I had so much trust, respect and affection. It is a chilling reminder of what Bev and Croyde would go through when the same thing happened to me in front of them.

But we all made it to the trials. Matt and I won but I still didn't want to compete in the pair. Despite winning the right to be in the top boat, whether that was the pair or the four, the other two didn't agree with me.

I still thought I was right; they were sure I was wrong and kept pointing back to our results the year before. I didn't spend the season in a sulk, I trusted Jurgen and Matt and genuinely believed that we could win. At the World Championships 2003 in Milan, the truth was only too evident. We believed in our own press – something that my pessimism usually never lets me do – and we hadn't moved on. In fact, it was the first time we hadn't lived by the adage 'treat every win as a loss', which forced us into the mind-set that we'd be moving the bar up even if we were chasing imaginary opposition. This winter, because we'd set a new world record, we'd created a new target for everyone. If we didn't move on we'd find they'd gone past us at the first race and there's no time to do anything about it once the season has started. The big changes are done session after session in the long winter months, not during the racing months. Plus in the past I'd always been able to coach myself out of bad form. But since swapping sides that instinctive ability wasn't there on bowside, or maybe it was and I'd somehow convinced myself it had gone. I guess I lacked the psychological skills necessary to free up my mind.

Some Sunday nights, I just cried, not out of pity but frustration and because I felt like I was pissing in the wind trying to convince Matt and Jurgen that something wasn't right. We couldn't always rely on power and fitness to get us out of trouble. The problem was that throughout our time in the four, and now the pair, I was always the questioning voice asking if we were doing enough and pushing us to to do more. Ultimately it must have felt like a negative voice. I guess I became a background noise that they eventually were able to drown out. Like the boy who cried wolf.

I began to hate going to training. It was terrible. It wasn't the physical aspect, which I'd always coped well with, enjoyed even, it was the fact that I didn't feel as though I was making any progress, that we were treading water rather than moving forwards and I was the only one voicing it.

Bev had to make me go rowing. 'It'll be all right,' she'd say in order to cajole me into the right frame of mind.

I'd never had a problem sacrificing myself physically during the four years up to the 2000 Sydney Olympics and knew that my technique would hold up whatever abuse my heart, legs and lungs were going through, but this was different. I had to think about the rudiments of rowing in a different and unnatural way. It was like learning to walk again but when one side of your body already knows how to walk; in the boat, Matt and I were powering one leg each. His hadn't changed since Sydney and he was doing the same thing whereas my leg wasn't always reliable. Which in turn meant he (understandably) wasn't able to relax in quite the same way and neither was I. I felt I was letting him down.

In Milan Matt and I – reigning world champions – inexcusably (no matter our problems) finished out of the medals. 'Saturday 30 August 2003: 'World Champs Final. Fuck, came fourth. Didn't just lose – weren't even at the races. The Aussies took it on and we were nowhere to be seen.' The misery stuck around with me.

'Monday 1 September 2003: Woke up still pissed off with everything and everybody including me.'

I've always said that if you've prepared well, mentally and physically, raced well and still lost, then you should be able to say to the opposition 'Well done, you were better than us today.' But I knew we hadn't moved on enough over the winter. Part of that was my mental block over swapping sides, spending four months single sculling when we could have been in the pair, not asking ourselves whether we were increasing our boat speed and not even exploring the possibility of a coxless four. Whatever the reason, we were relying on pulling a rabbit out of the hat on a big day by having the greater firepower. But as they say: 'It's not the size of your wave but the motion of your ocean, baby.'

To make matters worse, the GB men's coxless four finished second and the GB men's eight finished third. No longer top of the world, we were bottom of the domestic pile with the Olympics less than twelve months away. The lowest ranked athletes in the British team, what a horrible year. Not least for Bev, who was about to give birth to our first child.

[Bev]

Unfortunately, the run-up to the birth was hampered by James losing a major rowing race in a pair with Matt Pinsent. I can't remember the details. I was rather busy gearing up to give birth, but James returned home in a despondent fug that proved difficult to disperse. If there is one thing I cannot bear, it is sulking. I allowed him a couple of days to lick his wounds, walking on eggshells and offering platitudes designed to soften his mood. But my potential for such compassion is pretty limited. So I soon issued the northern directive that he needed to 'put his face straight' and get the fuck over it. The race was done – history – there was no point dwelling on it. He had to appreciate what he had and move on. But that was probably a bit like telling an alcoholic to stop being dramatic, pull up a chair and crack open a bottle of wine. Olympic gold medallists are not like normal people – and thank God for that – their truculence is what drives them on to provide great sporting drama for the rest of us sat on the sofa eating crisps.

My waters broke at 5.30 p.m. on 26 September 2003 as John Leslie was about to be interviewed for the first time by Richard and Judy following allegations of sexual impropriety with Ulrika Jonsson (a claim which he always denied and for which he was never charged). It was *such* bad timing. I managed to sit on the loo with the door ajar watching TV, a voice in the back of my mind suggesting I switch it off and call James. We hadn't quite bought all the bizarre paraphernalia we needed for the birth but fortunately he was at the local Waitrose so he could pick up the required bucket and sieve.

[James]

Croyde arrived two weeks after those World Championships, in a hypnobirthing pool near Tooting. Two weeks after that defeat and ten months before an Olympics, I discovered something. Going through a life-changing experience with someone you love unconditionally and ending up with someone else you instantly love unconditionally places sport where it should be in the pecking order of life.

Luckily for both of us, Bev got herself mentally in the perfect place. She had no gas and air, nothing. We'd gone to hypnobirthing lessons beforehand. Hypnobirthing is all about pain control. We were taught not to call contractions 'contractions'. They were 'surges' instead and the midwife told me (in language I could understand) not to 'piss in Beverley's bucket' by ever mentioning pain or anything negative. As if I would . . .

We'd also gone to ante-natal classes, which in our area happened to include the American film maker Tim Burton and his partner the actress Helena Bonham-Carter. At the fathers' evening we were told seventy-seven per cent of women could give birth in a field with no intervention whatsoever and yet sixty per cent *have* an epidural. Even my poor maths skills could spot the flaw in that. 'Why?' I asked intelligently.

'Because it fucking hurts,' said Helena.

Her husband only had one question from behind his fantastic sunglasses. 'When can the kid fly?'

I thought that was brilliant. All he cared about was getting the hell out.

When the time came for Croyde to be born, I was as ready as I'd ever be. I'd probably have made sure I was better prepared if I was the one actually giving birth, but I trusted Bev a hundred per cent and was willing to battle on her behalf – asking, demanding and being a pain in the ass to anyone in the vicinity – if she needed me to. Bev was amazing. I think I could have been better at my head-cradling role when she was in the birthing pool. She'd been in there a long time, and I was massaging the back of her head when I noticed that the hard callouses on my hands that normally caused shop assistants to drop the change in them rather than risk catching leprosy were peeling away like old scabs.

'Bev,' I said, somewhat heedlessly. 'My hands are falling apart.' Understandably, that didn't go down too well and was one of those points where I needed a slightly slower connection between my brain and mouth.

A few more hours went by, then I had another one of those moments. 'Bev,' I said. 'What happens next?'

'Read a fucking book!' she replied.

I learnt to keep my mouth shut after that and stuck to my main job of sieving Bev's poo out of the pool, only putting my hands in the water when necessary, and taking on the vital role of making toast for everyone. Or, strictly speaking, for me.

Through it all Bev was incredible – the way she controlled it all and knew exactly how she wanted it to be. It was a very special experience.

'Saturday 27 September 2003: Then we could see the baby's

head. I was shown with a mirror. Being somewhat tense and emotional I forgot about our red-haired midwife looking on. "Thank God, it's not ginger," I said.

'. . . Just before the baby was born, Bev got out of the pool and I held her in my arms as she pushed the baby out. It was the most amazing feeling. It was a crazy, amazing, wonderful day. I was so proud of Bev. She had the baby in exactly the way she wanted. I'm an incredibly lucky man.'

When it was all over the Birth Centre asked what I thought of the experience for their brochure. I said: 'It's like a ten-hour game of Twister trying to get a pineapple out of your arse.' I don't think they've used the quote.

[Bev]

We had a rather relaxing evening watching *Sex and the City* while I tried to remember my hypnobirthing breathing. We went to bed to get some sleep but at 2 a.m., I decided the time was right to call the midwife, Caroline Flint, who came round and agreed that we should follow her to the Birth Centre. Getting in the birthing pool was utter bliss and at 9.30 a.m. – after only once shouting at James, 'Don't *ask* me if I'm all right! *Tell* me I'm all right!' (while thinking *he should have read the bloody book!)* Croyde Turner Cracknell was born screaming and furious to promptly do a wee all over Caroline Flint and the second midwife, Pam Wild.

By ten o'clock that night, I was lying on the sofa, breastfeeding Croyde while watching the American Grand Prix and taking notes for *The Pits*. I think it's fair to say I was still in denial.

Reality hit home within the next few weeks as James and I struggled to come to terms with the monumental changes that a first baby brings. The problem with becoming parents is that there are just so many ways you can disappoint your partner on an hourly basis. James went to training as normal the next day (I was actually grateful that he'd been prepared to miss a session on the day of Croyde's birth) and life for him continued pretty much as normal. I am yet to meet a woman of my generation to whom this doesn't come as a complete and utter shock. In my case, at this stage anyway, I could at least rationalise that it was necessary because of James's Olympic preparation. There would be plenty of time after the Games for him to take on a greater share of daddy day-care.

My ante-natal mates and I would exchange supportive emails raging against our ineffectual husbands; despairing at our lack of sleep and pondering how it was possible to love something that requires you to wipe poo off the back of its neck at three in the morning.

James and I moved everything to our home in Henley, where he was training at the Leander Club and where having a spare room enabled my mum to move in – thank God – thereby helping to ease the burden of responsibility. Living in Manchester, but desperate to be close to their grandson, my parents even bought a second home, a small 'Park Home', a type of glorified caravan on an up-market trailer park (yes, they really do exist) that suited them and us just perfectly.

But after a few weeks, when Mum had gone back up north and I was left to cope alone, the pressure became almost too much. James would leave at 7 a.m. to go training and I'd struggle to feed Croyde, throw in a load of laundry, unstack the dishwasher, make the bed and settle him down for a nap in the garden while I spent a couple of hours writing. James would return home from training, exhausted and grumpy. Sometimes he might take the baby out for a walk while I got some more writing done, but more often than not, he too would have work commitments to honour and our home became a battleground of passive-aggressive comments that started with the line 'Why should I . . .?' And all the time – bubbling away like a malevolent cauldron – was the spectre of the Olympics and everything that that would mean.

[James]

2004. This was it. Olympic year. But after our disastrous result in Milan, everything was up in the air. Obviously the GB four – Toby Garbett, Rick Dunn, Steve Williams and Josh West – were wary of us crash-landing in their boat; even a group of rowers can work out that six into four doesn't go. Meanwhile, Matt had badly gashed his hand in an accident at home and then slept through burglars raiding his house and driving off in his Merc. So now he couldn't row, cycle, do weights, swim or drive to a doctor.

The rumours were still racing round about our possible switch to the four but we knew nothing would be decided until April. Jurgen doesn't listen to rumours. He is the one coach or sportsman you can believe when they say they don't read the papers. Steve Redgrave (Sir, by then) stuck his oar in, saying: 'If they [Matt and I] switch to the four, it's like they've run away from the challenge.' I thought of ringing him to ask why he'd changed to a four after Atlanta in 1996 and rowed with two younger blokes, but wisely I'd learnt plenty of things from the big fella and one was not to say anything impulsively – like announce your retirement! I decided against it.

In the middle of all this we went on a warm-weather training stint to Seville in February. While we were there, Jurgen called six of us (the four plus Matt and I) into a room after a training session.

He dropped the bomb.

'I have made a decision,' he said. 'You two are going to be in the four,' looking at Josh and Steve. 'You're going to be in a pair,' directed at Toby and Rick. 'You two are in the four.'

That was it.

I was shocked. Everyone was. I remember the look of devastation on the faces of the Bayern Munich team when Manchester United came back in the last minutes to win the final of the Champions League in 1999. Rick and Toby wore the same expression. They accused us of cooking it up between us, which wasn't true. We weren't expecting it any more than they were. It took a long time to get friendly with Dunny again because, to him, I'd stolen his Olympic dream. The reality was that he could have done better to make sure he stayed in the boat. It wasn't done on favouritism. It was done on results. Matt and I had just won the long-distance trailside and come top of our own side of the boat (stroke side and bow side) in a pairs matrix, but I didn't feel good about it having to be done. Especially as it felt like running away after being beaten at the 2003 World Championships, whereas a year earlier it would have been more of a tactical retreat. Not only was it too close to the Olympics but it meant that Jurgen didn't consider our average performance quick enough, which was hard to both hear and realise.

It made headlines. 'Ruthless Grobler Throws Two Crew Overboard' and 'Athens Bomb Dropped: Six Into Four Won't Go'. Dunny was quoted as saying: 'I'd rather lose to the Australians in the pair than win an Olympic gold medal with James and Matt,' which even he admitted later was 'freakin' stupid'. I probably didn't pour oil on the choppy waters by telling a journalist: 'I think friendships have definitely suffered but I can't be bothered to justify what I know is right. If they've got a problem with it, they should have performed better in the winter.' I'm married to a journalist – you'd think I'd know better.

But it was done now and all we needed was a smooth sail to Athens. What we got was almost a shipwreck.

We only had three regattas in which to get good enough to win an Olympic gold medal. Josh West had already been thrown out of the boat for doing badly in the pairs trials and Alex Partridge was put in his place.

'Friday 16 April 2004: It's Alex! I'm happy with that decision. It's now massively important to gel as a team.'

'Monday 26 April: Went to Leander to do some weights. Found it really hurt. My side killing me.' Sure enough I'd broken a rib.

'Sunday 2 May: There have been rumours that I broke my rib having a fight with Toby Garbett. A nice idea, but off the mark. Toby and I haven't exactly spoken much over the last couple of months, but there have been no blows.'

'Wednesday 5 May: Not what I expected to be doing on my thirty-second birthday, cycling in an altitude chamber while hockey players I used to go to school with walk past giving abuse – not much has changed in fourteen years.'

While Matt, Alex, Steve and Ed Coode (my replacement) raced, I was in Radio Five Live's studio in London, lending my expertise to the nation and answering texts. One of them was from a physiologist who'd been overseeing my cycling. The text said: 'What film d'you want in the chamber tomorrow, *The Rock* or *Forrest Gump*?' The selection at the English Institute of Sport wasn't that extensive so at least the public can be sure money isn't being wasted. So I said *The Rock*. Apparently, this was a bad choice because as I left the studio I bumped into Mark Kermode, Radio Five Live's high-profile film critic. '*The* fucking *Rock*!' he said in mock-horrified contempt, at least I hope it was mock contempt as I really liked his reviews and now he knew I had shit taste.

[Bev]

With a lot of childcare help from my mum and Jennie, I'd some-how submitted *The Pits* on time and it was published in spring 2004. The *Independent* newspaper ran a whole back-page splash on my revelations of sexism within the sport (it has always struck me as odd that despite being twelve chapters on different themes this was the one that caught the media imagination). Thanks to a smart publicist and supportive publisher, the book received some good reviews and I was wheeled on to various TV shows, feeling a little discombobulated due to the fact I was still breastfeeding and no longer sure about the morality of writing about a sport I had been paid to present in good faith. Bernie Ecclestone said something about me not being a very nice person. I'd never even met him. One former TV presenter colleague explained that I'd never been made welcome as I 'didn't love F1'. Apparently this meant I 'didn't deserve to be there'. And of course, most interviewers wanted to brush over the book and quickly get on to the topic that interested them most: what *must* it be like being married to James Cracknell? It sold about five copies.

That's not strictly true. But, let's just say, it wasn't a bestseller. I'd hoped the book might position me as a broadcaster who was unafraid to tackle some big issues, but every meeting I went to (having organised childcare and rushed out of the house smeared with puke from a screaming baby) started with, 'So . . . we're wondering if you'd like to make a programme with James . . .?'

[James]

In the middle of all this came Croyde's naming ceremony. We decided on a trip on a party boat to an island in the Thames. Our excuse for it being in May was that we'd been waiting for better weather but the truth is we were two predominantly selfish people having to adjust to the shock of having a baby and were rubbish at organising anything.

Although Bev will say my lifestyle didn't change one little bit after having Croyde, the reality was I had no option but to keep focused on the Olympic goal. I wasn't in the driving seat where rowing was concerned; I wasn't in the driving seat at home either. As for changes to my life, I appreciated the quiet and boredom of long-haul flights and training camps like never before.

Bev and I weren't religious and having decided against getting married in church, we didn't want Croyde to be christened in one either. We looked around for venues in Henley and seized the opportunity to have it on Temple Island in the middle of the Thames, which I had rowed past ten times a day for the previous five years – plus Bev, being a swimmer with a first-class English degree, couldn't resist the idea of a water-based naming ceremony with an alliterative title: 'Croyde Cracknell's Christening Cruise'. Game on. The date was set so that it didn't collide with one of the summer's regattas, so that the father could actually make it.

The uncertainty surrounding our boat was making me incredibly difficult to live with. I just couldn't switch off, not only in the build-up to the christening but during the first months of the little man's life. I believed that my result in Athens would have a really significant effect on Croyde's, not just financially but emotionally. How would we cope as a family if I didn't win? Or, if I'm being honest, how would *I* cope if I didn't win and what effect would that have on the family? As Bev has always said, she didn't care whether I won or lost. To her, I was the same person.

The weather was fantastic on Croyde's big day and the mile-long cruise down the river from the town to Temple Island was very special. There was a big contingent down from Manchester, including a crowd of Bev's mum's mates. 'I hope we get stranded,' one of them said. 'Then we can not only get rescued by strapping young rowers, but they'll be very polite while they're doing it.'

Matt Pinsent was one of the godfathers – or mentors if I'm going to use strict civil naming ceremony terminology – and I suspect was not the only member of the 'congregation' that day with half his mind on rowing. The whole crew and Jurgen were there. And as our champagne corks were popping, the Canadian world champions were having their first race of the season in Germany.

Obviously the day was not quite special enough to stop all the rowers getting texts from the outside world. I could hear the subtle 'ping' of texts dropping every few minutes giving people updates of the Canadians' race in Germany. Inexcusable as it sounds, I was glad to know the information was there when I wanted it, which made it easier to keep focused on this bit of water rather than a lake in Germany. I didn't need to ask for the result to be confirmed. The serious looks and conversations told me they'd won and won by a long way. Luckily I had my speech to distract me.

Actually, I read a speech written by Croyde. Well, the speech he would have written if he hadn't been six months old. It gave me the opportunity to push the boundaries of taste and acceptability while using the little man as cover for innuendo, piss-taking and risqué jokes that don't normally get an airing at a christening. Sorry, christening cruise.

I had to train the next day so it was for the Mancs and Bev's mates to make the most of the bars and nightclub (singular) of Henley-on-Thames as I headed home to babysit and, sadly, analyse the rowing results on the Internet.

I was fit for the next race in Munich, so Ed was out again. It was like musical boat seats. We were quicker than Canada in the heats, both won our respective semis but then I was ill for the final and got pulled out at 7 a.m. Tom Stallard, the spare, came in manfully at the last minute. They finished fourth.

We only had one more race to get it right before the Olympics. Lucerne. This time we were all fit and well (we thought) and we came third behind not just Canada but also the USA. The next day we met up for a debrief and Alex wasn't there. He fractured his rib and punctured his lung during the race. A flustered-looking Jurgen responded to the news with a simple 'Oh shit!'

Alex was out of the Olympics and Ed was in. We'd never rowed together before and our first race would be the Olympic Games in Athens in six weeks' time.

'Saturday 26 June: The Olympic Flame is in London. 70,000 people turned up in the pissing rain to watch the flame being lit by Steve Redgrave or it might have been for the free concert that accompanied the big fella's firelighting skills. Croyde fell asleep, then got woken up by Rod Stewart singing and threw up all over me. Much to the amusement of those Olympic fans Ronnie O'Sullivan and Martine

McCutcheon.'

'Sunday 1 August: Yet again managed to have an argument with Bev on way to the airport so a shit goodbye. Hopefully after all this is over, we'll start to get on better because at the moment it sucks like you wouldn't believe.'

One thing we had decided in those six preparation weeks was we wouldn't settle for silver. The Canadians were favourites for the race (not in Britain, but everywhere else in the world) but we would go for gold or bust. There would be no playing safe but we all had to buy into that strategy one hundred per cent for it to have any chance of working. If one of us was prepared to settle for silver, we'd end up not winning. We also made a decision to look up and enjoy what we were doing. We'd race better as a result plus we weren't in a torture chamber – it was supposed to be an enjoyable hobby that we were so lucky to be part of. In that mood, we boarded the plane to Athens.

Ed was my roommate this time. I'd roomed with him before in 1999 when he was in the four for a season when Tim Foster had back surgery. Then I'd been very amazed by his organisation. He used to iron his rowing kit. Annoyingly he refused to do mine. At one point, I caught him ironing his pillowcases. He was a man with a very positive outlook, which made him a strong contrast to me. But there were times, for a guy who went to Eton, Newcastle and Oxford Universities, when he could be really clueless.

He came into our room one day in Athens and said, 'I think I've annoyed one of the Canadian guys.'

'Why?' I asked.

'Well, I was being drug tested and there was this other guy

there. So we got chatting while waiting to have a pee and at some point I said: "What boat are you in?"

'"The Four," he said.

'I said: "Oooh, I think we're racing you."'

That was terrific. If the Canadians, the world champions, needed any extra incentive to row hard against us, the fact that a member of the British four couldn't care less who was in their boat was it.

I was amazed by his lack of awareness. But he was great to sit next to on a plane. He had this habit of twitching in his sleep a lot. Being a well-read Eton old boy he'd always be devouring a solid hardback, either that or being like Mussolini and pretending to. So I'd watch him doze off and just wait for the great moment – which would happen without fail – when he hit himself on the head with the book as he twitched. I loved it.

I'd ruled out Steve Williams as a roommate after waking up one night and finding him at the foot of my bed shouting: 'I've got it! I've got it!' He was having a bad dream and thought the ceiling was falling in. I didn't really want to deal with that the week leading up to the Olympics, so Matt got him (after I switched the room allocation at reception – there's an advantage to being first off the bus). Matt could sleep through anything – remember the thieves driving off in his Merc?

Steve was a quiet guy (with the exception of his nightmares), another vicar's son, like Matt. Every word was a prisoner. So it was pretty amazing in an interview before the Olympics when he was quoted as saying: 'I don't want to sound melodramatic but I've been through the greatest intensity of every emotion there is: excitement, passion, determination, regret.'

Bev, Croyde and my family were out there to watch – I like

to say me, but that's not quite true. Bev's brother, Adi, was in the British swimming team, racing in the 200 and 400 individual medley, which were not the best events to choose if you wanted to win because Michael Phelps – the greatest swimmer of all time from the US – was in them too. Adi's 200-metre race was on the same day as my heat. His 400-metre race was on the same day as my semi, with the result that Bev, Croyde, her mum, dad, sister and my mum and dad all chose to watch him instead of me.

'Well, you'll be all right,' Bev said. 'We'll watch you in the final.'

I pointed out that we hadn't got a bye to the final.

Mum and Dad had been to two Olympics and never seen me race and now they were choosing not to watch me.

As it happened, Bev was right. We made it to the final. We were up at the crack of sparrows again, just like Sydney, but this time very definitely not favourites. Canada had not been headed, or beaten. I don't remember being as emotional as I was in Sydney, mainly because we had a specific task that was taking all my focus. We had decided to make sure that after one minute's rowing we'd be in the lead. We thought it might just throw the Canadians off. We wanted to put them in a position that they hadn't been in before so that they might begin to doubt themselves.

According to plan, we were leading after a minute. Commentators always tell you that it's the last minute that hurts the most in a race, but for us it's the first minute that hurts most. Before the end of it you're already knackered and you've still got over five minutes to go. So we were ahead, we'd knackered ourselves already, but we had put the Canadians in a position to doubt themselves – but they didn't. They came back and overtook us. They were over half a length ahead (twenty feet), a long way.

'Crank it,' came the call from Steve. What he was shouting in reality was 'Panic!' It meant that every stroke we pulled had to be harder than the one before. We'd have the ability to keep doing it for 200 metres at the most. Steve called it with 500 metres to go.

We all thought the same thing when we heard the call. 'Shit, it's *too* early.' There was still a minute and a half to go. But even though we all thought it, we all gave it everything we had. That's when you really have to have trust in each other. If we hadn't all done it, we'd have lost.

We'd made the big move, pegged them back, drawn level and gone ahead but still they hadn't given up. They must have had a sniff that we'd blown, not surprising as the wheels had well and truly come off our wagon, and came back at us. In the end it was luck that we had a surge at just the right moment to take us over the line first. But working as hard as we had got us in the position to benefit from luck.

I thought we'd lost as the Canadian boat had drifted ahead of us, then I heard a Canadian-sounding voice shout: 'Who won?' We didn't know until we saw hundreds of Union Jacks suddenly waving in celebration on the bank.

What better way to be told, by people who genuinely cared whether you won or lost.

I held Croyde in my arms on the landing stage before the medal ceremony.

'Bring him with you,' said Matt as the presentation party were heading towards the podium.

'No,' I said, handing him back to Beverley, smiling, 'he hasn't earned it. Yet!'

[Bev]

I remember very little about the Athens Olympics except that the heat made it almost impossible to settle a ten-month-old baby. I do, however, have fond memories of watching my brother Adrian swim for GB in the 400-metre individual medley. Unfortunately, his heat and semi-final times clashed with both James's heat and semi. It's a mark of how confident we were about my husband's succession to the final that the whole family, James's parents included, came to watch Adi at the pool. Swimming had formed such a huge part of our lives. In fact, butterfly swimmer Steve Parry had been a friend since aged nine and lived with Adi in the run-up to the games. It was awesome to watch him win a medal behind Michael Phelps.

On the day of James's final we friends and family members piled onto a bus and nervously made our way to the stands. As the boat crossed the line, we waited for the photo finish and I literally felt my life flash before my eyes: if James, Matt et al lost, I did not know *how* I would ever shake James from his sense of failure. My life literally turned on a dime as we waited for the result. The whole GB section of the stand stood in deafening unison, throwing our arms into the air as their boat was announced the winner. If James had lost, he would have unfinished business and would surely want to aim for Beijing in 2008. Now, at least I had a chance of something resembling a 'normal' life. Didn't I?

[James]

As I watched the Olympic flame flicker and die in the stadium the Sunday night of the Closing Ceremony, I felt incredibly sad, not that sixteen amazing days had come to an end but that as the flame was extinguished, it was like being released from a cryogenic state. I was going to have to return to the real world and with that came some tough questions and decisions. Would I be in Beijing when the flame would be reignited in four years' time? The honest answer then was that I didn't know.

Competing and being successful at the Olympics is incredibly special. But there is more to the games than competing and more to life than the Olympics. My memories after our event – being at parties with the likes of Ian Thorpe and Michael Phelps, seeing them value their golds as much as I did mine, even though Phelps has a few more (seventeen more to be precise) to replace one if it gets lost under the sofa – was a first-hand demonstration that it's worth the sacrifice.

I race to win for myself and my teammates and I'm immensely proud to represent my country. But for me, the memory I will savour most was walking into the arrivals hall at Gatwick Airport to see hundreds of people waiting to welcome us home. It was humbling that the performance of the British team meant so much to them. Most of all it told me that if Britain one day hosted an Olympics, they would be the best Games ever.

5

[Bev – post-accident]

'But James, you can't! You just can't!'

'Why can't I?'

James's PA Emma sighs, taps a pencil on our kitchen table and looks from me to James and back again. She's stuck in the middle of yet another argument: wanting to advise James in a professional capacity, protect him as a friend and support me. It's less than three months after the accident. He's home – in body, but not yet in mind. Bizarre business ideas have been pouring in and his increased talkativeness means he's spending hours pacing the garden on his mobile phone. I watch worried from the window, wondering what he's cooking up next.

Now he's desperate to honour an existing commercial relationship with Bupa by competing in the upcoming Great North Run. But the foot that he broke running through Death Valley is still sore. His solution: to race in a wheelchair or handbike.

I hold my head in my hands, thinking of all the things I'd rather be doing than talking him down off the precipice once again. 'If people see you doing the Great North Run in a wheelchair, knowing you've had an accident, they're going to think you're bloody paralysed!'

'No, they won't. I'll do an interview with Sue Barker beforehand.'

Emma and I exchange a collusive look as my blood runs cold. It's too soon to put him on TV in front of a million people and risk him saying something odd, embarrassing or downright inappropriate.

I think about everything I've read about the world of TBI (traumatic brain injury) sufferers and how it is littered with tales of bankruptcy. Frontal lobe damage can cause compulsions that commonly include excessive spending (a good friend's mother had a skiing accident and blew $250,000 online before her husband noticed). John, as James's father and accountant, is keeping a close eye on his bank accounts to check that he isn't about to plough all of his savings into one of the many business schemes which keep cropping up in conversation: running a bicycle shop and cafe; investing in a line of nutrition bars . . . the list goes on. But my biggest fear is that he will return to work too soon, fail to manage his fatigue and, as his neurologist puts it, 'make a cock-up'.

I'm sure he'd make a lovely pot of tea to sell in his bicycle shop-cafe – but he's just not ready to think any of these ideas through logically and practically. I keep hearing the words of the psychologist in the hospital, 'You have to let him make his own mistakes', but they sound so cruel when those mistakes can be made on national TV. I watch him fidgeting, wanting to get up from the table and finish this annoying conversation with these two women telling him what to do.

Through smart business decisions, hard work and long-term goal-setting James has made the transition from rowing to a new and exciting career better than almost any other athlete I can name. He's worked too hard to fuck it all up now. But it is impossible to reason with him. Thanks to his wonky frontal lobes, he's wearing his 'concrete shoes' and no amount of conversational trickery will change his mind.

After several days of discussions, Emma and I have to go behind his back and phone Bupa. They are unequivocal that his recovery is more *important than his commitment to them (and they can't let him use a wheelchair). He looks pissed off. I've spoilt everything for him – again.*

[James]

So there I was, double Olympic gold medallist. After the triumph in Athens, I was at a loss as to what to do next. Well, where I went from there might sound like borderline insanity. I rowed across the Atlantic – most of it spent 'commando' – with a bloke I hardly knew. Then I raced to the South Pole, with the same bloke and another bloke I hardly knew, this time suffering from pneumonia and blisters so extreme I couldn't take off my boots without cutting them open, which at least gave me an excuse for my appalling skiing. After that I ran the Marathon des Sables, essentially six back-to-back marathons, over 250 kilometres in fifty-degree heat up ridges and down sand dunes in the Sahara Desert.

I'm not sure I can fully explain my motivation at the start of this process, even to myself. I know this much: after the Athens Olympics I wasn't ready to throw myself into another four years of training. I'd found the previous two years incredibly difficult mentally and was aware of the impact this had at home primarily because of my inability to 'leave rowing in the boatshed'. It wasn't fair on Bev or Croyde.

The thing I've always loved about rowing is that someone else's dreams are in your hands and vice versa. For the first time since I'd left school fifteen years earlier, I wasn't sure I was ready for that responsibility and I didn't want to sponge off other people's motivation either.

Not being as big as Steve and Matt, I knew how hard I had to work and the extra training I'd had to do to extract every last joule of energy to have a chance of winning a gold medal. But I also didn't fancy hanging up the dodgy Lycra suit just yet, so Jurgen advised me to take a year away from rowing, to keep fit and only come back if I felt the required hunger return.

I felt purposeless without a goal. Until now I'd oriented my life around sport. I knew where I had to be and when for virtually every day of the year, often a year in advance. Now, suddenly, to use an apt boat analogy, my life was rudderless.

For the month immediately after the Olympics, I'd been invited to lots of cool parties. Then the immediate afterglow of the gold medal began to dim, the football season got under way and the people organising social gatherings thought of other people they and their guests would rather meet. The invites, in other words, were on the wane.

But the well hadn't yet completely run dry and I was at an ITV cocktail party with Bev one evening when a very nice, confident guy I didn't know came over and introduced himself as Ben Fogle. I guessed he worked in TV or at least publicity of some kind based on his social skills being far in advance of the sportsmen I usually hung around with.

He'd hardly told me his name when he blurted: 'I'm rowing across the Atlantic next year, do you want to do it with me?'

'Can you row?' I asked.

'No,' he said.

That made my mind up. I immediately had respect for him having the guts, as a novice, to ask someone to team up with him who had scarcely done anything *but* row for fifteen years and for having the intelligence to try and team up with someone who could at least row a bit.

'Er, no, thanks,' I said.

Had we left that exchange as it was, I would not have spent Christmas 2005 in a tearful, hairy, malnourished and dehydrated state with a broken desalinator, bobbing up and down on the twelve-foot waves of the Atlantic Ocean, with an ass pockmarked by boils. Karl Marx would have been proud. He took great pleasure from the fact that the original manuscript of *Das Kapital* was smeared with pus from his boils because it meant he was in touch with the proletariat. I felt slightly differently as I was in absolute agony when I sat down, which was pretty much all day and all night. Plus the book Ben and I wrote about our experience didn't quite receive the critical acclaim of Karl's.

But I did not leave that exchange with Ben Fogle where it was.

A lot of thoughts were whirring round in my head about 'retirement'. It's an impossible word to grasp when you're thirty-two years old and have yet to have, as my dad would call it, a proper job. And I certainly didn't want to be seen as 'giving up' either.

I'd seen a sports psychologist when I fractured my rib before the Olympics. Although the rib was healed, Jurgen and I wanted to ensure I had one hundred per cent confidence in it and didn't hold back from fully loading it. She helped me use visualisation to increase my confidence in the healed bone. But as interesting as ribs may be, we also spoke about other things, including 'retirement'. It seems that on average it takes two years for elite sportsmen to fully retire and be able to look at events or results without feeling a pang of regret or wondering if they could make a comeback. The feelings you might have in the immediate aftermath of an event might be very different a few months later.

I learnt so much from Steve Redgrave: how to race under pressure, his podium advice ('Drop the flowers and don't cry. You don't want either in a photo!'), and, significantly, not to announce your retirement straight after your Olympic race. I remembered his plea to be shot should he ever go near a boat again in Atlanta. It was a great line but came back to haunt him in pretty much every interview from 1996 to 2000.

Steve clearly didn't mean it. Either that or he very quickly realised that rowing, training and the pressure of the Olympics was a walk in the park compared to looking after three kids. Opting to climb aboard the fun boat for one last ride seemed infinitely preferable.

I struggle to understand why athletes such as Lance Armstrong and Michael Schumacher came back. They had both had more than two years away from the sport but had they not asked themselves the tough questions like: Why am I doing this? What have I got left to prove? Or had they not found anything to fill the gap? All I know is that there is no way Bev would let me carry on without answering those tough questions, and many more. Do they not have anyone around them to challenge them?

It's probably because Bev isn't shy of challenging anyone (least of all me) and getting them to justify their actions that I didn't initially discuss with her the small matter of rowing across the Atlantic with Ben. I guess there were questions I couldn't answer and knew, quite rightly, that that wouldn't be acceptable to her.

[Bev]

There is one thing worse than a professional athlete: a professional athlete who has just retired. There were thirteen rowing gold medallists in Sydney, September 2000. By Christmas of that year, only three were in the same relationships. That is the toll the transition from top-level sport takes on love.

I'm very grateful that one of those relationships was James's, otherwise I couldn't have married him. But, in 2004, with Croyde now one year old and James very much in demand as a double Olympic gold medallist, we hit a low point.

I'm keen to get back out into the workplace and look to James to support that. He does . . . but we're at a loss with childcare. My own mother was completely fulfilled by motherhood and looking after kids – which was lucky for me and my siblings – and still is. She ran a playgroup for toddlers and our summers were spent at a playscheme for 250 local kids that she developed and ran with a team of fifty young staff. But I'm shocked that although I adore Croyde, I'm unavoidably bored and dissatisfied. My brain is turning to mush as I sing 'Twinkle Twinkle' for the sixty-fifth time in a day and discover that guilt can feel so overpowering. Each time I look at nurseries I feel like a bad mother for even considering institutionalising my son. Friends talk of their 'nannies' but such beings belong to a Victorian age in which children were presented to their parents for a goodnight kiss in a ruffled collar. And I detest not earning my own money. I feel actual shame when I tentatively approach James to say that my sole account has run dry and that day, pushing the pram down the road, I felt I couldn't stop to buy a coffee.

But I make a guest appearance on Eamonn Holmes's BBC Radio Five Live Saturday morning chat show to promote *The Pits* and the friendly Ulsterman asks me back on the following week. The job rolls on until I am a regular alongside Eamonn and I discover that I love radio almost as much as writing. I'm paid a typical BBC radio pittance but the sense of self-esteem is priceless and this gig only demands childcare every Saturday morning. When he is around, James happily obliges.

The first I know of the Atlantic Rowing Race is a leaflet left in our flat. There is a picture of a yellow boat surrounded by massive waves. I flick it from front to back. It's one of the rare occasions on which James and I can exchange a few words without being interrupted by a mobile phone or a crying baby. 'What's this?'

'Oh, nothing.'

'Really?'

'It's just a race that that Ben Fogle guy suggested I do with him. It's not worth talking about though. Nothing's decided.'

I do one of those wifely pauses, waiting to see if he's going to offer more information. He doesn't. 'Aha . . . so, do we need to talk about anything before those decisions are made?'

'Nah.'

[James]

I believe there's a gulf mentally between 'not carrying on' and 'giving up', even if, practically, it amounts to the same thing. (In fact, there's a third option, which is called 'growing up and deciding what you want from real life', but I was nowhere near ready to contemplate that one.) I wanted to be sure I gave myself time. It would have been too easy to slot straight back into the Olympic cycle. Let's face it, if somebody asks: 'What are you up to?', no issue can be taken with: 'I'm training for the next Olympics.' It's clear, it's concise and also acts as a Get Out Of Jail Card for being grumpy, tired and away – both mentally and physically – for four years.

I needed to buy myself some time without a goal for the first time in a decade and Ben Fogle's casual question was beginning to gain a foothold in my thoughts, especially as it would mean I'd have time and space to think properly when we were at sea. Alternatively, what a great way to postpone the big questions, keep myself fit and have a goal.

It gave me the option to come back and still row in Beijing or I could come back and move on. But in Bev's eyes I'd be engineering a situation where I'd leave her to juggle her career with family responsibilities while I went on a cruise. A cruise that actually meant rowing 2,930 miles across a stormy ocean in the middle of winter.

I didn't know Ben well – he was a presenter of daytime TV programmes, many of which seemed to centre on Longleat Safari Park. He'd made his name on the BBC show *Castaway*, where a group of thirty-six men, women and children built a community, under the watchful eyes of cameras, on an island in the remote Outer Hebrides. This was in 2000 and I was otherwise occupied, so had never seen it or him until the evening he came over and spoke to me. He may not be able to row, I thought, but he's clearly good in his own skin and gets on well with strangers. I sent him an email suggesting we meet up.

At this point, with a wife and a ten-month-old baby to consider, I should have opened negotiations at home. That way, whatever happened, it would have been a joint decision and there would have been fewer arguments and resentment.

I may have been thirty-two at the time, but I wasn't a grown-up. I'd spent half my 'adult' life with other hairy rowers, avoiding a real job in the real world. I had a baby and a wife who'd put her career on hold to have Croyde and give me the time to pursue my Olympic goal. Quite rightly, she felt it was time for me to support her. I knew that was right. But I was scared of making that decision.

So rather than talk about it I used something that seems to work (to a degree) in pretty much every situation – the ostrich technique. I buried my head – and waited for things to sort themselves out. I met up with Ben and we agreed to enter the race, plus sort some of the simple details like planning the logistics, plotting the course, arranging sponsorship, getting a boat and teaching my partner to row. Easy.

And yet, I still hadn't talked it through with Bev. (I blame that bloody ostrich.) Instead I left a brochure about the race on the kitchen table for her to discover. I thought at least that would get the conversation started. It certainly got the conversation started but it didn't go quite as I'd hoped. Understandably, Bev assumed that I'd never contemplate doing something like this without discussing it with her, and I assumed because she hadn't said anything she must be happy to let it progress.

Eventually the 'discussion' had to happen. What hurt Bev was that I hadn't given her the opportunity to make this a joint venture. It was a solo project (albeit with Ben) and a secretive one at that. That is the last thing it should have been as it impacted so much on our family.

Funnily enough the same happened in my relationship with Ben. We were both so busy working, and preparing for the race, that we somehow never spoke beforehand about our shared or divergent goals for the race. All our discussions had centred around the manifestly urgent matters of boats and sponsorships and food.

[Bev]

At about the same time, I'm deliriously happy to be offered a new TV show by Sky One, *Taste*, a food magazine programme that wants an 'enthusiastic but non-foodie' presenter to string together bits of chat with guest chefs and VTs about grub and booze. We'll film sixty-five hours and I'll finally start to make some money again. We'll shoot in two-week tranches so my mum will granny-nap Croyde to spend some time in Manchester. It's the most fun I have ever had in television and I get to sip cocktails at 10 a.m. and utter phrases like 'Pâté is enjoying a renaissance' with a semi-straight face.

Then suddenly (like most of life's greatest shocks, the details have become cloudy) James is going to row the Atlantic with Ben Fogle. It could take two months. There will be no support vessel. The BBC will film a documentary and he'll write a book. I'll be left home alone with Croyde, who will then be twenty-seven months old. I am blind-sided, especially when he says, 'But I *told* you about it.'

'James,' I answered, 'I think I would have remembered that conversation . . .'

In order to promote *Taste*, Sky asks me to do an interview with the *Daily Mail*. I know they'll ask me about James and Ben's adventure, which is already garnering many column inches. 'You have to be honest,' says James.

I say that I'm pissed off. I say that I didn't marry 'bloody Sir Ranulph Fiennes'. I say that sportsmen are inherently selfish. But I am only able to say these things because I know our marriage is fundamentally intact. I love my exasperating husband and I would never deprive my son of his wonderful father. But somehow, I forget to say those things and I don't anticipate how vitriolic my words will sound on paper. My put-upon-wife hysteria (with a mild comedy element) suddenly sounds as though I'm waving a rolling pin at James as he heads for the door. People start to say that there's no wonder he's going away for two months, I must be hell to live with. I *am* hell to live with. I'm dumbfounded that having a child has barely left me able to take a bath in peace while James is free to row across *the Atlantic*.

What James doesn't tell me is how worried he is about providing for our future. He fails to explain that he loves us but is lost and uncertain about his career: should he row in Beijing or retire? He needs time to think. He says macho stuff about 'testing himself' but I'm always ready with a quick comeback about how he can 'bloody well *test* himself' by having sole care of his son for more than a day. Let's just say, things in our house are not good. Reluctantly, I agree to take part in the BBC documentary ('Be honest,' says James.) On screen, I am entirely the seething mass of bitter resentment that I have become.

I meet Ben's girlfriend Marina at the boys' leaving party. I do not understand her at all. She is *so* supportive. I dash to the party from filming *Taste* and the BBC camera asks us for our feelings of anticipation. Marina springs into life, gushing about how proud she is of Ben. Today, it's a clip that never fails to make me laugh. You can literally see me tut and roll my eyes at her. I feel like a complete outsider. This is not my adventure. I don't support James. It's dangerous and I don't want him to die. I haven't had enough of us yet.

[James]

There was a key moment in the crossing when I found out that I was somewhat differently wired to other men – well, at least to Ben. He told me that in his darkest moments, slogging away through the Atlantic all by himself midway through a rowing session, what kept him going were thoughts of Marina, his girlfriend, to whom he would propose as soon as he hit dry land.

'Oh, you know,' he said, when I asked him what he specifically thought about. 'Marina, our weekends together, trips to the seaside, walking the dogs. I tend to relive memorable moments – my trips to the Amazon and travels in South America . . .'

But I didn't know. What did I think of to get me through the dark times? Thoughts of Bev and Croyde would make me ache from missing them, so I reverted to type as a sportsman and thought of the things I could control. Our speed, how better to take advantage of the winds, whether or not we're following the right course. How to improve our chances of winning, basically.

I'd been around competitive beasts all my adult life – and they don't get more competitive than Steve Redgrave. I remember once playing a water polo game against him (one of Jurgen's little training/bonding ideas). I was only nineteen but figured I'd dish out some under-water retribution for his off-the-ball fouls as Jurgen was more interested in his beer than his referee's whistle. There was an under-water skirmish and Steve surely wouldn't notice if I gave him a bit of a slap round the chops to warn him off the rough stuff. Plus I was sure he wouldn't know it was me. How wrong I was. We both roared to the surface, me in a headlock squealing 'sorry' more times in thirty seconds than you would have thought linguistically possible.

So it was pretty self-evident that I'd been mixing with highly competitive people for years and mistaking them for normal. I'd embarked on our Atlantic crossing to get there as quickly as we physically could. If I'd wanted a leisurely Atlantic voyage I'd have gone in a bigger boat, preferably one with an engine. Ben, on the other hand, just wanted to get there. It was a huge, fundamental difference and one we had neglected to talk about at any stage getting ready for the race. A massive mistake.

That was my biggest discovery on this adventure: that you need to discuss every issue – inflammatory or not – with the relevant people. A good example would be the person you are married to, especially if you are dashing out for two months on a transatlantic venture, leaving her with home, life and baby to look after. Another example would be the person with whom you are going to have to share intimate deck space, not to mention a mattress, a rowing seat and a poo bucket.

I think Ben was truly astonished by and could not relate to the apparent inhumanity of my will to win. There were times when it made me so frustrated and depressed and I'd sob down the phone to Bev, who would have been well within her rights to tell me to 'pull my face straight' but she never did. She was nothing but supportive.

I am ashamed to say that those phone calls coincided with periods when we weren't making as much progress as I thought we should due to infuriating storms, a capsize, getting thoroughly knackered, the state of my arse, Ben's non-competitiveness, his heatstroke from refusing to wear a hat, and running out of food and water supplies. We had been, I have to admit, pathetically bad at preparation, partly because I had thought more about reducing weight in order to give us the best chance of winning the race, partly because we hadn't given ourselves enough time and partly because, for the first time, I didn't have a team of people – coach, physio, nutritionist, boatman – helping. But our primary aim should have been getting there rather than racing there.

The greatest gap in our preparation had been mental. Ben isn't competitive on land and wasn't competitive in a boat. He was, however, resolutely determined to finish and that never wavered, whereas I wasn't honest with myself before we left. I thought I could control the competitive monster within me, and I thought that I was only competitive in a pure sport situation. Turns out I was wrong on both counts.

But it wasn't all frustrating or excruciatingly boring. Sometimes we experienced unwelcome excitement too, like the threat of being run down by an oil tanker. There is not much that makes you feel more vulnerable at sea than when you are a tiny rowing boat coming up against a massive seagoing craft lit up like a Christmas tree that has been on your bearing for the last two hours and looks like a floating Canary Wharf on the horizon. Ben was on the radio repeating: 'Big vessel, big vessel, big vessel, this is small rowing boat, small rowing boat, over!'

Then, out of nowhere, we heard: 'Don't worry, we are awake, we see you,' in heavily accented Russian. It was a bit like God actually answering a prayer for a change.

It was funny how swiftly our happiness – or otherwise – came to depend on food. The snack bags had been randomly packed by Ben's girlfriend Marina and so each opening was greeted by cheers if there was chocolate or boos if it was pork scratchings – a good source of fat and protein but not that appealing, at least in the first half of the voyage. Biltong never got the reception I felt it deserved although that too changed after 2,000 miles. There was a point when I'd lost so much weight and was so hungry that I was happily munching swollen pork scratchings saturated with sea water that I found on deck.

But 'happiness' is not really a word I associate with the trip. We descended into a fairly serious spiral of desperation at times and instead of supporting one another, we'd lash out. We suffered from not knowing each other and therefore not being prepared to open up in front of each other. We wouldn't show our true feelings or voice our concerns through a fear of looking weak. Blokes eh?

Christmas in the boat was a horrible time. The batteries had lost charge so the desalinator wasn't working. Rather than the ten litres of water we needed a day, Ben and I lived off one litre of water every twenty-four hours. Dehydrated and missing home badly, I called up Bev who was on her way out to a party. When I spoke to Croyde, he said: 'Hello, Daddy', followed immediately by 'Chocolate, Mummy?' because Bev had to bribe him to talk to me. What the hell was I doing out here? What was I trying to prove? What was I avoiding? How selfish an idiot am I? And those dark thoughts were not helped as news filtered through that one of the other boats in the race had been attacked by sharks.

When we opened our Christmas presents, Mum had bought me a reindeer key ring. I reasoned that it had to be edible otherwise it was a completely useless gift at sea. I took a hopeful bite. Into rubber. What was the woman thinking about? Leopard-print pants come to mind. Bev had been more practical and given me a two-inch-square M&S Christmas cake. I so wanted to scoff the lot myself, but out of the corner of my eye, I could see Ben (using all the wiles he'd learnt from his animal programmes and a year on a Scottish island) making a silent and desperate appeal. Clearly some bonding had been going on as I chose to share the cake with him and broke it in half. That was noble of me, except half an hour later I'd have thrown him overboard to get that half back again.

But by far the worst moment was the capsize, when I was fast asleep in the tiny cabin only to be summarily woken by a fiendish crashing, smashing noise, a bang on the head and water gushing over me. It was pitch black and I seemed to be lying with my face pressed against the small hatch in the cabin's roof. I intelligently deduced we'd been flipped upside down and while my mind wrestled with that thought, the boat rolled and seemed to stick at forty-five degrees. Thank God for the ballast.

And then I thought: Ben!

I leapt into the glimmer of daylight through the cabin hatch. The boat was listing dangerously but that was irrelevant. Ben wasn't on board. I shouted: 'Ben! Ben! BEN!' And added: 'FUCK! FUUUUCK!' All I could see was our stuff floating away in different directions but no sign of Ben.

'I'm here,' eventually came a small voice, which I followed. I found him and threw a grab line into the sea. I grabbed his hand and armpit to pull him on to the deck. 'I knew you shouldn't have been rowing, you were far too tired,' I said; it was my poor attempt to be caring and empathetic not vindictive or judgemental. He didn't speak. He just huddled in the boat, shaking with fright, tears streaking down his face and in shock.

We salvaged what we could but just one look at two bearded, emaciated, miserable, wild-eyed creatures would have been enough to tell you we weren't in tip-top condition. I would say it was then that my attitude – which had driven me insane and Ben to despair – came into its own. I didn't let us contemplate giving up for a second. If we wanted off this boat we needed something on which to focus. Rowing and making progress, however slow, would be better than just sitting there.

For times such as these Bev had given me a special letter. It said that she was proud of me, glad we were married and would be waiting for me when we reached the other end of the journey in Antigua. She ended with two impossible requests. One to call her night or day if I needed her (now a no-go area because the phone had bust) and just to get my 'sexy arse' to the Caribbean (that arse now being covered with horrendously painful boils and sores). I didn't deserve such a letter.

Ben, fearing I'd need some medical attention in the backside area, kept playing down the symptoms when I asked him to look (for which I do not for one minute blame him). But I was in so much discomfort that I decided to start taking some extra-strong painkillers on board for emergencies. As they made me drowsy, I had the brilliant idea of combining them with caffeine tablets to keep awake.

It was when I stuck my head through the hatch while he was on the oars and asked: 'Am I at Freddie Flintoff's testimonial?' that Ben realised I'd overdone the dosage.

Let me tell you in what state I presented myself to my loving wife and little boy when we eventually made it to the other side. My bum wasn't the only area causing me grief. I had blisters on my hands and feet with yellow pus inside them plus numerous cuts on my arms and legs which had now become infected and not healed because of the malnourishment and massive weight loss – over three and a half stone.

My tongue had a layer of scum on it, I had cold sores on my lips and the lymph nodes in my groin had swollen to the size of grapes. Added to that list I was confused, not making sense and who knew what I smelled like. Bev, I have to say, is a brave woman.

Funnily enough, though, it wasn't the physical hardships that most upset me, or even the drugs I had to take, it was the shocking discovery that the body I had trusted throughout my rowing career could let me down so badly. Once I'd realised we were close to land and within sight of my goal to win, my mind let its guard down and my body just fell apart. It's normal; I understand that. I just hadn't expected it to happen to me.

One good thing came out of it though: I discovered that I didn't want to go on rowing any more. Cancel my subscription to Beijing. That was it. Olympic career over. I was moving on. I did, however, make one selfless contribution to the GB rowing's Beijing campaign. When I told Jurgen I wasn't going to carry on to Beijing and he spent an annoyingly short amount of time trying to persuade me to carry on, he also asked me what I had learnt. I told him I was surprised how much pain the body can endure and that he hadn't really trained us that hard. He was delighted to receive this information and apparently implemented a few 'tweaks' to the training programme. I subsequently received a text from Steve Williams, who was in the Beijing four. It comprised just one word. 'Bastard!'

So I'd moved on . . . but into what? Somehow I had to earn a living which didn't involve a boat again, plus look after and spend time with my family without driving them mad. On the face of it, that left the field pretty open but as the trip across the Atlantic had shown, I might not be a normal person.

Most important was the repair work I needed to put into our marriage. I found out on the trip how much I relied on Bev's support. I vowed never again to underestimate her support or exclude her like I had. The experience had shown me we were far stronger as a team and even though she will challenge me, it always comes from a place of love and unconditional support.

So great was the assumption that we were getting a divorce that photographers had been camped outside our house to get a picture of the new man in Bev's life. They must have been a bit disappointed when a cross between Robinson Crusoe and Barnacle Bill came shambling back into view.

Ben and I had no immediate plans after the Atlantic crossing to do something together again. We did say that *if* one or other of us decided on a venture we'd speak to each other first. A couple of years later I heard about the Amundsen Omega-3 Race to the South Pole. It would be the first time in a hundred years that teams would race one another to the pole.

My excitement centred round the fact that we would be isolated and self-sufficient on the ice, hauling our stuff to survive on a sledge, and every minute would count. We would be in a race to reach the South Pole, in the footsteps of the Norwegian polar explorer, Roald Amundsen, back in 1911. I invited Ben to meet me in a coffee shop to see if he fancied the idea. The race was 800 kilometres across the plains of Antarctica, subject to raging storms at minus fifty degrees at a punishing 9,000 feet above sea level. What was there not to like? There wasn't going to be a boat!

Predictably he loved the idea – more long-term job avoidance for both of us. We decided to go ahead, and this time we would bear Amundsen's own words in mind, in theory at least. 'I may say that this is the greatest factor – the way in which the expedition is equipped – the way in which every difficulty is foreseen, and precautions taken for meeting or avoiding it. Victory awaits him who has everything in order – luck, people call it. Defeat is certain for him who has neglected to take the necessary precautions in time. This is called bad luck.'

One of the first things we realised we needed – apart from learning how to cross-country ski – was another member for the team as it had to be three people. Our first choice, actor Jonny Lee Miller, had to drop out because of a potential filming commitment that brilliantly for him came through but not so fantastically for us as the time we'd spent together showed that he would have been a great influence on both of us. So we set about finding his replacement.

After a process that involved a public appeal and the rubbish offer of a prize trip to the South Pole with two novices, dirt, pain and sleep deprivation (as so much in my life seemed to involve), we settled on Ed Coates, a great guy, a doctor (albeit obs and gynae) and someone with a decently high threshold for the cold. What more could we possibly need?

This time, when I said goodbye to Bev, she was wonderful. She told me to go and have an amazing time. By now Croyde was five and she was pregnant with Kiki, but she assured me they would all be fine and looked forward to having me back, safe and well, when the expedition was over. She wrote me a letter that made me cry.

She enabled me to go with such a sense of well-being this

time. That, and the knowledge that the 'snack bags' for our endurance mission had been based on a snacking technique I'd developed over decades of Christmas Days. It involved nuts, sweets, crisps, cake, cheese, chocolate, cold meats and chutney. Maintaining that sweet/sour balance means I (or anyone) can eat pretty much solidly from Christmas Day to New Year's Eve, when obviously social etiquette dictates that I switch to drink.

[Bev]

After James and Ben had returned triumphant from the Atlantic row, and I'd made life-long friends in Marina, Ben and their families, I was happy to concede that I was completely wrong. It was the best thing James ever did. It was the first of many smart moves. I learnt to trust his decisions. He realised he'd had enough of rowing and had got off to the best possible start in a new career that he would love. The programme depicted him as a slightly psychotic over-competitive sportsman. But I knew better. He was competitive – of course he was! But he was also incredibly thoughtful and was now ready to become a fantastic husband and father.

By the time the Antarctic race came along I was much more chilled. Yes, James would be away for another Christmas but he was spending enough time with Croyde to make up for that. We'd moved house to be back in Chiswick, close to my sister, and I'd bitten the bullet to hire a great nanny, Maja, who'd pop in a few mornings a week to allow us the occasional tastes of freedom that meant we could exist as a married couple rather than merely two resentful parents. I'd finished the first version of a novel and with Croyde now four, we were ready for another baby.

James was living life at an incredible pace – so much so that in order to conceive I drove to meet him during the London to Paris bike ride. I was better at calculating my cycle by now and knew that if I didn't catch up with him in July 2008 he'd be away on the pertinent days until almost Christmas. So, with phrases about mountains and Muhammad ringing in my ears, I met him in a small hotel in a town called Coquelle and, shortly after stepping out of his Lycra and taking a much-needed shower, we conceived our gorgeous Kiki Willow.

She was born at home, in water, in the sunshine, on Mother's Day 2009, just in time for lunch. Midwife Pam Wild was once again in attendance; self-hypnosis (I knew better than to expect James to buy into it this time!) and the wonder drug that is gas and air got me through. James was incredible: supportive, strong, funny and entirely present. We had our daughter. I'd never loved him more.

[James]

If you'd asked me then what my greatest worry was likely to be once the race had begun, it was probably that being physically the strongest I might unrealistically expect the others to keep up with me. It probably never occurred to me that the member of the threesome who would most suffer and lag behind was destined to be not Ed, not Ben, but me.

Not long before we'd left England, I'd been to a charity ball with Ben and changed out of my black tie into training kit at midnight so that I could run home from Central London to Chiswick. It was the easiest way of combining life at home with training properly for a selfish trip. Bev was at the same ball. We'd gone together but I chose a different method of getting home which killed two birds with one stone – time-efficient training that didn't impact on the family. The only downside was the affirmation (in Bev's mind and that of the other guests as a Lycra-clad nutcase emerged from the toilets at 12 a.m.) that I wasn't quite right in the head. Irony, eh?

I assumed my extra fitness from years of endurance training would be needed on the trip and I wanted Ben and Ed to be confident that they could rely on that extra strength should they be struggling. I, for one, was confident that their skills in other areas would be called on during the trip. If my extra energy and fitness reserves were needed to carry some of Ben's or Ed's kit on my sledge from time to time, I wanted to be ready and for them not to have to worry about it for a second. I guess I made that assumption in the same way that they might have mentally prepared for surviving with an obsessively competitive tent mate.

I even used to climb over the fence into Richmond Park at night to do a good session of tyre pulling. Climbing the fence was a necessity as these sessions coincided with the park's six-week deer cull. Adrenalin spurred me on during these nocturnal adventures. It was enlivening to know that some-where in there was a guy with a rifle. I just hoped he was a good shot – and didn't easily confuse a deer with a bloke and his tyre.

All this preparation and, in the event, it was me who needed the most help. We'd had a conversation before we left about being honest with each other and leaving our egos at home. It was all about getting ourselves and our kit to the South Pole. It didn't matter who pulled what weight. We thought it would vary as we all had good or bad days. The important thing was that we all work at the same intensity, easier if we left our male egos behind. We insisted that none of us would be afraid to say when we were struggling.

Easier said than done. In the event, I hated being the one who had to suggest we stop to put up our tents and get rest while imagining our Norwegian competitors racing ahead of us.

If Ben and Ed had said the same to me – 'Can I make a suggestion that we stop early?' – I know that I'd have questioned them. Couldn't they go a bit further? How bad did it feel? When I said it, Ben made light of it. Even made it sound like a good idea. But there was no denying I was suffering with health problems.

Even though we had those discussions about teamwork, being open with one another, I couldn't bring myself to announce what deep down I perceived as weakness. I was coughing, especially at night. I'd cough until I was sick, bringing up whatever precious dinner I'd just eaten, and I was finding it hard to breathe. After a week my face had become so swollen that it was almost unrecognisable. Perhaps the worst affliction of all, however, was my feet – made worse by the fact we were on them for over eighteen hours a day. They were wrecked by blisters that turned into ulcers and poor Ed, thanks to his doctor's training, had the pleasure of slicing and repairing as best he could amid the stench of rotting flesh. At least his role in future births would be a piece of cake compared to dealing with stinking, pus-infected seeping blisters at minus fifty degrees.

At least it made Ben retch just to look at them, which strangely gave me a certain sense of pride.

I understand why this made good television. Humans being stretched beyond their normal levels of tolerance behave in mysterious ways. Occasionally those ways closely resemble a toddler. Croyde and I would have agreed on a number of issues, if he had been there, not to mention an unhealthy fascination with al fresco crapping. At other times, the team was just emotional, angry and knackered. But it was over the incident of the crevasse field that I was labelled a tad unreasonable.

Without the cameras we wouldn't have raised sponsorship, without the sponsorship we wouldn't have experienced an amazing continent. But I felt the television condensed us into caricatures of ourselves – which I admit was better than boring footage of watching three blokes trudging through the snow.

All dramas need a villain and that villain was played by yours truly on the day the other two thought we'd entered a crevasse field. There is a very good reason to fear crevasses in the Antarctic – because they can kill you. The majority were near the coast, a thousand miles from where we were, but we still had to be on alert for them. They offer clues to their existence like unusual noises and a horizon that looks nearer because the stress underneath the ice causes the surface to bend upwards.

Nothing on this occasion told me that we were in the middle of a crevasse field. If you are, the first thing you'd do is rope up so that if one person does drop into the tight chasm, the other two can brace (if they have time), anchor and pull their partner out.

It was a noise that alerted Ben. I didn't hear it, or at least not the deep thundering sound he described. It was just a sound magnified by the perfect silence. It was an alarm bell, but also a dinner gong. Fatigue overwhelmed our fear. We camped – on a snow bridge or potentially in a crevasse field, our opinions as to which varied. Either way we had supper, which I coughed up and then swallowed again (sweet and sour chicken, which wasn't bad the second time round), and fell into a deep sleep.

The second time it happened, I felt more confident in my assessment of the situation. Ben shouted the warning: 'Crevasse!' He said he could actually see the snow falling away all around him – as he put it, 'like sand through an egg timer' – and he'd never been so scared in his life. It wasn't my position to challenge him but having been over the area first, I was less convinced. The reality was that none of us was an expert. Well, Ed was, but his obs and gynae skills weren't going to help in this situation.

It was 3 a.m. – we'd been up and skiing for nineteen hours and it was time to start thinking about putting our heads down. I wanted to make sure it was a place we were all comfortable with.

Ben and Ed suggested we rope ourselves together so that if one of us fell down the crevasse, the others – in theory – would be able to haul him up to safety. But I wanted to get away from this area and pitch up as soon as they were happier. Tent up, nosebags on, heads down.

I wasn't being foolhardy. There were no crevasse fields mapped in this area and the ice felt incredibly solid. 'I don't think we need to rope up,' I said. 'The horizon hasn't changed and I haven't seen or heard any changes underfoot. Why don't I lead and stop somewhere with a nice view?' This was my attempt at humour, given the plateau is thousands of identical miles of ice. 'If you or I hear or see anything change we'll reassess the situation.'

Ben and Ed were aghast but mostly in hindsight. They could have said something at the time but chose not to. I genuinely believed that the ground was solid and to give them, as well as

155

myself, confidence I made my way steadily across the ice, firmly testing the snow in front of me with my poles. But I admit the television edit makes me look somewhat – how shall I put it – 'unreasonable'.

With hindsight, Ben and Ed may have interpreted my actions as 'Don't worry, guys, if I'm wrong and I disappear, at least you'll know where not to pitch the tent.' That thought would make me a lunatic, and I'm not. Remember that 'safe, stable and secure' was Bev's rock 'n' roll pre-marital assessment of me.

I still think it was the right decision. The other teams in the race took the same route without a problem. But being right or wrong is secondary to having sympathy for people you care about, especially when you're all tired, cold, confused and not thinking clearly. Ben and Ed may not have been Antarctic crevasse experts but neither was I, and so nothing made my opinion more important than theirs.

The question I also ask myself is how much thought of home went through my head. I had so much to lose: a wife, a child, and another one on the way. It seems extraordinary to me now that the thought of the people I loved should not have made me more cautious. I can only think that the burning desire to be with them as soon as possible made me not want to waste any more time in pissing Antarctica.

It's interesting how you discover things about yourself under extreme provocation. I'd discovered that, thanks to blisters, pneumonia and frostbite, I wasn't the bulletproof guy of the trek that I had expected to be. It wasn't an arrogant presumption of physical prowess – as I'm clearly no Ranulph Fiennes (despite what my wife may think or say on camera) or Lance Armstrong – I just knew that my boringly relentless attitude to training gave me a higher physiological fitness level than the other guys. Instead, they were the ones having to help and nurture me to the finish line.

I was angry, secretly crying tears of frustration into my goggles which either steamed them up or froze them to my face. An infuriating situation but far more preferable – to me – than admitting my vulnerability to the other guys. In the end, it took Ed to insist we stopped for my sake to rest and I broke down and cried. 'I've let you down . . . I can't pull my weight . . . I trained so hard for this . . . I'm so sorry.' Ed put him arm round me, crying too. 'I love you,' he said. 'You haven't let us down.' Ben, by now in tears too, joined us in a group hug.

I suppose I learnt that to say 'I've got to stop' sometimes instead of 'I'll keep going' is not a pathetic failing. It's a practical necessity. Admitting weakness is a greater strength than I'd ever imagined in my Olympic days. I blame hanging around with that Redgrave bloke for too long. He didn't even believe it at first when the doctor said he had diabetes.

I told the guys that if I couldn't finish they should go ahead without me. They refused to do that. Well, in fact they couldn't go off anywhere without me as we had to finish as a team. So together we made it to the South Pole. We didn't win, coming second to the Norwegians. But at least it wasn't just me crying when we got there. We all chipped in tears caused by a mixture of relief, satisfaction and a sense of achievement at having come that far. That three polar virgins made it at all was something we could be proud of.

Even though we came second, which would normally enrage me, I learnt a few valuable things about myself on this trip. Things I vowed to remember and use in the future.

Admitting to myself that weakness takes more strength than relentlessly pushing on.

Creating an atmosphere where others aren't afraid to take a risk, push themselves and fail, rather than one where they feel pressurised and tested.

Taking a minute to sort a problem out early will save hours in the long run.

Being honest with yourself.

I didn't much like being portrayed as a the bad guy when the film went out, but more than that, I hated the idea that people thought Ben, Ed and I didn't like one another. True, they'd seen a lot of footage of the three of us arguing, crying, and sulking in various states of physical decrepitude, but the fact is I love both of them.

In fact, I was best man at Ben's wedding and he was one of the people who flew all the way to see me when I had the accident in Arizona. Now Marina, his wife, may hate me because whenever he and I get together we always seem to decide to enter another extreme hell . . . but Ben is one of my closest mates. And it helps that Bev and Marina have such a good relationship too.

After losing nearly four stone in Antarctica, I did the best I could to put it all back on by enduring the hell on earth that is Cape Town in January. I made peace in my mind by telling myself that it was worth delaying seeing Bev and Croyde a few days if I looked vaguely human for them (especially having left the South Pole at the same weight I was when I was fourteen). It is safe to say I didn't leave Cape Town the same weight as I arrived.

I couldn't wait to see Bev and Croyde as seeing them was going to be a totally different experience to that of stepping out of the boat after crossing the Atlantic. They had been a part of the journey from its conception to its delivery, they'd followed our progress across the continent and Croyde knew things about Antarctica that his friends and a worrying amount of adults don't know. For example 'Is that where the polar bears are or penguins?' Or 'Antarctica, is that the one in the north or the south?' At least the little man knew these facts at the age of five. But more importantly, his daddy was coming home safely with his nose and all his digits in place. I had also learnt the true definition of humility and a huge amount about myself that I believed would make me a better father and husband.

The importance of the latter point was hammered home when I saw Bev at the airport. She was eight months pregnant and looked beautiful.

I'd done water, I'd done ice so it seemed only reasonable that my next trip would involve fire.

There are a lot of weirdos at the South Pole – it seems to be the sort of place that attracts them. An English guy came to our tent at one point and said about my blisters, rather unsympathetically I thought, 'Ah, you think those are bad, you should do the Marathon des Sables.' If I heard a gentle popping, that was the sound in my head of a seed being planted. It might seem like a strange place, but being in a tent at minus fifty degrees made the appeal of running marathons in plus fifty degrees pretty strong.

Bearing Amundsen in mind, the preparation to race six back-to-back marathons across the Sahara Desert in temperatures of up to fifty degrees had to be pretty special. It's considered the toughest foot race on earth and at six foot four and weighing ninety-five kilos I was built for comfort not speed on the running front. Plus that comfort lasted for about five miles not over one hundred and sixty. A fact strongly reinforced when I met the reigning champion from Morocco, Mohammed Ahansal, in London to test our relative strengths.

He was literally half my size. A tiny guy just over five foot tall and weighing sixty kilos, brought up in the heat of North Africa. He'd been acclimatising for over thirty years and would definitely have been at a disadvantage on a cold, rainy river in England where I'd spent a long time acclimatising. It soon became clear that the Sahara wasn't going to play to my strengths. We did some heat tolerance testing, running at twelve kilometres per hour on two treadmills in a lab at over fifty degrees. He lost 500g and I lost 3.5kg in an hour. That made my mind up: I was going to spend as much time as humanly possible in that heat chamber.

The Marathon des Sables, or MDS, has a fifty-strong medical team in attendance and uses 6.5 kilometres of Elastoplast, 19,000 compresses, 6,000 painkillers and 150 litres of disinfectant per race. The dropout rate among the 1,000 runners is high. Two people had died in the race's twenty-five-year history.

You had to carry all your kit and food for the entire race. I'd worked incredibly hard to make my pack as light as possible. For example, only taking a paper police forensic suit to wear after the day's run and enough food for energy, but even so, I'd still be in calorific deficit each day. The one thing I didn't have to carry was water. Each competitor was given six litres a day regardless of their size or, crucially, how much they lost in sweat. Basically, Mohammed could be bathing in it while I'd be rationing it like . . . well, like a man dying of thirst in the desert.

As we gathered at the start, I was aware of the laughter my bulk (at least I hope it was my bulk!) provoked, especially when it became known that I was aiming for a place in the top fifty. The general consensus was: 'No chance, mate.'

This latest escapade was being filmed by the American-based Discovery Channel. They had been down the list of entrants, seen my name on there and thought: 'Ah ha!' For the reason that I was an iconic adventurer once more pitting my wits against the elements? I think not. Probably because there is a degree of dramatic interest in watching an ex-sportsman descend once again into self-inflicted hell.

Due to my training and heat acclimatisation, I had no doubt in the ability of my internal engine to cope with the day-on-day challenge of running that far and coping with that heat. What I wanted to prove was that I could make hard decisions in a competitive situation. Yes, my finish position was going to come down to running speed but more important was my ability to make the right decision at the right time.

Days One, Two and Three were marathons in the desert. There's no way to dress it up. That is what they were and twenty-six miles on tarmac is a walk in the park compared to twenty-six miles on abrasive sand and rock. One would be bad enough but waking up knowing you've got to run further that day while already dehydrated, calorie deficient and sore is what kills you. That's where the ability to stay positive and to remember how privileged and lucky you are to be running through the Sahara Desert is vital, despite the blisters and fifty-degree temperatures.

Day Four was the utter bastard, the twenty-four hours in

which you have to run essentially two marathons together, over eighty kilometres, through the most inhospitable, barren landscape you can imagine. The 'prize' for being in the top fifty after Day Three was to set off a few hours behind the rest of the field in the midday sun, hmm. My vocal sense of injustice at this curiously coincided with the organisers suddenly not being able to understand a word of English.

Going into Day Four I was the leading Briton – but I had to fight and dig deep like never before. It was brutally hot even when the sun eventually went down and the laser guiding us to the finish seemed to permanently be on the horizon. I was concurrently battling heat, dehydration, deep sand dunes and calorific deficit while trying to view the situation in a positive light. I came in late, in the dark and confused with dehydration. Also, as I subsequently discovered, I had two broken metatarsals, although at the time I was just aware that my feet hurt amongst many other more pressing ailments.

They laid me on a stretcher and set up the saline drip. But in the recesses of my wandering mind, I dimly remembered that a drip meant a two-hour time penalty. 'No drip,' I forced myself to say through blistered lips. They looked concerned, but these guys understood the mentality of ultra-marathon runners. We did a deal. If I sipped some water and kept it down, they might let me try and rehydrate myself naturally. On cue, I threw up the water they gave me. But the medics must have decided that I wasn't in danger, and they let me rest without attaching the drip.

With a couple of broken toes I had two stark options. I could either carry on or pull out of the race. But if you pulled out of the race there was no immediate transfer to a five-star hotel and fluffy pillows. Far from it. What you get is the dubious pleasure of staying in the Sahara, driving around with the support crew and becoming an odd-job man tasked with things like putting up the athletes' tent. They basically make it as rubbish as possible so nobody will pull out and become a Sahara tourist until the race is over. I knew if I carried on it was going to hurt, but everything hurt anyway. What difference would it make?

With no two-hour time penalty I just had to survive two more days' running/staggering. If I did I was guaranteed to be in the top fifty but it's funny how your goals change. So by now I'd refined my ambition. In the event's twenty-five-year history, the highest a Brit had ever come was thirteenth, so I was going to readjust my goal to come twelfth. I wanted to be the fastest-ever Brit.

I didn't cross the line with a triumphant sprint, more a hobble with a bandaged leg. Apparently, two broken toes weren't hampering my already-Neanderthal running gait enough, so I managed to pull a hamstring as well.

But I'd finished twelfth and I am genuinely as proud of that as anything I've achieved in sport. I made the right decision at the right time, toughed it out and dug deep when necessary, never stopped believing and found an ability to find the positive in (almost) every situation. A far cry from the negative attitude I had adopted in my rowing days. I also found that I was more relaxed than ever before on camera; able to get my feelings across easily under the tutelage of talented TV director David Harrison.

It was great to catch up with the people back at the hotel who'd doubted my ambition of finishing in the top fifty. Not because I'd proved them wrong but because it showed what work you have to put into building an engine capable of winning rowing races. I've always felt it's a sport that's been undone (especially in this country) by the Boat Race and the class-based perception of it being a sport of hooray Henrys mucking about in boats. I'm not suggesting it is the sport of the working man, but that doesn't take away from the work, dedication and determination it takes to be successful in it. Even though there was a huge personal victory for me in the Marathon des Sables, I like to think I stuck one in for the idiots in boats as well.

[Bev]

I was having a great time hiding Easter eggs in the Devon sand dunes when James finished as the highest-ever Brit in the history of the race. I had never been so impressed. It was unthinkable that a man of six foot four and weighing almost a hundred kilograms should beat the gazelle-like desert runners of Morocco and Kenya. By getting up early (and, unbelievably, running home from nights out at 12 a.m.!) he had organised his training around us. There was no doubt that he possessed one of the strongest minds in the history of elite endurance sport.

He came home happier than I'd ever seen him. There was a gentle calmness that had settled across him: a twinkle in his eyes born of immense personal satisfaction. David Harrison produced a documentary of the race that was nothing short of brilliant. The Discovery Channel loved it. Minds turned to the next challenge. They had an eye on introducing James to a wider audience – namely the American territories in which the channel was so successful. Those viewers would love this handsome Brit with his charming accent and sparkly eyes; a man with two Olympic golds and a hunger for tough challenges. The programme makers devised a trip: crossing the USA using four Olympic disciplines of running, cycling, rowing and swimming. He was literally the only guy in the world who had the necessary skillset to do it all in a suitably impressive time.

James was more excited than he had been before any other project. I didn't question the safety of the journey. He'd cycled Land's End to John O'Groats several times and had ridden across France and Spain to Gibraltar. With such experience beneath his belt, I trusted him entirely. With the trip pending, we sat down and talked about his hopes. Six years after retiring from competitive rowing, he finally felt he was approaching a secure place financially. This trip could move him to the next step – one at which he would be able to take the pressure off himself; see more of his friends and take more holidays. Kiki was 15 months old. We'd both love one more baby. We toasted all of our hard work and felt immensely lucky. Life had never been better.

6

[James]
So, there I was on Santa Monica pier in the summer of 2010, about to set off on my bike, attempting to cycle, swim, run and row across America. I can't say a tickertape parade was there for my send-off. This was lucky as Mark, my physio, had just put the finishing touches to my cycling leg shave-down fetish and once again my backside was on display. Apparently Mark felt that my 'furry hot pants' would mix badly with sweat and saddle-friction-reducing cream.

So no parade, but the TV presenter Vernon Kay who'd I met at Heathrow on the way out stopped by. He was hosting a show in Los Angeles and in the middle of rehearsals to not only get the format nailed but to 'refine' his Lancashire accent so the audience could understand what the hell he was talking about. (Apparently, his brilliantly enthusiastic first words on set –'Hiya, y'll riii-ght' – made the director call a halt requesting the same enthusiasm but a little further 'refinement'.)

He knew Bev from TV and modelling in the past. It was great to see him on the way out and even better of him to come down. He wished me luck, saying he was very glad he wasn't coming with me. I'm not sure whether the transcontinental journey or my company put him off, but either way, it was a damn good premonition.

My plan was to cross the States from California to New York in sixteen days under my own steam while taking in some of the amazing sights the US has to offer. This would mean swapping modes of transport between running, swimming, rowing and cycling. A change, in this case, was not going to be as good as a rest. I hoped the views and people I'd meet would take my mind off the inevitable sore butt that was heading my way.

I'd cycle to Death Valley from LA, run through the 'Valley of Death', bike along Route 66, row across Lake Erie and then back on the bike to New York, finally swimming fifteen miles of the Hudson River to finish under the stern eye of the Statue of Liberty. The worst hundred miles of which (or so I thought) were going to be the run in Death Valley, not just because of the temperatures of well over fifty degrees, but because my metatarsals still weren't loving my graceful running style. In fact I hadn't run since the Marathon des Sables so as to give them the most time to recover and I wasn't intending to set a land speed record across the hottest place in America. It was going to be uncomfortable but I had confidence in my support team. For humour and motivation if not sympathy

I was met at the airport by Bernie Shrosbree, who was ex-Royal Marines and a guy I completely trusted, having met him on a training camp in Lanzarote in 2000. He'd been whipping Mark Webber, Jensen Button, and Fernando Alonso into shape for Renault at the time and the production company filming our journey for the Discovery Channel had hired him to lead the team that would ensure I was able to keep safely moving on.

Bernie and I had done the Devizes to Westminster canoe race together and I was given some insight into the way his mind worked when at 2 a.m., after fourteen hours of non-stop kayaking, I suggested grabbing a cup of hot soup from the support crew before we cracked on for the last four to five hours of the race. He just looked from side to side and then said: 'Where are they?'

Thinking he was starting to hallucinate, I reassured him: 'Bernie, mate, there's no one here.'

'Exactly, nobody is shooting at us,' he said. 'Get in the fucking boat.'

So that was his baseline. If there is no danger, get on with it. He was hired by the production company on my recommendation, as I knew he would do two very crucial things: stand up to me and look out for me. It wasn't a race: the primary object was to make it across, and he's someone you would always want in your corner.

The rest of the support crew included Dr Fred Wadsworth, a nutritionist, and Mark Perkins (ex-military so understood about discomfort and the limits of the human body), who was with me on my Sport Relief trip to Africa when I rowed across the Channel, cycled through France and Spain and swam the Straits of Gibraltar. He was the physiotherapist for the trip and I had absolute faith in him.

And so with Vernon waving me a fond farewell, I pressed on the pedals and got going. 'I'll get a plane and meet you in New York,' he shouted.

I felt lucky to be testing myself in a way that I genuinely enjoyed while making a good television programme and hopefully inspiring people to be more active and test their limits. Perhaps I had found my niche, doing television documentaries like this. No rower has been able to retire on their earnings from mucking around in a boat, and I was no different. I'd been paid in a lifetime for my sport what Carlos Tevez earns in a week, and I felt the pressure and responsibility to earn a living now I had a wife and family. How I, or in fact we, achieved that was still a work in progress.

Bev and I had really talked about our future and come to a far better understanding than we had ever had before. When I came back from this trip, there was going to be – and needed to be – a big change. We (or more accurately, I) would make much more effort to stay in touch with friends and have a fully involved social life because there are only so many times you can tell people that you're away or busy before they drift into other friendships and – understandably – leave you alone. Bev was again completely supportive of this trip. She didn't get involved in any planning; simply assumed that what I was doing – with a support team and a production company, on the open road, through a country with working telephones, shops and motels – was as safe as you could get.

I had a police escort out of Los Angeles and at one point they broke the speed limit keeping up with me (admittedly, that was downhill with a following wind), which had the combined benefit of amusing me and making the next few miles pass more quickly with a smile on my face. Then, rather than looking after a masochistic English guy, they went back to proper policing and I started a lovely twelve-mile climb in thirty-eight-degree heat as we entered the desert. It was like cycling into a hot fan. An ideal appetiser for an eighty-mile run through Death Valley, It was so hot I remember saying to

Bernie that you could poach an egg on the ass of my shorts. 'No thanks, I prefer scrambled,' he said.

Soon the laughter stopped, as after only a few miles of running I had hobbled to a walk. My right foot, or more specifically the dreaded metatarsals in it, was killing me.

Bernie had said before the run started that I might like to use a couple of running poles. I told him to get stuffed. 'I won't be using them; I'm below sea level, not going on an alpine walk!' I said, confident I would be able to run (after all, it was only one run and then back on the bike). The problem was that it may have only been one run but it was seventy-eight miles in blistering heat. When he hung them out of the truck only a couple of miles further on, I said: 'Oh give them to me then' with that particular type of ungraciousness that comes with eating humble pie. Thankfully they took enough of my weight to ease the pressure on my toes and I was able to carry on.

It was hard, hot, horrible work but there were two great incentives to cross the run's finishing line: Beverley had flown out to see me and there was an ice bath waiting for me to help my aching legs recover – which apparently I was going to love.

Somehow, I managed to finish three marathons, from 18:00, through the night to 13:00 the next day, at an average of 105 degrees. I drank thirty-five litres of fluid but lost 3.5 kilograms. What a lovely day out! The crew gave me a round of applause. I seem to remember them shaking their heads a lot. It may have been disbelief, or perhaps they were just recoiling from the smell of me.

I have to say that a hug and a kiss from Bev were way more enjoyable than immersing my body in ice-cold water. Ice baths are never fun, but having run for nearly twenty-four hours in horrendous heat and then switching from a temperature of fifty degrees to less than five was so horrific I begged them in an octave I didn't think my voice could reach to let me climb out again.

This is where Bernie and Mark's knowledge of interrogation techniques and human limits came in handy, as they weren't letting me out. Bev didn't appear to be listening to my cries for help. She handed me some sunglasses, although burning eyeballs were the least of my worries.

Getting back on the bike after a few hours' rest, I grudgingly admitted it was a good plan to keep the legs moving as the bike wasn't going to get down Route 66 on its own. We began ticking off longer and longer distances. I was in a good place as we entered Arizona, recovered from the run and feeling as upbeat as I had done at any stage of the trip. I'd met a few interesting characters on the road, who sometimes biked beside me for a while to wish me luck. A couple of bikers (this time Hell's Angels who sensibly had bikes equipped with a motor) checked me out. 'Have a real safe ride,' I remember one of them saying as he tore off up the road.

Going over the continental divide, I could see the plains stretching out beneath me. It was an amazing sight but it wasn't just the landscape change that was astounding – I could also see a few tornados swirling on the horizon. A buffeting wind started up around me, so I called a halt to the ride for the night. There was no point going on in those conditions. I hoped it would die down by the following morning and we'd have a few hours' sleep in a motel to get us ready for the next day.

That worked out as planned. The next morning one of the

guys gave me a lift in the RV back to where I had stopped cycling the night before. We could have started at the motel – it was along the route I'd be taking and now we were doubling back on ourselves – and nobody would ever have known, but I couldn't do it. It would have been cheating and I wanted to do every mile.

It was about 4 a.m. and very quiet. The road was almost empty at that hour. This was a safe, wide public highway. I felt fresh and was riding with lights, front and back, as the sun rose over the wide Arizona plain.

I felt fantastic. All I could hear was the rhythmic buzz of the pedals turning and my steady breath in the sharp morning air as the road stretched out in front of me . . .

7

[Bev]

I know that something is wrong the moment the hotel phone beside me rings. It's 6.30 a.m. Even though I'm checking out in a few hours, Las Vegas's receptionists know better than to interrupt the sleeping dawn of nocturnal gamblers. Still on UK time, I'm already awake.

'Bev, mate, it's Bernie.'

And I know. I just know.

'There's been a crash. You've got to go to Phoenix.'

It struck me as an odd word to use even then: 'crash'. It spoke of impact: bones against metal; the skid of a bike across tarmac. But it's also the slightly macho word used by army-types like ex-marine Bernie Shrosbree who had known James for several years. Bernie has seen many traumatic things in his life. He is one of those blokes who gets dropped in the ocean and scales the side of a warship to hold a gun to the enemy's head. But Bernie's voice wavers and cracks. He is scared. I am scared.

It's a brief exchange in which I long for information that I don't want to hear. James is physically strong. He'll be fine. But then he says that James has gone to hospital from the roadside in a helicopter. My stomach lurches – I know that Americans don't do expensive medical helicopters unless someone is seriously injured.

Sure that I'll forget, due to the ringing in my ears, I scribble 'Phoenix' on a note pad and call James's PA, Emma, in London. We have known Emma for a long time and I feel incredibly fortunate to have her support. As always, she is calm and competent while also sending her genuine love and concern. She keeps asking, 'How? How has that happened?' But she hangs up, assuring me that she will get me on a flight from Vegas to Phoenix as soon as possible.

I throw the last of my few things into a suitcase, not knowing that the clothes I've brought for a weekend will have to last me for the next month. You imagine that in the eye of a storm, you will crumple, but I've come to understand that the human spirit is deep and courageous and makes sure you don't forget your toothbrush.

Waves of nausea wash over me as I take the lift down to check out. I can't be sure, but the way that I've made the most of the all-day Vegas buffets suggests that I might very well be pregnant again. If James is going to be dead by the time I get to Phoenix, I have to hold it together for the sake of his unborn child. I cannot control what might or might not be happening to James's body right now, but I have a responsibility to my own, and to the one that might be growing inside me. The maternal instinct is a powerful, self-preserving and life-affirming thing.

There would be many days to come in which pregnancy and traumatic brain injury made very poor bedfellows, but on 20 July 2010, the possibility of a baby sibling for Croyde and Kiki makes me stronger, less emotional and fiercely pragmatic. I buy a banana and a muffin, and add four sachets of sugar to a large cup of tea to stop my hands from shaking.

On autopilot, I check out, drive to the airport, return the hire car, and find the check-in desk. Emma has found me the first flight available and she's also called my sister, Cal. We decided not to tell James's parents until we had more news, but Cal would travel from London to Henley-on-Thames where my parents were blissfully unaware; taking care of Croyde and Kiki. Someone calls from James's agent's office. Her facts are scant, but she seems to think that he was conscious on arrival at the Winslow Hospital, Arizona. This would prove to be nonsense, but it does at least offer me a little optimism for the two-hour flight.

Fastening my belt I suddenly have time to think. I'm OK – until I consider the kids and having to explain to Croyde that Daddy isn't coming home. That image strangulates me and I have to dab at my eyes with a paper napkin. I try to finish a book I'm reading but the words slip off the page. Like most atheists in a crisis, I say a little prayer.

Bernie meets me at the airport and we drive to James. I'm still clinging to the news that he had been conscious at the hospital.

Bernie looks at me. 'Bev, this trip is over.'

The faces that meet me in the hospital waiting room confirm the severity of the situation. The all-male TV and support crew are ashen. I walk in and make a joke about who's to blame but it's greeted with an eerie silence.

James is in Intensive Care. I wait for a doctor to come and see me. Dr R. Odgers is a blond-haired, six-foot-three twenty-something with a name from a Carry On film but the kindly manner of Dr Green in ER. Expertly, he explains that James has no broken bones; he is not paralysed.

It's a beautiful piece of bad news delivery: get the good news out first. Dr Odgers explains that my husband has sustained a massive blow to the back of the head. This had caused a 'contrecoup' injury, a French term, literally translated as 'against the front'. The brain swung forwards, smashing against the inside of his skull. He has 'subdural haematoma and sub-arachnoid blood and frontal contusions', which means that although his brain is seriously messed up – bruised and bleeding all over – the significant damage is to the frontal lobes, the part that controls our personality. He has a 'basilar skull fracture' – a massive crack down the back of his head that they'd shut with a clutch of metal staples. My husband, he says, is not breathing on his own. He is in an induced coma as this allows them to keep him still, minimise the risk of seizures and regulate everything that goes in and out of his body.

Dr Odgers assures me that they're watching very carefully to see if the swelling continues. If so, they will have to open up the front of his head to release the pressure. Brain surgery, in other words. I take it all in as he advises that James's parents fly out as soon as possible.

The Intensive Care unit is oddly familiar thanks to my many wasted hours watching American hospital dramas. Around a central, circular doctors' station there are roughly eight individual rooms containing inert bodies, beeping machines and nurses in smart navy blue outfits quietly going about their business.

My knees buckle when I see James and I collapse into the plastic chair beside his bed. If he'd been awake he'd have been impressed, no doubt quipping, 'Finally! I've been waiting years for you to go weak at the knees.' A nurse asks, 'Mrs Cracknell?' and hands me a clear plastic bag containing his blood-covered wedding ring.

Except for the clumps of dry blood on his face, a hefty bandage around his head, a tube down his throat and small pipes up his nose, electronic pads on his chest, a sturdy blood-covered neck brace and the fact that he isn't moving, he looks fairly normal. I've always been a sucker for a pretty face and even after ten years James could still walk into a room and surprise me with his good looks.

This isn't one of those moments. But it is the perfect introduction to brain injury: the hidden disability. In just his blue hospital shorts, lying on the bed with his cyclist's tan (brown arms, white chest), he looks incredibly fit and healthy. Nevertheless, the reality of the situation finally hits home. I shake my head in disbelief, kiss his eyelid – a small part of his face not obscured by plastic pipes. 'Hello, baby,' I say softly, and hold his hand. I sit down and rest my chin on the edge of the bed as Bernie comes in and puts an arm around my shoulder.

I have always hated bicycles. Of course, I know that they are good for the planet, cheaper than cars and a great way of exercising. But in a room of cycling enthusiasts I always feel like the lunatics have taken over the asylum: how could anyone get on a bike when an engine-powered ton of metal is always going to win the battle against a human being in cotton shorts?

In 2006 James took me to Richmond Park in preparation for a triathlon I had decided to enter. The race itself would be on the beautifully smooth tarmac around Dorney Lake without a car in sight. I'm a decent swimmer so, I reasoned, I could be out of the water first and coast along enjoying the view. And I didn't want to win it – with a three-year-old boy I just needed a good excuse to do some regular exercise. But somehow I'd acquired a pink thin-framed drop-handlebarred racing bike that scared the shit out of me. Much to James's disgust, I'd prefer a bicycle with a basket on the front and a seat that is lower than the handlebars. On the surprisingly busy roads of Richmond Park I was reduced to a quivering, crying, petrified wreck as James shouted at me to stop being such a wuss.

He was right of course, I was being ridiculous. Bicycles aren't inherently dangerous. I've even started to use the basketed variety myself to nip to the local shops.

Whenever people asked how I could 'let' James go on his extreme trips (i.e. all the time), I'd answer that although I know he's a careful and considerate cyclist, I was most scared of him riding a bicycle on the open road. I'd only agreed to him doing the trans-America trip because he would have safety vehicles in front of and behind him at all times. But as I sit at the hospital bed, listening to the machines beep and watching the wires snaking in and out of his face and his chest rise and fall at the whim of a ventilator, I don't consider any of this. The most pressing issue is to call James's family. I can't yet speak to my own mum or the kids – that would have burst an emotional dam that I was managing to hold back.

Thankfully, my sister Cal has already prepared James's sister Louise (we all live within a one-mile radius of each other in West London), his mum Jennie and dad John, who had, coincidentally, been visiting Lou.

They too have been encouraged by the erroneous news that James had been conscious on arrival at the hospital. So the enormity of the situation comes as a blow. I explain to John that they should get on a plane as soon as possible. He's in shock. But in typically dry style, he sighs, 'T'riffic.'

My first day at the hospital is simultaneously cataclysmic but strangely uneventful. I drop off my numbers with the nurses in case they have to call me in the night and leave with Mark and Bernie for our hotel. After the chill of the ICU, I'm longing for the relief of fresh air, but Phoenix in July is an oppressive forty-six degrees. Despite the great expanse of desert sky, it's suffocating to leave the air-conditioned hospital.

Home for the next month would be a basic American Marriott hotel that caters for travelling salesmen and the families of patients in hospital. The reception is full of the TV crew – cameramen looking shocked and appalled; executive producers huddled over pieces of A4 paper and looking worried, doubtless not only for James but for the impact of what had just happened. I'm not worried about blame and responsibility. I just want James to open his eyes, say, 'Wow, that was weird,' and we'll all get the plane home. Nothing else matters.

The hotel has a small business centre in the reception area that would prove to be a lifeline to the outside world. When not at the hospital, I will sit here with a cup of bad coffee from the instant machine and manage things with Emma in England as best I could. But the problem with mass communication is that people grow hungry for information that might otherwise remain private. Physiotherapist Mark Perkins had been updating James's Twitter feed with snapshots and comments during the trip. It had gone strangely quiet. The charity page set up for the event was suddenly not being updated. I knew we were living on borrowed time with the outside world.

James's parents, Jennie and John, arrived. They were calm and stoic and I was hugely relieved to have their support. There is no doubt that James has inherited his toughness from them. I think, like me, the first sight of James in the ICU is almost too surreal for them to take on board.

The nurses are constantly reading digital screens around James's bed; taking his temperature and replacing an IV filled with a heavy diuretic that courses into his veins, removing excess fluid from his cranial cavity. The ventilator breathes for him; a feeding tube pumps in nutrients that emerge pale yellow into a bag attached to a catheter. As a journalist, I'm accustomed to dealing with steep learning curves. If the phone rings at 10 a.m., I might have to research, rethink and regurgitate a topic I know nothing about for a thousand-word article five hours later. And I was always the girly swot who weirdly enjoyed the discipline of revision. But suddenly I was cramming for an exam I didn't want to take. Normally a lover of new words, I was taking them like bullets I would have to carry for the rest of my life.

A neurosurgeon arrives to brief Jennie and John about their son's condition. His contrecoup injury is officially a TBI – traumatic brain injury – and as long as he doesn't succumb to pneumonia or other infections that are extremely common after such an accident, he will henceforth be known as a TBI survivor. He's only alive because there has been no damage to his brain stem, the part at the back of the head on top of the spinal cord that regulates breathing, heartbeat or other involuntary functions necessary for life.

The Cracknells have to hear that their thirty-eight-year-old son has extensive damage to the frontal lobes: the area of the brain that governs speech, memory, movement and personality. The doctors talk about 'outcome' and how it is unpredictable – one of the hardest aspects for families of TBI sufferers. The neurologist says that when James wakes up he will be 'impatient and unable to concentrate'.

Soon we are back to considering the symptoms that we read about in leaflets handed to us by the team looking after him. 'Short- and long-term memory loss; slow thinking; short attention span; inability to process information; problems with planning, organisation and judgement; mood swings; depression; confusion; irritability and restlessness.' I raise an eyebrow at John. 'Blimey, do you think we should let him stay asleep?'

As James's parents and I absorb the magnitude of events, nurses come in to prod his hands and feet with little steel rods to check that he responds to pain stimuli. We share thank-God expressions as he instinctively draws back his feet and grimaces deep in his sleep. Even though the doctors have said that James is not paralysed, seeing his feet move brings indescribable relief. If he can walk, I think, he can run. If he can run, he can be James.

After a couple of days, the doctors decide to ascertain whether he can breathe unaided. Switching off the noisy ventilator attached to the thick pipe that snakes down his throat is tense to say the least. But I know that if James is good at anything, it's breathing – that cardiovascular system has made him one of the world's top endurance athletes. But desert marathons are suddenly small-fry compared to this: this is his big moment. We leave the doctors to perform the procedure and wait – holding our breath while hoping that James doesn't do the same.

Seeing him without the pipe down his throat brings another episode of relief. He's still wearing the thick bandages around his head; a neck brace to keep the spine still and an oxygen mask, but seeing him breathe on his own is a huge step. The irony is unavoidable: we're used to James pushing through some of the world's toughest physical boundaries; snapshots of his puffed-out cheeks powering rowing boats in world-famous finals are the norm. And here we are grateful that he is able to draw breath. For several days we keep a bedside vigil, watching as nurses try to elicit a response.

At times, it's futile – lovely Intensive Care nurses loudly speak his name, hoping that he might open an eye, squeeze a finger. I hold his hand, urging him to grip. Jennie, John and I take it in turns to wander down to the basement cafeteria to return with huge, American-sized cups of tea. Together, we're just about coping.

Someone in James's agent's office – in a well-intentioned attempt not to 'sensationalise' the story, has down-played the severity of the injuries. Jennie is being impressively calm until a TV executive from the production company hands her a copy of the *Daily Telegraph* in the hospital lobby. It contains a piece about the accident. According to the report (lent unfortunate credibility as it's the paper that both James and I write for), James is 'sitting up and chatting to his wife'. Jennie bursts into tears. Like me, she knows we are facing a massive uphill battle. That journey will be made all the more difficult if people around James have high expectations of his recovery. Sure enough, a steady stream of chirpy texts, calls and emails arrive from friends and strangers relieved that James is A-OK. Sponsors call Emma to request appearances with James in a few days' time. *GMTV* want to do a live interview. Jennie's builders ring to say they are relieved to hear James is fine and which type of handles did she want on her new kitchen cabinets.

Meanwhile, in Intensive Care, we sit by James's bed, waiting to see what will be left of the man we love if he decides to come back to this world.

Horrendous dark blue and yellow bruises have appeared across his lower back and down his legs. One calf is completely black. It is an absolute miracle – and testimony to his incredible skeletal strength – that he hasn't broken any bones.

After a few days of being completely unresponsive, James begins to wake. It starts with the odd grip of a hand, his knees jerking upwards, feet pushing against the bottom of the bed. An arm will suddenly bend and try to remove his neck brace or the various cannulas out of his forearms. It's terrifying as his actions are so erratic and quick. Plus his considerable strength means that it can take two of us to hold him down and stop him hurting himself. His eyes are still closed but his determination is already evident. With me pushing hopelessly to hold his arm down, he lifts it and hooks a long finger into the edge of his neck brace in an effort to pull it off.

The nurse nods. 'Look. His actions aren't random. They're purposeful. That's good.'

I use all my body weight to push his arm back to the bed, 'Purposeful? Ah, you've finally met my husband.'

Soon sounds begin to emerge: dry growls that are croaky and angry. These moments disappear as quickly as they arrive and he'll fall yet again beneath a cloak of heavy, dark sleep. He hasn't yet sat up but from time to time Dr R. Odgers appears to carefully turn James's head to the side to inspect his fractured skull. The white pillows gradually turn red as blood continues to seep through the thick bandage and from between the metal staples holding his scalp together beneath his mass of thick, matted hair.

One afternoon, while James lies motionless, Dr Odgers pulls up a chair and sits beside me. 'So, remind me what he was doing when he was hit.' I tell him about James's many achievements: two Olympic gold medals; the Atlantic, the Antarctic; the highest-placed Brit to finish the epic Marathon des Sables race; the marathons he had just run through Death Valley a few days before the accident. It feels odd because I rarely meet anyone who isn't fairly familiar with James's exploits. I spend a lot of time on the sidelines, rolling my eyes and childishly mouthing 'w-h-a-t-e-v-e-r' as people gush about his achievements. James laughs at my attempts to keep his feet on the ground, but now I'm able to be proud. 'He's a pretty impressive guy.' Dr Odgers casually gives me a little time to ask him a few questions about the longer term: will he recognise me? The kids? Will he be able to live normally? But he doesn't have any conclusive answers. 'His brain,' he says, 'is running the show.'

Happy with James's physical observations, the Intensive Care doctors eventually decide it's time to ramp up their efforts to awaken him. They reduce the medication he's on to keep him sedated and wait to see what happens.

'Jaymes . . . Jaymes.' The angelic Intensive Care nurse is about fifty years old with a shiny brunette bob and a drawling Arizonan accent. 'Can you hear me? You are in a hospital. Squeeze my hand, Jaymes.' She speaks loudly but kindly and it reminds me of the tone I use to wake Kiki from an afternoon nap.

'Do you know where you are, Jaymes?' When he doesn't respond, she smiles at us, shrugs. 'He's not ready yet. I'll come back.' My in-laws and I are all being terribly English – twiddling our thumbs nervously, none of us being particularly comfortable with talking loudly at a prostrate James in a silent room. We share a smile when John returns with coffees – the canteen has reported a shock run on sales of English breakfast tea.

The next day I come in to find the nurses chirpier than usual. 'He's awake!' I drop my handbag, look at James snoring and think, 'Really?' But they raise his bed to a sitting position, shout his name and pinch him in the crook of his neck. His eyes roll open; slowly he focuses; raises a tiny smile and purses his lips to blow me a kiss. Then he's gone, back into the black. 'Did you see that? Did you see that? Did he blow me a kiss?' I can't be sure I haven't imagined it.

'Yes, he did! He recognised you! That's a really good sign.'

He is still in there. All I can think about are the children. How do you explain to a child that even though their father looks the same, his brain is broken and his personality changed for ever? I stick photos of the kids on the wall in front of his bed. He may have recognised me, but there is no guarantee that they will elicit the same response. If his eyes are going to start opening, I'm going to fill his head with as much normality as possible.

Inspired by his reaction, the nurses are now on a roll. 'Right, we're going to get him sitting on the edge of the bed. Come on!' This strikes me as a big step for a man who has been lying flat out for several days and only started breathing by himself very recently. But two nurses and a 'sitter' (usually a student nurse) hurry themselves waking him up, shuffling him forward and swinging his legs over the side. 'Jaymes, Jaymes. How are you, Jaymes?' His head lolls; the thick white bandage dark red at the back. He already looks thinner thanks to muscle-wasting steroids and the brain consuming massive calories in an attempt to heal itself. 'Jaymes. Jaymes! How are you, Jaymes?' And as though steaming drunk with an extraordinarily posh accent he slurs, 'Maaarrvellous.'

Relief and adrenalin collide. I can't stop laughing. It is classic James: mock-posh humour and a dash of sarcasm. I thought he might croak 'OK' or 'fine'. But 'marvellous' was bloody hilarious. He'd never been less marvellous!

His new sitter arrives: a Russian woman; stocky and squat with short brown hair and an accent I will never forget. Despite her enthusiastic warmth, she possesses the demeanour of a James Bond baddie. I can't quite think who she reminds me of until Jennie arrives and whispers, 'Oh good God, it's Rosa Klebb.'

We suspect that 'Rosa' is the Intensive Care unit's secret weapon. Her voice could wake the dead: a man in a brain-injury semi-coma should be a push-over. 'Rosa' sets about harassing, stalking and pestering James. Jennie, John and I know that although it's probably wrong to be laughing at the afflicted, one of us regularly has to leave the room whenever 'Rosa' turns full throttle on James. 'Mr Jamez! Mr Jamez! Zee must vake up now, Mr Jamez!'

Poor James fleetingly opens his eyes to be greeted by a James Bond baddie poking a finger in his arm and shouting down his ear.

Perhaps in a desperate attempt to escape 'Rosa', James becomes much more active. Although this is incredibly positive and allows us the relief that leads to moments of humour, it also means that he has to be physically restrained. It's awful to watch him straining against the white leather straps that tie his wrists and ankles to the bed. All we can do is offer him words of reassurance that mean nothing to his damaged brain.

After the American adventure, James had been due to embark on another trip with Ben Fogle. This would be the third of their jaunts together for the BBC and would have involved mountain biking in America for a three-part series and a book. One of the hardest calls I had to make was to Ben and his wife Marina to say that the trip would not be happening. Like us, Ben and Marina's life is always at the mercy of the next project, the next TV commission, the next opportunity to make money as a self-employed freelancer. There is no job security in our lives. I'm not looking for pity – we are all ridiculously fortunate and Ben and James have chosen these careers – but they are also both haunted by the very real possibility that the phone could stop ringing tomorrow. And I know that the next BBC trip was to be especially important for Ben.

As I suspected, the Fogles instantly dismiss my apology: TV programmes and income and lost projects are utterly irrelevant. I adore Marina. Not only is she criminally beautiful, she's also smart and strong and together we've been through a lot as the wives left holding the babies. There was not a hint of disappointment in her voice for Ben. More than anyone, she could have been walking in my shoes. In fact, she put the phone down and minutes later Ben rang back to say he was getting the next plane out.

Without the ventilator tube, the nurses are keen to see if James can swallow. I'm shocked that nobody has mentioned this to me before. Along with breathing, I consider swallowing a fairly vital life skill. They bring a plastic cup of water and a straw, and as Rosa Klebb shouts at James I awkwardly offer him the drink. He takes a sip as his eyes, liquid and blank, open for a moment. A little escapes from the corner of his mouth but he definitely swallows. They suggest we try some ice. I take a little crushed ice on a spoon and gingerly move it between his lips. He obviously hasn't showered; his face has been wiped but there are still bits of dirt, patches of dried blood and a small indentation on the side of his nose but I'm amazed that his teeth are intact. Not only does he swallow, he also crunches. Now it's the nurses' turn to be amazed.

He recognises his parents and after an agonising pause is able to tell the nurse the names of his two children: Croyde and Kiki. But when he sees Mark, the physiotherapist, James assumes he's waking from a nap and must get back on his bike. We have to explain over and over that he is in Phoenix, in a hospital. He has had an accident. His brain is bruised and is playing tricks on him. His speech is still slurred and bizarrely posh but he's just about stringing sentences together. I feel so lucky – many TBI sufferers have to learn to talk again.

But James is also determined to recommence his trip. It's as though his brain has switched back on at exactly the moment it turned off. But of course it hasn't – we don't really understand it at the time, but he will recall nothing of these days. His insistence on carrying on where they left off is so intense that he is once again tied to the bed. He's still sleeping for perhaps twenty out of every twenty-four hours, but when he's awake, he's like a drunk heading back to the bar only to be turned away. 'C'mon mate, c'mon mate,' he keeps urging Mark. 'Let's go.' When Mark – yet again – explains that he is in hospital and the trip is over, James's disappointment bubbles over into anger, but he quickly runs out of steam, shaking his head at the room, disgusted with us all for spoiling his fun, before falling asleep again.

He can't stand up and there's a worrying slackness about one ankle that turns inwards when he is sat on the edge of the bed. But if left to his own devices he would try and walk out of the room. 'Rosa' continues to shout at him and turns on the local TV news to show us a story about a British sportsman called James Cracknell being in the hospital.

I manage to push thoughts of a possible pregnancy out of my mind except for mealtimes, when I force myself to eat healthily, and in the evening, when I stop short of the extra-large glass of wine I'm craving to take the edge off the day's tension.

Ben Fogle arrives as the doctors decide that James can be moved from ICU into a neuro-recovery unit where he will still be closely monitored but won't require the life-saving measures of the immediate post-trauma phase. I'm nervous about the change of scenario but Ben is so confident, well mannered and considerate that his arrival is a breath of fresh air. I joke with him that he should have his own TV show in which he interviews the ill and infirm while also checking that their wives have all the comforts they could ever need. 'You could call it *Ben at your Bedside* or *Fogle Talks to Old Fogies*, something like that.' He spots a nicer room in the unit where James arrives on a gurney and, as a well-spoken British man in Arizona, asks if we could possibly have that brighter room, if it isn't too much trouble, please, thank you.

After being fairly alert in the ICU, James starts to sleep even more and is literally awake for mere minutes simply to eat and drink easily consumed soft food. When he does see Ben I have a little chuckle to myself: this is *really* going to confuse him. One minute he's doing his Discovery TV job, the next he's faced with the mate he was meant to be starting his BBC gig with three weeks later. But he merely manages a 'hey buddy', before drifting back to sleep.

It's five days since the accident and almost ten days since I saw the kids. I'm starting to miss them enormously and although I've spoken to them and my mum several times, I feel a strong, instinctive need to hold them. I also think that having them here will signal normality to James. The TV crew have all drifted home and there isn't much for me and the in-laws to do all day except stay by James's bedside anticipating any speech or movement. James may not be up to much daddy day-care but I feel a stronger need to see the kids than ever before. Unfortunately, nobody told me that James's sleeping stage is simply the calm before the storm.

The Discovery Channel are fantastically supportive and organise a flight for James's sister Louise, my mum Joyce, Croyde, who is six, and Kiki, just seventeen months. I reorganise the hotel rooms and the Marriott kindly finds us a suite with an adjoining double room. The hotel runs a complimentary shuttle service to and from the hospital and Jennie, John and I sit in exhausted silence as we chug back and forth in the white minibus.

The lady on reception knows me as the-woman-who's-husband's-head-was-hit-by-a-truck and never fails to ask how he is doing. So far, Jennie and John and I have been eating at a nearby restaurant, but now we have a small living area with a microwave, a fridge and a sink. We can stock up on a few essentials and it's bliss to simply return to the room after a day at the hospital and veg out in pyjamas before collapsing into bed.

The press are hungry for more information about James. Emma

has been staving them off but we conclude that with a week gone by already, we should probably update them. A British journalist has been hassling the hospital press department and insinuated that they'll send a photographer if we don't release some information. I couldn't care less if they get a photo of me looking like crap in my dirty clothes with big bags under my eyes. But I feel fiercely protective of James and want to retain some control over the information that is printed. We have a ten-year relationship with the *Daily Telegraph* so I speak to my editor there and explain that I'm sorry but I can't write an article at this time and we agree that I'll give a brief interview to one of their staff writers. I'm cautious but it seems a good compromise. On email I select photos of James looking strong and sporty on his bicycle days before he was hit. I want to be by his bedside but I also need to do this for him. The copy is sent through for me to approve and I hit the roof when I see that not only is it unusually mawkish, it is also written in the first person with my by-line – as though I've had the time and inclination to sit down and compose a large piece on my seriously ill husband!

I'm furious and shout down the telephone to my lovely editor, who pulls the piece amidst a mass of apologies. I'm so tired. I feel totally alone in handling the media. I don't know if I'm doing what James would want and more than anything I long to discuss it with him. I set about composing a small press release with a few details about James's improvements. I email it to the paper and sit, exhausted, with my head on the desk of the business centre.

'James, where are you?'

'Merseyside on Sea.'

'No, you're in Phoenix in the hospital. You've had an accident.'

'Oh.'

'Where are you?'

'The Tour de France.'

'No, you're in Phoenix in the hospital.'

'Is this Cal's wedding?'

'No, it's a hospital.'

James looks around the room where his parents and I observe his coming back to life. He is able to feed himself and bites a raw carrot. 'I'm very partial to the chilled crudités,' he slurs in his newly acquired ruling-class accent, 'but I feel dreadful taking the most comfortable seat in the room.' Then he closes his eyes and goes back to sleep.

I thank God that we're in America. The medical care here at this stage of recovery is the best in the world. A team of physiotherapists, speech and language therapists and occupational therapists are assigned to James and set a timetable of activities. They arrive in brown cotton trouser suits, full of energy and smiles, asking James how he is and whether he knows where he is yet. They tell us that he is typically disorientated and fretful; agitated easily and very confused. And that they want to see if he can walk.

Mark and I have been to buy him some new shorts and T-shirts as we were tired of the flap in the hospital's regulation shorts that allow him to inadvertently expose himself at inopportune moments. James, of course, couldn't have cared less – in fact, he has to be coaxed back into bed several times completely naked – but we need to make some small effort to preserve his dignity.

So, while wearing his new pyjama pants and T-shirt, three physiotherapists hoist him off the bed and tie a colourful belt around his waist. I haven't seen him standing up for a week and I'm shocked by how skeletal he looks. His cheeks are sunken; his eyes have a zombified stare. With one guy holding the belt and the other two supporting his weight, his left foot drags uselessly across the floor as he manages seven steps towards the nurses' station before falling back in bed exhausted.

Jennie, as a physiotherapist herself, is encouraged. I, however, am floored. It's the first time that I have cried in public. A week earlier I'd watched this same man finish a triple marathon in Death Valley. Now he was spent after seven supported steps. The palsy in his deadened left foot is terrifying. I realise – perhaps for the first time – that in layman's terms he is seriously fucked up.

I'm scared that when I see the kids and my mum I will start crying and not be able to stop. But when they run towards me in the airport arrivals hall I instinctively know that I have no right to burden them with my emotion. If they see me calm and happy, they too will weather the storm that is about to hit them.

I tell Croyde that Daddy has bumped his head and it's bruised – just like he gets on his knees – and the bruise needs to get better, but while it does, he looks different and will say some funny things. I have no idea if I'm doing or saying the right things. This sort of information is not provided in any parenting book I've read.

BMW in England have heard about James and offered us the complimentary use of a car for the stay. It makes a huge difference and means that I can drive to collect my family from the airport, take them to the hotel, whipping the kids into an excited frenzy about the outdoor pool and, even more exciting to Croyde, the Burger King next door.

I can't stop hugging and kissing them. It's hard to know what Kiki, at seventeen months, understands, but she always seems to have a very intuitive look in her eyes. I'd bet anything that she knows this isn't a normal holiday.

As always, my mum is amazing and insists she has the kids in her room as they'll all be jet-lagged and awake at 3 a.m. I share the double room next door with Louise, which is actually lovely as we rarely get to spend that much time together. I'm grateful for Louise's analytical brain and emotional intelligence to help me pick my way through the minefield of medical jargon to come. The next day I take her to the hospital.

'James, do you know where you are?' I ask.

'Big ball airport.'

'You've had an accident. This is a hospital. Look, people have sent so many lovely cards. There's a letter from the prime minister.'

'Right.'

'And a basket of fruit with love from Paul O'Grady, his partner and the dog!' I want James to smile. He hasn't smiled yet and he's always been really fond of TV presenter Paul O'Grady.

'Nice to know they are thinking of me while they're shagging their dog.'

'James!'

The sitter, Denise, laughs as I apologise, 'He isn't normally like this.'

'It's normal around here,' she says. 'By the way, does he always sound so English, so . . . la-de-dah?'

Tentatively, I take the children to see their daddy. The nurse suggests we go in one at a time so as not to overstimulate his brain. Mum and Lou stay outside with Kiki while I take Croyde into the beige room with its one window above the vast car park, a bed, a couple of chairs and Denise watching over my husband. James has pulled the stretchy bandage from around his head down over his eyes – like an aeroplane sleeping mask. He's on his side and I'm thankful that the pillow is freshly changed and Croyde isn't faced with any blood. We tiptoe around and I try to make a game of it with Croyde. 'Ssh, we have to be quiet. Daddy is asleep.'

We sit by the bed and I explain a few of the things to Croyde: the way the bed can move up and down; the cannula in James's arm where the doctors can give medicine; the fact that there is someone with him night and day to take very good care of him. Our talking wakes James and for a moment his eyes open but he doesn't have the energy to lift his head from the pillow. 'Hello, bunny rabbit.'

'Hi, Daddy.' Croyde looks to me for reassurance. 'Will he say something funny now?'

James manages to cuddle Croyde on the bed for a couple of minutes but then seems to forget he is there and turns away to go back to sleep. I tell him he's been such a good boy and usher him out with a little packet of hospital biscuits.

Kiki is more reluctant to go near James. Without much speech, she seems more tuned in to the non-verbal changes that I suddenly start to see: Daddy smells different, his movements are completely different, he lies on a strange bed with a beard and a white thing around his head. His voice is not the same. Where once were large muscles, bones are visible beneath grazed and bruised skin. But more than any of the above is the startling new look in his eyes. Seeing them through her, I realise just how vacant, frightening and lost they are, roaming the room as though looking for someone who isn't there. James wants to cuddle Kiki but she won't go near him. Eventually, I coax her with a biscuit and she snuggles her head on James's chest for a moment. His eyes are shut but he smiles and pats her hair.

It's been nine long days since the accident but James still has absolutely no idea where he is. He keeps asking to go 'outside the room to the master bathroom'. He strikes up a friendship with his sitter, Denise, and when I arrive she has given him a shave. I'm relieved that he's able to start showering with the aid of a chair

194

and two people to move him, but he now has a little goatee beard that rather adds to his eccentric persona.

His bed is raised to a sitting position when his tray arrives. He's on a finger food diet and it's dreadful: limp burgers, sugary yogurts, white bread. The only redeeming quality is the 'veg cup' or 'chilled crudités' that James is so appreciative of. But he shovels everything in at once: burger dipped in yogurt; orange juice poured over the vegetables. Denise sees my slack-jawed stare. 'Don't worry. That's normal. TBI patients eat crazy, jumbled up stuff.'

Apparently James has been telling Denise about his time at the Olympics. This is great news: he can remember something! But then it becomes clear: he told her he did decathlon in the 1984 Olympics, adding, 'I didn't win. I'm not a natural hurdler.'

He tells tale after tale about football and keeps talking about 'productivity' and 'efficiency' and banging on and on about 'John Dillinger' who turns out to be an American bank robber from the 1930s that I've never heard him mention before!

One morning, he calls me as I'm about to leave the hotel. He speaks with a sense of urgency and says that I have to bring him the right outfit as he's representing Holland in the 'world synchronised pooing championships'. For obvious reasons, that makes Croyde laugh a lot.

But after several days of normal food, without a visit to the toilet, the nurse and I discuss whether he could indeed be entered into a world pooing championship. He still can't go to the loo alone so we decide to offer him a bed pan. Thus ensues one of the most bizarre episodes in which James swings from moments of apparent clarity – 'Beverley, I am thirty-eight, I know how to poo' – to off-the-scale nonsense. He talks in his plummy accent about the time he was a 'member of the Household Cavalry' and had to 'doff his cap'. He looks at the bedpan and announces, 'This is precisely what the WC was made for. It's a wasted opportunity to harvest some top-quality arse gravy that may be served at breakfast tomorrow.' The nurse and I give up, not because he's especially recalcitrant, but because we are laughing so much we can't concentrate on helping him.

The physiotherapists are doing an amazing job of improving James's balance and working on the palsied foot. He is still officially a 'fall risk' but they start him on a Zimmer frame and it's cute to see him walking along the corridor with Kiki (who took her first steps in London in our absence) using the lower bar to totter along beneath him. He can only manage a few minutes at a time but he's upright and moving and that gives us huge hope.

It also gives us nightmares. Because a few days after James starts moving, he literally does not stop. His medical notes record that he 'cannot be still for more than thirty seconds'. We arrive in the morning to find the nurses swapping stories about how this British guy paced the hospital with his sitter 'all night'. It's extraordinary to witness. He will walk into a room, sit down, scratch his head as though working out where he is, say, 'Right, then, let's go,' and stand with his Zimmer frame and leave – 'purposeful' again, but utterly illogical and disorientated.

His behaviour also teaches us another new word, 'perseveration', which is frankly a synonym for torture if you're a family member of a TBI survivor. It refers to the action of becoming 'stuck' on an issue, thought or task and persevering with it. James 'perseverates' on trying to get somewhere but he doesn't know where. He becomes convinced that his laptop has been left in a lift and must walk round and round the hospital with Mark (who I have begun to kneel before in complete admiration of his patience with James) in order to find it. Of course, when he doesn't find the laptop, he becomes increasingly agitated until he can be distracted onto another 'hook'. Louise describes it as like seeing an old LP stuck on repeat.

Having left in such a hurry, Jennie and John have reluctantly had to go home to the UK. Although it's lovely to have the kids with Mum and me, it's also hard work – I feel pulled in different directions, wanting to give time and emotion to both James and the children. I make the effort, along with Mum, to lug towels and sun cream down to the hotel pool so that the kids can go for a daily splash, all the time fearing sunburn or cracked heads on slippery tiles.

Mum and I take the morning off from the hospital and visit the zoo, but as it's July in the Arizonan desert, the animals do the sensible thing and stay inside their huts. We have a brief half hour of relief standing under a fountain with our clothes on.

But then it's back to the hospital where for a few moments James is able to show the children some affection before packing all his belongings into a pillowcase and heading for the door. Apparently, it's about the hundredth time he has packed and unpacked that pillowcase that day. Louise and Mark look knackered. At midnight – after he's been awake (except during brief naps) for more than two days – the doctors give him a sedative.

It's twelve days since the accident and the date on which we were meant to be starting a rare family holiday in Portugal with a group of friends. I am no longer able to ignore the nagging voice in my head telling me that I must do a pregnancy test. While on the daily supermarket shop (James is munching his way through mountains of snacks) I stop at the appropriate aisle and the next morning confirm my suspicions alone in the hotel toilet.

I go into Mum's room. 'You know the phrase "it never rains but it pours"?' She cries; I cry. Kiki looks at us like she's missing something. I'm happy and bemused and sad all at the same time. It's a miracle (especially as James was only home for a couple of days the month before!) but I can't help but feel cautious and anxious about what this will mean in the coming nine months.

At breakfast, where we eat little boxes of raisin bran every day from polystyrene bowls with plastic spoons and drink tea from paper cups, everyone nearly falls off their chairs. Louise says, 'Jesus! Congratulations!' and we shake our heads at the ridiculousness of throwing this into the mix.

But of course I can't tell James. I will have to tell him over and over and that would be really sad. I sit in the room with him later that day as he sighs, wanting to pace about, not listening to a word anyone says, not relaxing for a second, always moving and snapping at me if I don't do everything exactly as his brain says it should be done. I miss him so much.

We all start to dread going to the hospital. James has become an evil caricature of himself: impatient, restless, judgemental, angry and irrational. He has been moved to the rehabilitation unit, which is a happy step forward; a step towards going home; but also a rather grim building that feels more like a hospital ward than the lovely 'pods' of the previous areas. But he'll be kept on a tight schedule of treatments that will hopefully tire him out and help him sleep.

But with these new demands comes a change in mood. And it seems that I am the focus of his anger. The therapists tell me this is normal, 'They always take it out on the spouses,' they say, but I'm struggling to rationalise that it is entirely the brain injury talking. Maybe it's just James being horrible?

We are desperately in need of some new energy in the camp when James's friend, actor Jonny Lee Miller, arrives from LA. He seems to bring out the best in James, who is delighted to see a friendly face. Jonny sits with James while he attempts his therapies: card games, word searches and some gentle sessions on a hand bike. James oscillates between being strangely talkative and suddenly asleep. The occupational therapists try to play 'I went to the shop and I bought . . .' but he fails to list more than two words at a time.

Mostly, he now knows where he is but he is still keen to start the trip from where they left off. He is incredibly persuasive and pesters and pesters to use a phone (we were advised to confiscate his mobile in case he caused all sorts of trouble at home). I allow him several calls but have to pre-empt each one with a warning call that he isn't yet capable of making decisions. He spends half an hour pacing up and down reception trying to persuade the Discovery TV boss to bring back the camera crew.

Mum and I take the children to an aquarium but we are both so tired from worry and jet lag that we spend most of the day in a subdued mood. At over forty degrees, it is too hot to go outside with the children and Kiki grizzles all day. When we arrive at the hospital, James is furious that I've been absent and his manic, agitated demeanour starts to scare the kids. Except for a small waiting room, there isn't really anywhere in the rehab unit to spend time with James. Mark appears and tells us that a social worker has recommended two to three weeks in rehab followed by one-on-one care at home. My mum bursts into tears and I snap at her to go around the corner as I don't want the kids to see her so distressed. I'm only worried about James and fail to realise that Mum is sixty-five years old and worried about her daughter, her son-in-law, her grandchildren and her unborn grandchild.

I feel like a total shit and apologise. We talk about Mum flying home with the children as she can manage them more easily at home and I can give my full attention to James. But I worry about her attempting the long-haul flight alone with two children under the age of six and we arrange for my brother Adrian to fly out and then home with them.

Jennie arrives back in Phoenix, regretting that she left at all as she did nothing but worry about James, and I take her to the rehab unit. It's a pretty depressing place where old ladies paint little stained-glass windows and teenage boys with patches shaved out of their hair play with Lego. James's face is still expressionless and he isn't sleeping at night so when they try to perform his treatments, he falls asleep. He must catch and throw a large ball while counting but he can't do both at once. It is a great indicator of his brain starting to fire up as he gradually improves over the next two weeks.

However, I'm struggling with his complete lack of empathy. The doctors did warn me, but one evening, after a ninety-minute discussion about why he can't send emails, I walk into the bathroom, rest my head on the windowpane and sob. It's my own fault – running around all day I haven't eaten for seven hours and I don't have the necessary resources of energy needed to handle him. Once I start crying, I can't stop. I feel dreadful: this is the last thing he needs, but I literally can't get my breath. I splash water all over my face and try to compose myself before going back into his room, where the sitter nods sympathetically at me as though she has seen this a thousand times.

I try to leave, but suddenly James is kind and beseeching, asking me to stay and eat something, and I feel bad to leave. All he has in his cupboard are revolting pots of instant microwaveable macaroni cheese which he heats in the communal kitchen and covers in ketchup. We sit on plastic chairs at a plastic table as James eats plastic food and huge tears fall down my face. He doesn't even notice. He even tries to make 'normal' conversation for the first time in two weeks. I need a hug. I need *him* to make me feel better because he is so badly injured. It's a paradox that I'm too exhausted to figure out. I have nothing to give him. And I am so scared.

I am beyond relieved when my brother Adi arrives. He is strong and optimistic and funny. He helps make some of the daily decisions about who does what and who goes where. Adi is also Croyde's favourite person in the whole world. He swam at the Athens Olympics and he's an actor now – the perfect mix of fun and competence to take the kids to play in the pool.

The next perseveration to hit us lasts for the remainder of the stay and involves James wanting to send emails and have his mobile phone back. No amount of rationalising, reasoning or cajoling can make him see that this is not a good idea. In England, Emma changes the password on his email account. Part of his occupational therapy involves writing at a computer and he seizes this moment to tap into an old Hotmail account that we didn't know about. From there he contacts the *Daily Telegraph* and the following day I arrive at the hospital to be told that a photographer is coming to take pictures of James in rehab.

When I suggest that is not such a good idea (he still keeps asking why the 'girls on reception' – nurses – won't let him go home), he freaks out: 'Who do you think you are trying to control my life? What the fuck has it got to do with you anyway? I can make my own decisions you know! It's all organised so you can just piss off.'

I'm actually tempted. But instead, I call the newspaper, who tell me that James has already given a 'fairly lucid' interview to them and the photographer is on his way. I take a deep breath. 'Do you understand,' I say in the calmest voice I can manage, 'he is a patient in a hospital with a serious brain injury. He won't remember any of this. You are abusing him as a human being – *and one of your own journalists* – if you run any part of this story.' The debacle takes up a whole day as editors speak to subs and everyone tries to work out what the hell happened. I actually feel sorry for the paper. They don't know how badly injured James is, and on a brief chat, I imagine he did sound 'fairly lucid'. But once again they are apologetic, call off the photographer and rip up the interview.

I question whether I'm doing the right thing all the time. Would he want photos of himself in his pyjamas in a hospital ward surrounded by old ladies doing jigsaws? Maybe he thinks this is OK? Maybe he is better than we think? And then I come in to find him absolutely convinced that the *Telegraph* has commissioned him to ghost-write Gary Lineker's column on the Ryder Cup. 'And,' he says as an aside, 'his girlfriend told me because she slept in my room last night.'

My boobs are killing me. I'm bloated and knackered while the occupational therapist gives me and James a talk on life at home. James won't be able to have sole care of the kids. He won't be able to drive for at least a year. He will have to be watched while cooking or boiling a kettle. He won't be able to go back to work for several months. James says that's bullshit and besides, he'll be going to Chelsea Football Club's rehab centre. We explain over and over that he has a brain injury: Stamford Bridge does not have a specialist neuro-rehab unit!

The occupational therapist says that once back in the UK, it will be important to keep James's stress levels down. 'In that case,' James says, quite matter of fact, 'I shouldn't be going home. The only thing that stresses me out is Bev.'

To say this is upsetting is an understatement and is the biggest test of my resolve so far. I want to hand him back his phone and laptop and allow him to make an enormous pile of complicated shit that he then has to clear up. I want to get on the plane with my mum and the kids the next day and let him deal with everything on his own. I want to scream, 'Fuck you! I'm pregnant and have spent four weeks doing everything for *you*, you selfish bastard!' but I look at him rubbing his forehead, not sure what's really going on, and think about the song I walked down the aisle to: Sade's 'By Your Side': the words were all about not leaving your lover's side, not even when times were tough – especially when times were tough. It feels like we've had a row and I want to make up – but he isn't there to make it up with. I don't know where he is. But it isn't here with me.

8

'Just tell me straight. Did my husband die on 20 July?'

Bev, to neuropsychologist at the Wellington Hospital, September 2010

[Bev]

As we leave the hospital in America, the grandfatherly neurologist shakes my hand and says, 'Just don't let him make any big decisions for a while.' It isn't until I watch the bleak concrete monstrosity disappear in a heat haze that I think, 'What the hell did that mean? What qualifies as a "big" decision? And what's a "while"?'

I am dreading the journey home. We have been cocooned from the outside world and therefore other people judging the new James. He has moments of 'normality', during which we might get into the lift to fetch lunch from the basement cafe, and for just a second it feels that everything is going to be OK. He makes a reasonable comment on the weather ('unbelievably hot'), but then the moment's gone. He spots a poster advertising the canteen and insists that the smiling woman in the photo is BBC sports commentator Jill Douglas. He looks me straight in the eye

204

and asks how I know it isn't Jill Douglas. It isn't just the lack of facial recognition that is chilling, it's the fact that he can't see how ridiculous it is that a BBC rugby presenter might be advertising the Phoenix hospital's canteen.

Emma and I have spent hours on the phone trying to establish the safest way to get James home. He is still at risk from seizures and the insurance company finally concede that a business class seat and a medical escort – a Dr Aled Jones – is the most cost-effective solution. At the airport, a porter arrives with a wheelchair. 'I. Am. Not,' James says as he looks at the apathetic bloke pushing the chair, 'Sitting. In. That.' Aled Jones (who's already tired of James asking if he's coming with us or 'walking in the air') sensitively advises that it might be a long walk to the gate. I am less sensitive, pleading in hushed tones that he 'use the frickin' chair as it will get us to the front of the queue'. Between us – with laptops, medical kit and holdalls – we seem to have more hand luggage than a passing school of exchange students, so using the excuse that pregnant women shouldn't carry heavy things, I dump it all in the chair and politely ask the porter if we can keep it with us, 'in case my husband wants to sit down'.

Prior to the flight, James was allowed a few hours at our hotel. You might imagine an emotional reunion in which we tumbled under cotton sheets thanking our lucky stars that he wasn't dead. Instead, I sat on the edge of the bed open-mouthed at how much he talked. For years I had regularly whined the female marital mantra, 'Why don't you tell me more about your day?' only to receive a grunt as he headed for the gym. Now, I simply cannot shut him up.

Somehow, outside of a hospital, I had expected more 'normal' interaction; as though the mask of brain injury would disappear along with the scent of disinfectant to reveal the kind, strong man that I knew and loved. But every time I opened my mouth to say something, he failed to pick up on the 'social cue' and carried on: a stream of consciousness that darted from topic to topic; meandering around the houses until he got to the point he was trying to make or simply tottered off in a different direction. His unassuming humility had been replaced by a type of aggrandising egotism. The doctors had said that he would 'exist on Planet James for a "while"' (that word again). They weren't kidding.

The problem was, I had some rather important news to tell him. 'James, listen . . .' We faced each other on twin beds, his cheeks oddly sunken despite the fact that he had gained a little weight; eye sockets deep and grey. I held his hands; the knuckles still bore scabs and scars from the tarmac on Route 66. 'You know how we talked about having another baby after Kiki? Well, you may not believe this, but I'm pregnant again.' He blinked, finally silent for a second, then turned his head to look at me through a half-smile, 'How long have I been out for? Is it mine?' For a split second, in a quick-witted joke, he came back. I was overjoyed. But I couldn't be sure that I wouldn't have to tell him again.

Rather like incentivising Croyde to behave with the promise of a portable DVD player, I have promised James that he can have his mobile phone once we are on the plane. Without something to focus on, I fear he will pace up and down for ten hours talking at strangers. Treating him like a child feels cruel and ridiculous but like decent parenting it comes from a genuine need to protect and nurture.

He reclines his chair and tap-taps away with quick thumbs, replying to the hundreds of well-wisher texts that have arrived. I wonder about the messages that will appear in in-boxes when we land. What on earth must he be saying? But there is nothing I can do about it.

I lie back and begin reading a book that will change my life, *Where is the Mango Princess? A Journey Back from Brain Injury* by Cathy Crimmins, an American journalist whose husband suffered similar injuries to James thanks to a speedboat that hit the side of his head. Like us, the couple also had a six-year-old child. Crimmins' book tells me not to panic, to roll with the punches, to toughen up and to be prepared for the future. She teaches me the most important lesson of all: it's OK – in fact, it's vital – to find the comedy amongst the desolate landscape of brain injury. I'd been thinking that I was the only one with a macabre sense of humour. The hospital's physiotherapist had given me the book as we left. But her helpfulness was somewhat undermined by the accompanying words, 'Seventy-five per cent of people who have a brain injury get divorced.'

Back in London it becomes even harder to find reasons to smile. I am swamped with relief that my parents have taken the kids to Devon, which means they don't witness James arriving home for a few minutes before being driven off reluctantly in an ambulance to the hospital in north London.

Thankfully, the TV company's insurance allows James the privilege of a private room – rather like a Travelodge but with a mechanical bed, a sandwich menu and an emergency cord in the loo. He still refuses to accept that he needs medical attention but reluctantly engages in their programme of rehabilitation.

It's important for TBI sufferers to start a period of 'formal' rehab so as to maximise improvement within the first six months. Sadly, this window of opportunity is often neglected due to inadequate NHS resources in the UK. The majority of patients are simply returned to their shocked and frightened families where they have become an impatient, confused and angry stranger in their midst;

a person who wears the face and clothes of a person they loved but who they no longer know. Is it any surprise that so many marriages fail? That so many families fall apart?

The therapists around James will attempt to develop some of his diminished cognitive abilities including short-term memory, planning, organisation and word finding. They aim to 'soften' his 'rigidity of thought', to introduce shades of grey into his simplistic black-and-white view of the world.

The programme offers James 'structure' to his day – something that he always preferred but is now an absolute necessity to keep his mood stabilised.

The hospital stands on a busy intersection and I worry that James will be allowed out on his own or with a visitor who won't know his limitations. It is extremely common for TBI sufferers to pick up another injury within six months – especially on roads – as they may not be able to judge speed and distance or may become easily distracted. James has been in a hospital for four weeks and I worry that the nurses on reception will see this walking, talking, athletic man and underestimate just how badly he was injured. If we get this far and he falls under a bus I will not be responsible for my actions.

The first three months of pregnancy always wipes me out, but this time I'm drowning in a new fatigue that runs deep in my bones. I sit on the edge of James's hospital bed wondering if anyone would notice if I just curled up and disappeared for a few hours. I wake up each morning to a quiet house, thinking of the kids splashing in the Devon waves, and wonder about those women whose husbands suffer similarly tragic accidents but who don't have the unconditional love and support of their family. The sadness that must fill those houses makes me get a grip, climb out of bed and feel thankful.

In the hospital room, James wants to know when his bicycle will arrive. I'm suddenly less sleepy, looking from the psychologist to his dad and back to James. 'Sorry? Did he just say his *bicycle*?' The psychologist shifts awkwardly in his seat. James shoots me a dirty look. 'Don't start . . . yes, you heard, a bicycle.'

John sighs and shakes his head. The psychologist clears his throat. 'James has ordered a bicycle to come to the hospital so he can go out with the physiotherapist.'

I am past the point of being polite, 'He has ordered a *bicycle*? You *let* him?' James holds up a hand, appalled with me. But I won't stop. I am furious. 'And nobody here thought to tell me?'

Weirdly, I stop being angry. I just grip the edge of the bed and start to cry. 'We are here because you get knocked off a fucking bicycle and you're about to go out in London, on busy streets, less than six weeks later on a *bicycle*?' John comes over and sits on the bed, puts his arm around my shaking shoulders. James looks at me, utterly impervious to my tears. My emotion just does not seep through to his damaged lobes. The mechanisms that would enable him to understand my point of view are all mashed up.

The psychologist tries to speak a few times but James talks over him, angry at my 'overreaction'. When the psychologist does get a word in, he looks embarrassed. 'I can tell you from our written tests that James is performing well, but I'm afraid we don't have a test for empathy. This is very interesting. It's fair to say that a decreased capacity is clearly evident here.'

I blow my nose on hospital loo roll, adopt my most sarcastic tone. 'You think?'

But it's something, at least, an acknowledgement that this is not normal in behavioural terms. They have only my word that it is also not typical of James.

Over the next few months I will learn that frontal lobe damage exaggerates existing personality traits, tendencies and problems. Effectively, the 'brakes' that moderate and modify childlike behaviours have come off. James is an evil caricature of himself. It's like he's been through a time machine and come out as a stroppy teenager I would never have dated. Several times we relive arguments and issues that arose – but were resolved – eight years earlier. Some of his rants are so extraordinary that, if he lets me, I'm able to walk away but on tired and emotional days I snap back, which leaves me feeling like a bad person. Poking fun at myself, I sob to my sister through a rueful smile, 'It's like ten years of good work has been undone.'

If I don't go to the hospital every day, James is angry with me. When I do arrive, he's angry with me for having nothing better to do. Marina Fogle tells me to stop being so stupid and have a day off – she makes food and drives it round for him while I go for a swim with a slightly clearer conscience and see my midwife for an ante-natal appointment. But I cringe that James won't be sufficiently grateful of Marina's generosity.

Despite the loneliness of the situation, I read that he is by no means alone. In 2010–2011, 215,000 people were admitted to UK hospitals with an Acquired Brain Injury (ABI or TBI), with one million people living amongst us with disabilities caused by a brain injury. In the USA, 1.7 million acquire a TBI each year, with men in greater numbers across all age groups; such an injury is a contributing factor in 30.5% of all injury-related deaths. Witnessing James's unreasonable and aggressive behaviour, I am saddened – but not surprised – to discover that many studies of British 'offender populations' conclude that 50% of inmates have a TBI. In the UK alone, that equates to 40,000 imprisoned men with irreversible brain damage.

Shortly before James is discharged, I have a one-on-one meeting with the psychologist. 'Tell me,' the poor guy is used to my straight talking by now, 'did my husband die on 20 July?' I'm sick of woolly answers from 'experts' but I get another: 'It's hard to say.'

Written exercises are performed to assess James's 'cognitive executive functions' or 'thinking skills', such as finding synonyms for a list of words. As a graduate and a journalist, it once would have been easy for James to find other words that mean the same as those given to him, but his sheet of answers is frankly bizarre.

When asked to give another word for 'home', he doesn't choose 'residence', 'house' or even 'abode', but instead 'comfortable' and 'relaxing'. The word 'ship' is not followed by 'boat' or 'vessel' but 'hygienic' and 'top heavy'. For 'toilet' he writes 'clean' and 'kids changing'. It is as though his mind is merely playing word association: that very stream of consciousness that flows unchecked in conversation. My personal favourite is the word 'smash'. He doesn't jot down 'bang' or 'crash' but 'time efficient' and 'tasty', clearly thinking the test is asking him about powdered potato.

On the day of his departure, a pharmacist visits his room to explain his medications: anti-seizure pills and a mood-stabiliser that doubles as a sleeping pill. I ask if they might write it down in case James forgets and I can offer back-up if so. He snaps at me to shut up. 'I'm not an idiot, you know!' The young doctor doesn't challenge him and hands over a paper bag of pills – without separate instructions.

Other than that, we are packed off with a list of neuro-psychologists taken from Google. Apparently James should be 'encouraged' to arrange his own care. I am dumbfounded. They are asking a man with serious organisational deficits to plan his own rehabilitation – a man who still doesn't entirely believe that he's been injured!

Sadly, it seems, this is all too common. In the UK we are world-class at scraping people off the roadside, but looking after them long term? At that – the part that will stop a downward spiral of catastrophic consequences – we are pretty much useless.

There are no welcome-home banners or celebrations on James's return. I can't muster the necessary enthusiasm: James isn't really home. I turn the key in the door with a sense of dread. How will we cope? How is he going to fill his days? And my overriding fear: how is he going to act around Croyde?

Before the accident, James and I were pretty much united as disciplinarians with the kids. James needed the odd prompt to offer up a bit more affection, but I never once worried that we would have any major disagreements on how to parent. But it became clear in America that his 'new' fathering style had swung uncharacteristically towards the harsh and uncompromising. It was my biggest concern.

In an attempt to find some common ground, I buy a football book and a pile of cards, nonchalantly suggesting they sit down to fill it in. Croyde has missed his daddy and I'm trying to keep everything normal. But it takes so much concentration from James to order the cards that he is incapable of relaxing or having fun. Rigidly, he insists the cards go in a certain order, losing patience at Croyde's typical six-year-old boy approach: namely, to open each packet as quickly as possible and slip them in wherever the colours look nice. James won't let him open all the packets. He tuts and looks irritated. 'Try again,' he barks when Croyde doesn't read a complicated foreign player's name perfectly. It's awful to watch. Croyde looks up at me, confused about why Daddy is not smiling and being so strict. I sweep him up, leaving James insisting that Croyde was doing it 'all wrong'.

I'm reassured yet again by Cathy Crimmins' book, in which she describes the problems her husband Alan had with their young daughter: '*The normal, childish things Kelly does, such as forgetting where she put her sneakers, yelling with excitement, or turning up the volume on the television, irritate Alan all out of proportion. He calls her "stupid" or "an idiot" and when I confront him about it, he claims not to have said it.*' On one occasion Alan takes Kelly to the movies but after a misunderstanding about how many pick-n-mix sweets she is allowed, Kelly drops them on the floor and Al loses his temper. '*While she was bending over to pick up the candy, Al booted her smack on the rear end, hard, in front of everyone.*' James has never hit Croyde, but I can imagine how such a scenario might escalate. When Crimmins confronts her brain-injured husband he admits the kick. '*She dropped the fucking candy. And it cost a lot of money!*' This, she says, is '*A turning point . . . until now, I'd thought I could modify Alan's behaviour by giving him "feedback" and talking about strategies for controlling his violent impulses. Now I want to kill him.*'

At eighteen months of age, placid, calm Kiki doesn't cause James any anxiety. She sucks her thumb, giggles a lot and occupies herself dropping plastic coins into a pink piggy bank. It is almost as if she and James are on a similar mental wavelength. Croyde is noisy, boisterous, energetic and argumentative – everything that overstimulates and stresses James's recovering frontal lobes.

Friends pop in to say hello and I watch fascinated by the new James's lack of inhibition; talkativeness and 'emotional lability' (another new phrase I learn that describes a loss of control over emotions, manifested in excessive crying or – in James's case – laughing). Old mate Matt Dawson doesn't even have time to pull up a chair and James has dived straight into an anecdote about a friend's Special Forces training that culminates in a punchline (not for the faint-hearted) about the stench of a man's penis after several days in the jungle. Matt looks at me wide-eyed. It is not that James appears unwell as such. He is just so . . . *different*.

Of course, in the months after his accident, everyone who visits is so happy to see James and so interested in his story that he spends hours talking about himself. In his 'pre-morbid' life, he was known to spend whole evenings with people who would leave knowing nothing about his remarkable achievements. I'd tell him to 'Brag a little! You have so much to be proud of', but he never did. But suddenly he's a noisy raconteur, name-dropping and telling stories about his time in America that are always slightly (or wholly) incorrect.

I make Sunday brunch for Ben and Marina Fogle; plus Marina's two sisters and partners. He shows no interest in anybody else's news. Conversational cues to shut-up-and-let-someone-else-talk pass him by. When he clearly isn't going to offer to help me out in the kitchen, I ask if he'll pour some drinks, only to be met by a biting, embarrassing response: 'OK! OK! For God's sake!' in front of everyone.

Over the next few months I find myself becoming one of those wives, the type who apologises for her husband's behaviour. And I hate it. I never wanted to be one of those women.

Brain injury books explain that it is this self-centredness that is often the final blow for families integrating the brain-injured person back into their lives. It is a stark fact that the social network around the recovering person will reduce within the first couple of years as friends grow tired of calls never being returned or no interest being shown in their problems.

James never mentions the pregnancy and I barely give it a second thought except to take the odd vitamin. It is very different to the last two times. I can't leave him alone with the kids in case his memory and judgement of risk let him down. I worry that he will leave the front door open and Kiki will wander out. And, of course, I daren't leave him alone to bully Croyde.

Within the first week home, I'm coming out of the shower (always with one ear on what is happening downstairs) when the doorbell rings. I can hear a conversation but there is something about the unfamiliar voices that worries me. Wearing only a towel, my hair dripping on the floor, I find James chatting away to a couple I don't know, one of whom is carrying a large black camera. 'Baby,' he says, wide-eyed, 'these people are from the *Daily Express*.'

I barge past him to close the door. 'Do you mind? We are just home from the hospital.'

The female journalist looks affronted. 'Can't we even get a picture?'

'No! You bloody well can't!' I slam the door in their faces.

Old James would have beaten me to it. Now he looks cross with me. 'That wasn't very nice.'

'What did you say to them?'

'Nothing.' That seemed highly unlikely. James had always been a shrewd judge of the press and had clear guidelines about access he would and wouldn't give. But there was now a simplistic naivety about him that concerned me. 'Just be careful what you say to people. We don't need any more complications.'

By day, I become an evil jailer, stopping James from going to meetings and public appearances. By night, we lie side by side, alternately getting up to use the loo every hour (the brain-injured person's body must work hard to regulate its fluids. I'm just pregnant). He wants to make public appearances that are booked in the diary but it's unimaginable that he could deliver his usual motivational speech as he either talks too much ('verbosity'); talks around a topic ('tangential speaking') or talks only about certain hooks ('perseveration'). And he is unnaturally irritated by small things.

By lunchtime each day he looks exhausted, yawning and pacing aimlessly looking for something to do. He slumps to his office at the bottom of the garden but has insufficient concentration to write more than a couple of emails. And he has absolutely no insight to recognise or understand these changes.

The BBC – who can't fully understand what he's going through – hassle us to come round and film him at home in case he ever decides to restart the cancelled trip with Ben Fogle. His corporate partners, including Adidas, Bupa and BMW, are being wonderfully supportive, offering good wishes but insisting they don't need him until he is ready. We are asked on to lots of TV shows and the usual magazines request interviews. We say no to everything.

It's mid-September and the doctors advise that he doesn't attempt work until November. I'm sick of constantly having to explain why he can't do things and I don't know how I'm going to keep this up. Returning to work at the right time is crucial for TBI survivors. The subtle (and not so subtle) changes can easily upset any workplace. And TBI history is absolutely littered with bankruptcies.

Sixty-five per cent of people with a brain injury will suffer fatigue problems because the brain stem is damaged – the part that controls consciousness, wakefulness and sleep rhythms. I repeat over and over, 'You look tired. Go and lie down. You need to rest. You look tired . . .' All of James's 'new' behaviours are grossly exaggerated when he is tired. Fatigue management (or 'pacing' as it's called) becomes my very own hook. I think that if I can only get him to sleep, I can get him better.

Teatime with the kids is the worst. By 6 p.m., he is yawning and grey, snapping uncontrollably at Croyde. He towers over him at the table. 'Sit down . . . use a knife and fork . . . don't talk with your mouth full . . . clean your plate.' I try to cajole him to take a nap. When that doesn't work, I plead. Then I insist. But still, steadfastly he refuses to go and lie down. Desperate, I speak to Dr Fred Wadsworth – the nutritionist from the America trip. He is the only person, apart from me, who is unafraid to be firm with James. And, like a child, James seems to respect the clear boundaries that Fred defines. He seems to agree when Fred explains the value of sleep (although promptly forgets when he leaves). Fred looks through James's medication. 'When does he take this one?'

'Don't ask me. He's very protective of his drugs. And the hospital didn't give me any details.'

Turns out he had been taking the grey pill when he got up in the morning – it was his sleeping tablet.

Unfortunately, taking the pill at night makes only a small difference to James's daytime tiredness and still I battle on, a stuck record asking when he is going to rest. I come to regret Jurgen Grobler's maxim all those years: 'Rest is rust.' Now I have my own, 'Rest is a must', but I'm boring myself with it.

It becomes almost impossible to have Croyde and James in the same room. Unwittingly, Croyde does or says something that irritates James and instead of being the adult, James will engage in an argument. It is bizarre to witness my husband – formerly a calm and authoritative dad – try to 'win' a row with a seven-year-old. But Croyde is a smart boy who's inherited his parents' ability to fight their corner and James must resort to bullying, mimicry and mocking. Undermining James is the last thing I want to do, but if I don't intercept, Croyde ends up hurt, confused and crying, 'Daddy is laughing at me.'

Whenever I walk out of the room, I am inevitably followed by Croyde in tears at something James has said or done as soon as my back is turned. All too soon, I become Croyde's ally and protector. James and I are no longer equals to him.

Without the structure that work provides to his day, James begins to bounce off the walls. He is confused, agitated, rudderless. All the improvements seen in the hospitals seem to be slipping away. We have no clear guidelines about what work he might be able to do and when. He tries to sit on his exercise bike but quickly gets bored and then frustrated at himself.

And he has picked up another particularly hurtful hook. Every time conversation gets difficult he volleys, 'Why don't you stop interfering in my life and get a fucking job. I'm sick of making money while you do fuck all.' I don't even rise to it. If his damaged brain doesn't get the tragic irony of that sentiment, there's no way I can explain it to him.

We go for my twelve-week scan and I'm shocked to find that I start to cry. I've never felt especially emotional at a scan before. I realise that at the back of my mind I'd assumed that no unborn child could survive the sheer amount of adrenalin that I have been running on. But I'm also crying for the future of this little heartbeat because I have no idea quite what our family life is going to look like. James doesn't cry. He hasn't cried since the accident (a typical 'blunting' of emotions). But he does get out his phone to show the sonographer – who has no idea who he is – a photo of himself in Intensive Care. I shush him, embarrassed. 'It's not relevant, James,' but he insists and I wipe gel off my belly as he tells her all about his accident, as usual getting most of the facts wrong.

But despite the good news about the baby, the tension in our house is reaching boiling point. I'm with James almost twenty-four hours a day and although I am his greatest irritant, I am also his confidant. He seems oddly reluctant to talk to anyone else and can't make a single decision without consulting me. Fifty per cent of TBI patients suffer depression and days can pass without either James or me managing a smile. I've tried to set up appointments with psychologists but it feels futile without James's full cooperation. Each time I feel forced to tell him he's behaving irrationally, angry or looking tired, he snaps, 'Oh I'm sorry! I forgot – you're the bloody expert!' I point at him. 'I'm the expert on *you*!' But I don't want to be. I'm winging it. And I'm drowning. I want a real expert to control the rehab that I'm not qualified to do.

Every time I grab a moment to sit down and make the changes requested by a publisher interested in my fledgling novel, James comes into my office to talk at me. If I ask him to give me a moment, he either says 'no' and sits down anyway or is deeply offended, tutting and telling me to 'fuck off then'. It is simply inescapable.

One afternoon, two people from his agent's office were coming round to see him. Before they arrived, something – I don't remember the details – had set him off and a row started that I could not escape. I tried to walk away but he was wearing the 'concrete shoes' (the metaphor used by psychologists to describe his 'rigidity of thought') and no amount of reasoning would work. He followed me into every room. Eventually, I had to lock myself in the bathroom, sobbing. When the doorbell rang he answered as though nothing had happened, his manic laughter floating upstairs.

It was so confusing: how could he do that? Be awful with me one moment and then perfectly charming with others the next? Nobody told me that TBI families almost always report stories of patients who are polite at hospital appointments or while visiting friends and then become selfish, angry gits behind closed doors. The medical theory is that in a familiar, relaxed environment the person's brain responds more spontaneously and loved ones are 'safer targets' who won't reject them. Some experts go so far as to say that the TBI patient actually needs these outlets to vent their rage and frustration. But I was sure of one thing – I would not allow us to start a pattern of abusive behaviour that would take years to break.

Unfortunately, one evening when the kids are finally asleep, we are about to hit a new low. It has been another long, upsetting, difficult day that culminates in Croyde crying himself to sleep after another pointless and hurtful telling-off from James. Croyde can be a determined and demanding kid, no doubt about that, but James's judgement of situations is often way off the scale. I lose it. I say I've had enough. I say that he has to go and get better somewhere else because it is too much for us. But I'm not calm and beseeching. I'm angry and tired. I need to get out of the room and calm down. I go to leave but James stands in the doorway, refusing to let me past. Sick of being bullied, I try to push past and something within him flips; he grabs me round the neck with one powerful hand and holds me down on the bed. He tightens his grip until I can't breathe. I'd like to say that I couldn't believe it was happening, but I could – there was a terrible inevitability about it.

Except for well-meaning family and friends, we are all alone, drowning in a sea of fear, stress and confusion. I try to take a breath. For a moment, I genuinely think he might kill me. I pray that a flicker of empathy will ignite, just for a moment, amongst the broken neurons struggling to fire in his brain, behind his deadened eyes. He lets go. I grab my phone, and lock myself in the bathroom. I call my sister in a panic: 'Please come round. James just tried to strangle me.'

Five minutes later she rushes through our front door into the hallway where James paces, rubbing his forehead, looking lost, disorientated and remorseful. Cal walks straight up and hugs him. 'It's not you, James. It's not you. It's OK.'

'I'm sorry. I'm sorry, Cal,' he mumbles into her shoulder. She doesn't ask any questions; she just holds him and says it's OK. She says it's his brain playing tricks on him. Her words are perfect: 'It isn't you, James. It isn't you.'

I make tea and they sit on the sofa for ages while James talks about how he feels (although he doesn't use words that describe 'emotions'; he keeps returning to his 'hooks' – subjective versus objective; morality; honesty; not being trusted). But amongst the weird concentric circles, it becomes clear how much he desperately needs to talk to an 'expert'. And I vow to stop expecting him to arrange his therapeutic care, but to sort it out myself.

For the next few weeks, life is a daily battle to keep James rested and protected. He takes his first tentative ride on a bicycle (by allowing him to do so in the hospital, the 'experts' have made it impossible for me to argue it isn't yet safe). But he forgets his helmet and turns round after twenty yards freewheeling on the pavement to retrieve it. The next day, a paparazzi photograph appears in the *Mail* of James cycling without a helmet. I feel so sorry for him. He would never deliberately ride a bike without one. It was the helmet that saved his life in Phoenix.

An agent asks him to appear at an evening event showcasing motivational speakers. I tell the guy it's too early, he can't put him on a stage in front of people eager to see how he's changed. But I'm ignored and forced to humiliate James by briefing the interviewer on his communication difficulties. Thankfully, she listens and isn't afraid to interrupt him when he meanders off track during several long monologues. I watch with my breath held. He does well. But it wipes him out and at home we must suffer from his subsequent fatigue.

The Discovery Channel begins talks about editing and finishing the programme of James's American trip and subsequent accident. It's yet another huge, emotional decision. The result is a very complicated media situation and James takes the enormous step of switching to a different management team. The end result of all this is that, with our consent, the programme will be finished. We will have to support the campaign to advertise it, which will – unfortunately – be the week that the baby is due. It will transmit at 9 p.m. on my due date.

The stress of this upon James is immense. It is entirely typical of brain-injured people to undergo huge practical changes alongside the emotional and physical ones after an accident. But James had so many hopes pinned on this expedition. The reality that they may be shattered seems to hit him. One evening, he sits in the lounge and talks at me while I watch TV. But suddenly he is crying, openly sobbing into the crook of his arm. I should be sad for him and I am – but I'm also jubilant. He's crying! Real tears! Normal, human emotions! I almost offer him a high five, but decide to hug and console him instead. He's slowly coming back to me.

I do however make a suggestion: if the Discovery Channel wants to show the America programme, they must offer him one last documentary. I won't let the last thing people see of James Cracknell be a brain-injured man looking sad in his kitchen talking about the person he used to be. No way. He likes the idea. I go to bed wondering what the hell I've just done.

In December we attend the Headway Annual Awards Luncheon as special guests. It is an unexpectedly emotional experience. To a hushed room in a posh London hotel, the host delivers an account of our story so far. I feel my throat tighten and I manage to dab at my tears discreetly with a thick napkin.

But we are surrounded by incredible, brave people: women whose stories are so tough that I don't feel I even deserve to sit at the same table. There are those who care for immobile, incontinent loved ones twenty-four hours a day; those who will never walk or feed themselves again. My husband is able to hand out the awards. I want to apologise to every single person in that room for my moments of anger and sadness. Boo hoo for me. I want to say how in awe I am of every person who is worse off than us – and there are many. I take James's hand as we step out into the freezing air. He looks dignified and courageous. How could I even think about giving up?

I've started to see a local counsellor, a woman who I meet with the line, 'I'm going to give birth in three months. My husband has a brain injury. I need to feel a little more . . . *robust*.' The sessions help enormously. At the time of the accident, with a view to a possible new career, I was due to finish my own part-time two-year training as a psychotherapist – little did I know the irony of that. But along with all my other plans, it has disappeared down the rabbit hole of brain injury.

Entirely believing in the process of talking therapy, I'm able to vent my frustration without fear of upsetting anyone, or some-times I just go through the box of tissues and feel a bit sorry for myself. On other occasions, we discuss practical ways in which I can carve out some time for myself or talk assertively to James when he is being demanding. It's the psychological equivalent of 'flossing', and I'm able to take a breath, dust myself down and step out into the London winter air feeling slightly lighter.

James and David Harrison, the director of the Marathon de Sables programme, start to discuss possible options for another trip. Simultaneously, James starts to see a neuropsychologist and a wonderful NHS occupational therapist who comes to the house and discusses all sorts of practical solutions to help James's extraordinarily bad time-keeping, diary-planning and communication issues.

For the first time in five months, I allow myself to step back a little and let him get on with things – until one day I come home to find him at the table with David and Emma (who, although she is employed by his former agent, has agreed to carry on working as James's PA one day a week until he gets settled). There are sheets of A4 strewn everywhere. I've been Christmas shopping for the kids and am unusually relaxed. 'What's this about?' I pick up a sheet.

I see the words Yukon and bicycle challenge. Everybody is silent, hoping that someone else speaks first. 'Is this the trip you're considering?' Emma is trying to tell me something with her eyes.

I scan down the sheet. 'It's a bike race . . . on *ice*? Are you fucking kidding me?'

James looks slightly flustered but then resolute. 'It's snow actually.'

'Oh! That's OK then! *No*. Forget it. You *cannot* do a bike race *on ice*. You've *all* gone mad.'

David lets himself out. I stomp around a lot and go to bed in one almighty sulk, knowing that my oh-so-stubborn husband will end up doing a bike ride. On ice.

When Croyde breaks up for Christmas, we grab a few days in Devon. A change of scene might do us good. We never normally take our nanny, Monika, with us on holiday, but now I need her. Being at home with us during some of the day, she has become a huge source of support to me. But we leave late and I want to recline a little with a six-month baby bump, so James drives. Normally a careful driver, he can no longer judge speed or distance; he switches lanes erratically at 80mph and brakes at the last minute. By the time we pull off for petrol, just twenty minutes into a five-hour journey, I look over my shoulder to Monika, who is as white as me. I'm already in the driver's seat when James returns from paying for petrol. Amazingly, he doesn't argue, and within five minutes he is snoring, open-mouthed, in the passenger seat.

The week before Christmas, while on his way to visit Dr Fred Wadsworth for another dose of moral support, James picks up the trauma injury that the text books predict: in his case, a broken metacarpal, sustained while walking quickly up the Tube station steps, carrying a Brompton folding bike as he didn't want to cycle in bad weather.

At 6 a.m. on Christmas Day – so that he will be healed in time for the Yukon trip – he undergoes surgery to wire his broken finger bone back together. My mum is suffering with the flu and so I open Christmas presents with the kids and James's dad, who has dropped him off at the hospital. My sister and her husband Rick are hosting Christmas lunch, a short walk around the corner. James joins us, groggy from a general anaesthetic but unwilling to go to bed, and sleeps for much of the day on the living-room floor.

Two days later we fly out for a much-needed week in the Egyptian sun with the kids, my parents and some friends. On our return James ends up back in hospital – the wound from his surgery has become infected and must be re-opened. They think he may have a version of MRSA. I think we're cursed.

Somehow, after many antibiotics, several health assessments, arguments with insurance companies who won't touch James, and having been through the Health and Safety risk assessment with David Harrison about a thousand times, James is ready to go to Canada.

The stress is immense. I've never been much of a crier, but on one memorable day, I sob down the phone to five different men, only two of which I am related to. Idiotic doctors who know almost nothing about James's case make rash decisions about the medical support he will need. I am adamant that he can only go to the Yukon if he has two medics with him at all times – one of which will be Fred – and will be made to take regular sleep breaks. Everyone agrees. I think they just want to silence the crazy, crying lady.

The kids and I kiss James goodbye at the airport. They have made cards to wish him luck. Confident that he is in good hands and I can do nothing more, I practically skip back to the car: the freedom is immense. I am worn out from the 24/7 responsibility of watching his back. I need a break from him. And I have no doubt he feels the same about me.

9

[James]

My next memory is of lying down in a strange room. But I can see Bev. And there's Mark. That's all. One weird disassociated image and then it fades. They call these 'islands', sudden breakthroughs of conscious memory, in what is otherwise a total blank.

I remember Jonny Lee Miller coming to see me, but at what point I'm not sure. I just remember bits of him being there.

I was told Ben Fogle and Matt Pinsent came to see me early on and I have no memory of that at all.

At one point I was apparently convinced I had to file an article for the *Daily Telegraph*, ghosting for Gary Lineker who was living under my hospital bed while I was sharing it with his wife.

The islands developed into a series. More like an archipelago chain a long way from where you don't want to be. I remembered that I had been cycling but I wasn't sure where or why. It varied between the Tour de France and a trip across Africa. The only consistent feeling was my determination to get on my bike, wherever it was, and continue the journey.

Through my eyes, I seemed the same, and everyone else was being weird. When I saw Mark, I felt really well rested, and because he had been the first person I saw every morning on the road trip, I assumed it was time to get on the bike.

He kept saying 'The trip's over' but I associated him with moving so strongly, I felt compelled to be active. When I was back on my feet it was his fate to walk with me for eighteen hours a day, round and round the hospital grounds, holding me up by a belt he'd constructed around my waist.

Even now, I'm not sure if my memories of the hospital in Phoenix are genuine memories or they've been implanted through hearing the stories of my behaviour since then.

This is to my distinct advantage. I have no recollection, for instance, of enquiring whether one of my nurses had spent time training with the Pittsburgh Steelers (the American football team) due to her strong resemblance to one of their players, Jerome 'The Bus' Bettis. 'The Bus' earned his nick-name from the size and power of his gluteus maximus. In other words, he had a damn big ass. This is not a bad thing if you're a running back, and he was one of the best, winning Superbowl XL in 2006. As a nurse, however, it was less of a compliment.

Strangely enough, I look back on my comment as a positive. This is because it meant that my long-term memory recall (even if it was meaningless sports trivia) was still in some kind of working order, even if the insult filter system wasn't.

The hospital gave us a brain injury fact sheet to prepare us for common issues that arise. It mentioned that people with brain injuries might also behave as if they are at work. I didn't think I'd been guilty of that one, especially as I've always tried to avoid a 'proper job'. That was until I got home and Keith Perry, my boss at the *Daily Telegraph*, told me that I'd actually filed 1,000 words on the Ryder Cup, which I'd never seen and can't remember doing, especially as I have little knowledge of golf. Thank heavens I had Gary Lineker under the bed to give me some inside information.

I hated the fact that I was capable of such strange and random behaviour that even now I have no recollection of, but I was pleased that I could convince the medical staff that I had to write an article (in fact, I still don't know whether they believed me), and having cracked the password that Bev had put on my email account, could even send it off.

This strange and random behaviour stretched to all types of actions. When my food was delivered in hospital I'd straight away mix in my starter with my main course, shove my dessert on top then cover it all in ketchup, mustard and sugar. Apparently it's what TBI patients do and, to be honest, I could still do it now: over two years on I have no taste or smell. Which, according to Bev, lets her get away with murder, but is socially unacceptable when I drop a 'silent but violent' and can't understand the reaction to my bombshell.

I think this allegedly eccentric behaviour (although normal for brain injury patients) plus my lack of communication at the time made it impossible for the medical stuff to 'know' the real me. Then my reaction to a letter shocked them further.

One day the post came and the first letter I opened was from David Cameron, the prime minister, saying he was sorry to hear about the accident and wishing me and the family all the best for a speedy recovery. I said: 'That's nice of him,' whereas the nurses couldn't believe the British prime minister had written to me on official Downing Street letterhead. Presumably my response was a little muted.

By now I'd been taken from Intensive Care and initially tethered to a bed to stop me from trying to find my trainers (despite still having a broken foot), remount my bike, and carry on with the ride. I didn't know I was in hospital, let alone Arizona or the US (although I knew it was damn hot), and I didn't know I had suffered life-threatening head injuries from being knocked off my bike. Mercifully, even now I have no memory of the impact or the following weeks. It's amazing what the brain does to protect the mind, as I'm sure the memories would haunt me every time I took my bike out.

Seeing the film that Discovery made of the journey up to and including the accident, I have no emotional reaction to seeing the blood-stained shirt on the road that the paramedics cut off my body, nor the battered and bloodied helmet that saved my life. That may be because frontal lobe brain damage is likely to shut down some of your emotional reactions, or it might just be because I can't remember the moment of impact. It's gone.

What I do feel is sorrow for what the people I love have been and continue to live through. For them having to be called to the hospital to say goodbye, not knowing what I would be like if and when I recovered, for Bev not being able to tell me she was pregnant until weeks later, for being the different person I am today. In so many ways I'm the lucky one. They are more aware of the changes than I am.

Although I had other 'get well' letters and shirts from, amongst others, Becks, the English football and rugby teams and Team Sky, my main preoccupation seemed to be with writing not reading. I have no recollection of that Ryder Cup story I wrote for the *Telegraph*, it was entirely the work of my subconscious, but it made some sort of sense so I should try using it more often. I'd certainly rather be left with 'sleep writing' as a symptom of my brain injury than having to go to the toilet five times a night as it is.

I accompanied the story with a note in which I acknowledged the get well wishes I'd been sent by the prime minister and my mates. Apparently Bev asked friends and colleagues to send uplifting emails and she printed them off to show me.

Back in the hospital I clearly knew I had had something important to finish. The compulsion I had to keep going with things had not left me because of the accident. So being tied to a hospital bed to prevent me from wandering off can't have improved my mood. Going nowhere never has.

My dad said that he was able to have a conversation with me and then I would drift off into a totally different place (understandable if it was about tax or accounting but apparently it never was). There were recurring themes. 'I've got to get my bike. I've really got to crack on,' I told people over and over again, which must have been horrendously upsetting in the light of what had just happened to me.

Slowly the islands became a little bigger and I wasn't floating out into a sea of confusion as often. I can remember Mark, not just in his role as my minder in walks round the hospital, but as an amazing friend, and also because he was so good at entertaining Croyde when I wasn't capable of being a normal dad. Which was pretty much all of the time.

It was the nights that were most infuriating. I was awake most of the time because the blood pressure machine kept deciding I was just about to die. The machine could discreetly test my blood pressure, requiring no activity on my part and a minimum of intervention on the nurses'. But there was nothing discreet about the four-hourly performance we went through. Like many endurance athletes my resting heart rate is low, especially when I'm asleep. So the clever device also checked my pulse when it was checking my blood pressure, and if it was below forty beats per minute it assumed I was dead, causing the whole room to go into an emergency cardiac arrest mode. All the lights came on, the alarms sounded and an army of medics came flying in with defibrillators to kick-start my 'failing' heart into action again. Every time I had to persuade them that I was fine, this was normal. The whole process took ages, then it took me a while to go back to sleep – only for it to happen all over again a couple of hours later. It did my head in.

I heard this happened to Seb Coe as well when he caught food poisoning in Germany. He fainted and when he came to he was in a German military hospital just about to have the jump leads put on. Perhaps athletes should carry warning cards in their wallet: 'Leave My Heart Alone. We're Not Ill, Just Freaks With a Stupidly Low Heart Rate.'

At the end of a hot, weird, frustrating but strangely unemotional (for me anyway) five or six weeks, I was allowed to fly home, travelling with Dr Aled Jones (which I found highly amusing) and a cannula in my arm.

I had to be accompanied by Dr Jones not in case I needed an emergency rendition of a classical masterpiece about a snowman but because of the massively increased risk of having a seizure due to the brain injury. So I had this damn needle in my arm in case he suddenly needed to hit me with a shot of anti-seizure medication. I expect these doctors can usually relax in business class while their patient goes to sleep. It wasn't quite such a restful trip for Dr Jones. Not because I had a seizure but because it seemed to me the perfect time to catch up on movies, so I managed to stay awake the whole time and that was without intervention by the blood pressure machine. The sad thing is that I could have watched the same film over and over again as I would have no memory of ever having seen it before.

When we landed in London I had to go straight to the hospital for more poking around and intensive rehab. This didn't fit in with my plans, not that I actually had any, but I didn't think there was any need for it and desperately wanted to be at home. But everyone insisted. I can see now why Bev wouldn't have wanted me at home but I can vaguely remember feeling rejected and sentenced by her to an indefinite period of probing. That was when I first met my neurologist, who shared his name with a famous rugby player, and we had a slight misunderstanding.

For some reason, my mind had decided that this doctor was obviously the father of one of my friends who was part of the World Cup-winning rugby squad. I was sure (at the time) that his dad was a doctor. He's actually a retired geography teacher. But in my mind he was a doctor and I thought, this is going to work well. I definitely remembered being told that his dad's advice during a rugby match was: 'If you get a bang on the head, just say it was your shoulder. That way they'll let you play next week.'

So I am recounting this story cheerfully to my neurologist, saying: 'Look, you've got a relaxed attitude to brain injury, can I go home?'

His reply was not what I had hoped: 'I am not that person. I take brain injury very seriously and you're staying in.' If I'm honest, we haven't got on that well ever since, although my mate thinks it's one of the funniest stories he's heard. I did tell him he shouldn't laugh at the afflicted.

I know what happened to me and I know that I have suffered from the after-effects of brain injury when my frontal lobes were crushed against the inside of my skull. Or, as described by the Phoenix doctor delicately, 'you rang your own bell'.

I know that I went through a phase of 'post-traumatic amnesia'. I have read the fact sheets and I am genuinely so proud to have become vice-president of Headway, the brain injury association. But the day-to-day issues of living with the condition are harder to explain.

I thought I was all right. I thought I was making good judgements and it was everyone else who was behaving strangely. I've learnt over time that this wasn't the case, but it's hard to know whether brain injury is the culprit for a certain type of behaviour or just frustration at the people you love and respect doubting you and your ability to make any decision.

I know I was desperate to escape the hospital – I can't remember specifics, just the feeling I had – because one day my dad came to visit me and while he stood in reception en route to my ward, he heard my voice: 'Hello, Dad. I'm going out.' As I wasn't allowed out on my own, he made sure to come with me. It's a good job he was there because I looked at the traffic lights and was absolutely confident that red meant 'Go'.

Before I was allowed home from the English hospital, even

As much as Ben tried to convince me it was a cabin made for 2, I wasn't buying it, however good his company was.

Part way into our 50 days at sea. My beard was coming along ok, unfortunately so were the boils on my posterior.

2008: about to swim from Gibraltar to Africa with David Walliams for BBC Sport Relief. I'd just rowed the Channel, cycled through Europe and he's a much better swimmer than me – no wonder he's laughing.

The Antarctic race: not what you want to see looking in your tent in the morning!

Easter 2010: the brutal Marathon De Sables. Around 1,000 people gather on the start line ready to endure 151 miles over 6 days in the blistering heat of Morocco (inset). Finished 12th, highest ever Brit. Proudest achievement since rowing. Sun, sand (but no sea or sex).

Santa Monica pier, LA, at the 'end' of Route 66. Day 1 of my trip across America for the Discovery Channel. Never made it to the other end.

Riding into Death Valley, California, prior to running through it. Hottest place in America certainly lived up to that reputation.

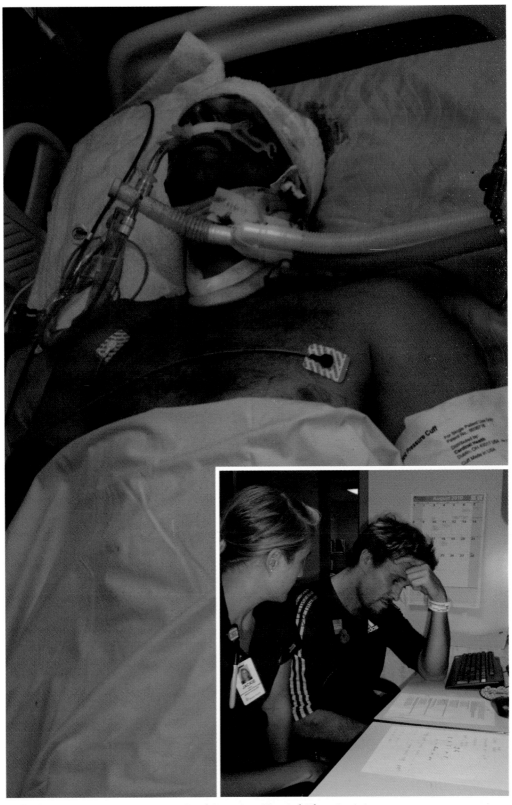

20th July 2010: intensive care, Banner Good Samaritan Hospital, Phoenix, Arizona.
Four weeks later trying the patience of a saint, therapist Jaclyn Knoll (inset).

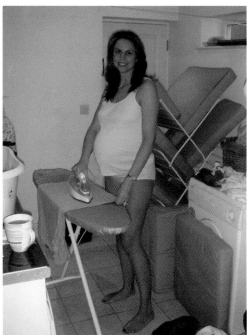

Left: at home, so happy with 20-minute-old Kiki Willow. Born on Mother's Day, 22nd March 2009. Amazing day.

Right: ironing in labour, 6 hours before Trixie Bea is born.

Antenatal check, March 2011. Kiki tries to guess if it's a girl or a boy. Mummy just glad of the lie down.

February 2011: the Yukon Arctic Ultra, the world's coldest race, learning to trust the new me. (You see, Bev, I told you it was snow – NOT ice).

December 2011: Victoria Falls, Zimbabwe, filming World Toughest Expeditions for the Discovery Channel. Annoyingly, Livingstone had already discovered it 150 years earlier.

I'm no Dr Dolittle, but I think he's saying, "Get off my land". Canoeing down the Zambezi in a hollowed-out tree trunk.

May 2009: Bev's parents' 40th wedding celebration lunch at Luscombes in Henley-on-Thames. Clockwise from front, Roger Turner, Rick Nolan, Joyce Turner, Cal Nolan (holding Kiki, 6 weeks), Bev, Abi Fogo, Adrian Turner, James and Croyde (6).

James's solution to losing his license: the tricycle! Comes in handy to get Bev, Nana (Joyce) and the kids round to Cal's on Christmas Day 2011. Croyde is hacked off because he doesn't get a seat.

24th July 2012: James ran
through Kingston with the
Olympic torch. Incredible
day. Croyde very impressed
and seriously proud of
his daddy.

for a trial run, I had to prove I could do certain tasks. I had to go to a shop with a list and buy the correct quantity of items on the list. Having managed that, I progressed to a list where each item had to be bought from a different shop, toothpaste from a chemist, for example, or pain au chocolat from a bakery.

The next step involved making a plan and following it through logically. Something that victims of a frontal lobe injury lose the ability to do. So I had to get a recipe off the Internet, write down the ingredients, make a shopping list and then head to the shops and get the right amount of everything on the list.

Next was to put that plan into action on a 'sleep over' at home but with an extra test – follow the recipe and make the delicious culinary delight myself.

I chose lasagne (why, I don't know – tasty but labour-intensive) and a Victoria sponge. I was convinced I'd always made a mean Victoria sponge. Months later I asked my mum about my legendary sponges and she said to her knowledge I'd never made one in my life.

I had to take photos of the food when it was cooked and bring them back to the hospital. I found out later the medics had checked with Bev to assess my behaviour. I was slightly disappointed they hadn't enquired about the outcome of the meal I whipped up, as I thought the lasagne rocked. There again, the Victoria sponge looked and (apparently) tasted like a relic from her reign.

Following instructions was awful. But not being allowed at this stage of my recovery to be left on my own, or be alone with the kids or be around sharp knives, hot pans or anything that was fragile was heart-breaking.

I remember doing the tasks and feeling like I was being tested – a feeling I still have two years on, but mercifully I don't remember being watched and constantly assessed. On the positive side, at least the watchers were people I loved: Mum, Dad and Bev. On the negative side, I needed and wanted them to trust me as they previously had.

I hated the fact that the neurologists, neuropsychologists and psychiatrists – the confederacy of '-ists' – were making decisions about me that might have been accurate medically but imposed a glass ceiling on what I would be able to do in the future. Worse was the fact that they only knew me as a patient post-accident but not the person I was or what I was capable of before the accident. So how could they impose these ceilings on my recovery based on results from generalised tests? Like being given a minute to name as many words as you could beginning with the letter D: dungeon, dragon, drachma . . . proper nouns didn't count. I had to follow numerical patterns (I should have asked my dad to do that one) and one day they came back to me and said they were really worried. According to my test results, I was in the ninety-ninth percentile for stubbornness. I asked what that meant and was told that 'out of every hundred people you're the second most stubborn'.

They thought that was abnormally high and concerning because it could be a limiting factor in my ultimate recovery. Apparently my unshakeable self-belief that I would get back to who and where I was before the accident would help me in the first six months. But after that they felt my lack of mental flexibility would be a problem. 'Mental inflexibility!' What on earth did they mean?

I told them my attitude to life was no different than that of the people I'd spent so much of the last fifteen years with. To which they shook their heads as though I'd just told them that gravity was a myth. Luckily Steve Redgrave came to visit me a day or so later and since visiting hours were obviously a hassle for someone with his busy life, combined with the sportsman's belief that 'time has no meaning for a man with no job', he just stayed. When they tried to throw him out, he carried on sitting there. The neuropsychologist came in and said: 'OK, so now I've met the hundredth.'

'I told you I hung around with stubborn people,' I said. 'And that I wasn't the worst!' My tests also revealed some interesting insights into how my brain works now, and how it had been damaged. I had a sub-normal facial recognition ability – in fact, I was in the lowest five per cent – but on the other hand I was in the top five per cent when it came to numerical recall, which is the level you need to join Mensa or get into MI5. This shows the extent of my injury, as normally there's no way that you can be that low in one area and that high in another. It was a superb illustration of just how badly my brain had been affected.

After two further weeks of tests and rehab I was allowed home. I felt both better and worse at this stage. My injuries were healing physically but the reality of what had happened and the effect it was going to have started to dawn on me. It became clear to me that there was stuff I couldn't do any more.

The power output that I used to produce for hours on a rowing machine or the static bike drained me after five minutes. If I was preparing for a challenge, I used to spend hours on a treadmill or rowing machine when the kids and Bev were in bed. Unsociable and slightly weird I know, but it meant training didn't eat into crucial family time. That was no longer an option as I needed more sleep than before. In fact, I now needed more sleep than the rest of the family.

Above all, self-motivation, a characteristic which had served me so well as a sportsman, simply wasn't there. I'd get on the bike, turn the pedals a few times and think: 'This is quite boring, I've had enough.' But I'd done a boring, repetitive sport for years. I couldn't understand why my motivation to keep going just wasn't there. That's something that before the accident I'd never had a problem with.

Then there was the dreaded question, the one I was faced with six years earlier with my retirement but thought I had finally answered. The trip across the States, it seemed, had been leading to a long-term relationship with the Discovery Channel and the chance to do things I genuinely loved whilst exploring and experiencing places I'd always wanted to visit. I had to face the fact that the niche I been carving out for myself as a documentary-making adventure/ endurance performer had been fatally wounded by what had occurred on that road in Arizona. So that question was once again doing the rounds in my head: What are you going to do now?

Who was I? I looked the same (in the mirror at least) but *was* I the same person? The honest answer was no. I had no consistent memory for well over five to six weeks after the accident. I had to relearn most tasks and physical skills, even the basic one of walking. I seemed short-tempered, frustrated and angry to those around me.

I hated that my accident was putting those I love through such a terrible time. I'm reminded every day of the changes others see by being unable to do things that I once took for granted. I tended not to hear compliments and positivity but retained the small criticisms for far too long. Bev could say a hundred positive words but I only heard the negative and heard it incredibly loudly.

What I needed was a challenge to prove to myself and others that I was capable of doing what I had done before. In conjunction with David Harrison (who I'd worked with on the Marathon des Sables programme and knew me before the accident), I decided what I needed was to cycle on ice over 700km through the sub-Arctic wasteland of Yukon, North America. Some might think this was a crazy reworking of what had gone before, putting myself back in a position to be hit. They might even think it was hypocritical, claiming to be guilty and heartbroken while preparing to put my loved ones through the wringer again. But the decision to tackle the frozen wastes of the Yukon hadn't been plucked from some random abyss. Some serious thought and reasoning had gone into it. And serious work would have to go into preparing for it to ensure that I would be strong enough for the challenge. But it was perfect: there were no vehicles, a safety and medical team would be there at all times and I'd be working exclusively with people I knew and trusted.

The Discovery Channel had put out the film (*Race Across America*) of my abortive adventure in the US and shown graphic footage of me in hospital. I didn't mind. I didn't think it was ghoulish. They had made the film and not showing it would have been a waste of time and money. I understood the commercial imperative. But I did not want the public's last sight of me to be lying flat out in a bed. It wasn't fair on the people who loved me, the medical staff who'd saved me, mates who'd helped me or anyone who's suffered from a brain injury. Other people in my position had survived and battled to show that you can recover. You can be the person you used to be, if not better. I wanted to do the same.

I needed to prove myself to myself. That I could plan, develop a strategy, prepare and motivate myself to train for something. Then show I could make the right decisions at the right time, something that wasn't the case at home. I felt observed and not trusted. If I could demonstrate that I still possessed that ability, to others as well as myself, it would have the combined effect of elevating my confidence and that of people close to me. Lastly, it had to be on a bike. I wasn't and wouldn't suggest starting from the point where I got knocked off but it was symbolic to me that it be on two wheels to show that my self-belief and determination to get back to where and who I was before hadn't dissipated. Plus, as I'd said, there were going to be no trucks where I was headed.

My motivations weren't all selfish. I wanted to be a better husband and father. I hoped that out there in the wilderness with nothing but my bike and my thoughts, I might finally rediscover my old self, which would help put my life back together.

It is highly significant that Bev thought it was worth it too. I felt that I'd learnt to be more considerate since the accident, and even before that from rowing across the Atlantic. So I was aware that saying I wanted to pop across to Alaska on a bike wasn't going to be an easy sell, nor would it be easy for Bev to comprehend. Funnily enough the words 'cycle' and 'ice' didn't fill her with delight but she came to understand why I needed to do this.

Perhaps the reason she agreed, as she said on the film of the trip, was not only because she trusted David and understood the safety measures we would take, and was going to be included every step of the way, but also because she wanted 'the spark back that he used to have'. I wanted that for her, for me, and our marriage, too.

Bev said she trusted me but I didn't feel as though she did. Frontal lobe injuries tend to make planning and rational decision-making harder. So this was my chance to prove that I could be trusted with both. I was being left alone with the kids by now, but I felt I was constantly being interrupted. I was more short-tempered; things that had rarely bothered me before now were hugely significant and I'd go on and on about them. Things like Croyde speaking with his mouth full, something I've never been saintly about myself. And he's an eight-year-old boy. But my newly raised levels of irritability and temper meant that he didn't want to eat with me any more.

We'd been close to never seeing each other again – and yet we reached breaking point over something as ridiculous as table manners. It was disturbing but at the time I couldn't see that I was the problem. I can see why Bev thought enduring the Yukon was worth it.

If the trip to Alaska could change anything it would be to never hear Bev say again 'You're not the same person I married.' She maintains that she used these words when desperate – to get me to rest. I didn't see the point in taking naps but she was obsessed about it. I hated hearing that I'd changed because it highlighted the stress and problems of our personal relationship. For her to say 'your sparkle is back, you're back' would mean I'd moved on but it would also mean other issues were back in place: trust, relationships with the kids, friends; even reactions to people I'd never met before were back and predictable. It would mean Croyde wouldn't say things like: 'You're much more shouty now.' Perhaps if I was him, I'd ignore me. If something like what had happened to me had happened to my dad when I was Croyde's age, I think I'd let it wash over me, which was pretty much what he was doing to the extent that he'd ignore me and not want to spend time with me. But Croyde is more sensitive than I was at his age, not to mention funny, sociable, musical, better coordinated and great at dancing.

There's no denying that I got on best with Kiki. She was so young when I came back from the hospital that all her problems could be solved very easily. She was either hungry or sleepy or shitty. She didn't judge me. The only thing we noticed is that she always cried when I left the house. Not out of an uncontrollable passion never to be apart but because she probably associated me going out with everyone becoming upset, as had happened the previous summer. I went to America and then suddenly everyone was crying, jumping on planes and her life was being turned upside down, spending weeks living in a hotel in the fifty-degree heat of Phoenix. Understandably, she didn't want that to happen again. She wasn't the only one.

So I had a brilliant relationship with Kiki but life wasn't fun for Croyde and Bev. I haven't asked, I don't want to know, but I would understand and forgive them for thinking: 'I wish that truck had hit you harder.' They wanted and needed some consistency in my behaviour and I wasn't able to give that.

It was bad enough that my wife had been phoned up in the middle of the night to come and say goodbye to her husband because he was in Intensive Care and not expected to live. It was as tough in a different way that Croyde had been uprooted to spend two months in the grilling heat of Arizona. But on top of that they also had to endure a 'different' person living with them who would snap, get frustrated and angry at things that had never bothered him before. I understood and even felt guilty about it then, but not in the way I do now looking back. At the time, I felt I was in a catch-22 situation. I wanted to be given some control back but I needed to earn that control.

Alongside this there were just a couple of practical bumps along the road to recovery, as I occasionally tested my limits. The *Daily Telegraph*, who I've written for since 1998, had been amazingly supportive and gave me a present of a fold-up Brompton bike. A stylish little number, which even has my name down the side. When I cycled alongside Croyde on his way to school he used to shake his head with embarrassment and say: 'Oh no, not Daddy's small wheels again.'

Small wheels or not, it was damn practical, as the DVLA had revoked my driving licence while they assessed my driving ability, so the folding bike was brilliant for getting around. I was on my way to Fred's a couple of days before Christmas to talk through how I would handle the chaotic, hectic and unpredictable nature (sorry, pleasure) of a big family Christmas. Fred had been a phenomenal support to me both practically and emotionally. I was carrying the bike up the stairs over a railway line footbridge when I fell up the stairs. Despite it hurting, I bounced straight up out of embarrass-ment. I clearly wasn't that badly hurt and as I'd just been riding the bike I still had my helmet on. I was just about vertical and busy working out my next move when a lady walked past and said jokingly, 'Ooh it's lucky you had your helmet on.' I assumed it was for the clown-like uncoordinated manoeuvre rather than a comment on the accident in Arizona.

I carried on to Fred's who now had some proper medical reason to advise me – my little finger had repositioned itself a centimetre or so lower down my hand and hurt. 'See how it feels in a few hours,' he said, 'and if it's not too swollen, ice it. If it hurts in the morning get yourself down to A&E.'

I followed his instructions to the letter and headed to Charing Cross Hospital on Christmas Eve, where it was confirmed I'd broken a metacarpal (a finger – like a metatarsal but not as famous). They casually informed me it would need pinning when the hospital re-opened after Christmas on 28 December. Ah. The only trouble being that Bev had booked a family holiday in Egypt just after Christmas, replacing the summer holiday that had been abandoned when everyone relocated to cheery Phoenix where I was lying unconscious.

I explained the delicate situation that I'd already caused one family holiday to be cancelled because I was in hospital. One cancellation can be put down to bad luck; two would look like I was deliberately avoiding them. 'Is there any way it can be done before the twenty-eighth because we're due to fly on the twenty-seventh?' I begged.

Their sympathetic response was 'theatres are shut for non-emergency operations until the twenty-eighth'. I was about to say that wiring my little pinkie may not have been an emergency to them but the battering Bev would give me if I caused another holiday to be cancelled surely would be. I tried a bit more charming persuasion, to which they offered at least one piece of practical advice.

'You'll just have to find a Jewish surgeon.' I guessed this was hard enough on a normal day, let alone lunchtime on Christmas Eve.

But at last some good luck arrived with the news that my brother-in-law's uncle's mate was a surgeon who knew another surgeon who was Jewish. I took a photo of the X-ray on my phone and texted it to him. He confirmed I did need an operation and tacked me onto the start of his theatre list.

My dad picked me up at 5.30 a.m. on Christmas Day and took me to University College Hospital where I had a general anaesthetic and they pinned my hand. The wires were left sticking out of my hand as when the bone had healed they would be pulled out rather than undergo another operation. By the time I got back home everyone had eaten Christmas dinner, played a few games and fallen down in glycaemic comas. The irony was that even having been up at 5 a.m. and been under general anaesthetic, I thought I was still the liveliest.

We made it to Egypt but I felt really shitty the whole time. I couldn't go in the water because I had an open cut where the wires were sticking out. A few days in, I discovered the hand was badly infected, the clue being the pus constantly seeping out. It turned out I had picked up an MRSA-type infection so I had to go under general anaesthetic again at the same hospital, the wires were taken out and the wound was fully cleaned up. Luckily, the bone had healed properly and I didn't have to endure yet another operation.

It was now vital I made a quick recovery. The plans for the Yukon challenge had moved on and I was due to fly to Alaska in less than a month to take part in the Yukon Arctic Ultra. Taking in the disciplines of skiing, running and mountain-biking, and invitingly described as the 'Coldest Race on Earth', the race covered over 430 miles of frozen wilderness, ice-cold winds, blizzards and temperatures of minus fifty degrees. Just what the doctor ordered. At least infections would be harder to pick up in those temperatures. Every cloud . . .

Now more than ever I felt it was a necessity for all our sakes that I did something to prove to people I could be trusted. I wanted to get back on a bike and having no memory of the collision made that easier. The simple fact it happened on a public highway – which could happen to anyone, any time – helped me. If I had been somewhere really remote or doing an adrenalin sport like cave diving or base-jumping, then I can see my accident could have been put down to a poor decision on my part. But on Route 66, riding safely where I should be, wearing the right kit and protective clothing, it wasn't my fault. I couldn't have done anything else to ensure my own safety.

Needless to say the production company and I had difficulties with insurance, especially as it was the first trip I'd done since the crash. I had to accept that I would be operating with different limitations. But I would have a film crew with me again – and Dave, who Bev knew, and who crucially knew what I was like before the accident which Bev wanted so that (I assumed) she could ask him how different I seemed when we returned. The crucial element was having the back-up of Fred and another doctor and Royal Navy cold weather specialist Kent Haworth, who had insisted that they would pull me from the race if I started to make irrational or dangerous decisions. I was happy to agree because I was confident and, more importantly, wanted to prove I'd make the right decisions under pressure, as I used to prior to my accident. It was the major reason for doing a self-supported event in the Alaskan wilderness.

I would carry my own tent and food while I cycled, they

would track me on skidoo and we'd meet up at various checkpoints. But for most of the race I would be on my own with my thoughts. In those conditions a tent and food would be fantastic company and a tremendous mood enhancer. I couldn't say the same about my thoughts.

Regardless of the medical support I had tracking me, it was a self-supported event unless they felt the need to intervene. I went into it dismissing the 'comfort blanket' they provided. Which was just as well because I swiftly discovered that doctors – as well as having rubbish handwriting – can't drive a skidoo either. They managed to flip it over while fully loaded with all their kit which scattered their stuff all over the deep snow. I fully appreciated the irony that they were supposed to be the ones keeping *me* upright.

Bev understood the reason behind why I had to go on the Yukon trip, though she claimed she did trust me and wasn't policing my decisions so didn't think I was going to prove anything new to her. What she did want was for me to gain some of the spark, life and confidence within me that had disappeared since the accident, and if I needed to go to Alaska to do that then so be it. It helped enormously that she was so involved because she asked questions of the medics, the production company and the support crew that I may not have found the confidence to ask.

So I set off, on a voyage of personal discovery. Hopefully. We congregated in the town of Whitehorse at the start, a small troupe of masochistic weirdos masquerading as athletes in thermals and windproof tops. Fewer than ten competitors in the history of the event had ever completed the course on a snow bike. The inviting cocktail of the cold, frostbite, impassable snow, injury, illness, exhaustion and the sheer hostility of the conditions ensured that most who tried had failed.

The day before the race a large crowd of people cheered the dog-sledders who set off twenty-four hours earlier and in theory compact the snow on the route, making it slightly easier for the cyclists and the runners to move over the frozen terrain. The huskies all had little booties on their feet – and it would be one of the small comforts of the race to find one of these doggie snow boots (not to mention a few hundred turds) discarded in the snow every few miles as at least it meant I was going the right way, although a collection of the latter wasn't quite as comforting when you'd got to pitch a tent.

I assumed the day of the race there would be few people to see some numpties on bikes and skis setting off. My fellow competitors and I weren't as cute as the huskies, but the fact that there would be less biting and shitting going on more than made up for that.

The film crew, Fred and Kent weren't put off by my lack of loveliness. Their presence served as a reminder, and a necessary one, that I had committed to this project not to win. If I am being honest, this was all about rebuilding my self-confidence, which was lower than I could ever remember. This was about seeing how much of the old James Cracknell was there and whether I could be him again.

Many would quite rightly ask 'Why would you want to be that person again?' I'm still working on an answer to that one.

There was enough of the old geography teacher in me to find the scenery on the first day beautiful. It was a balmy minus twenty degrees and the landscape stretched over frozen lakes and ice-trimmed trees towards distant mountains. Maybe not distant enough, given that we were going to have to go up some long steep inclines towards the end of the race. Even so, I could appreciate the sights. I was lucky the scenery was both spectacular and on an epic scale as I wasn't going to be lacking the time to enjoy it.

This appreciation of 'Narnia' lessened somewhat after twelve straight hours in the saddle. An exceptionally sore butt, a painful knee and an estimated six more days of this to come meant my attention was switched elsewhere.

There would be one mandatory eight-hour stop at a farmer's property after 300 miles and Fred and Kent also insisted that I would have to be off the bike for six hours every night. This effectively tied one hand behind my back and made it impossible to win, but as I've said, I was focused on a different prize. I was two hours in the lead at the first checkpoint and was in my sleeping bag when the guy behind came through, rested for a few minutes and was off. As I probably would have done before the accident. With only one mandatory stop in the race I'd have planned to spend as little time as possible off the bike and made the most of the long eight-hour break, and not stopped again until the finish. Which was exactly the tactic he used, his only solid sleep being the compulsory eight hours, although he was so exhausted at that point he lost 'bladder control' when the farmer sat him down and gave him a dish of piping hot lasagne. Which explained the waterproof boots the farmer was wearing and the wide berth he gave me when I pitched up.

With the neurologically enforced rest, I was effectively in a straitjacket. If I didn't want to be permanently wearing one afterwards through sheer rage and frustration, it was imperative I developed a new mental attitude before going on. 'Winning' was always such a failsafe motivation; now I didn't, and couldn't, have that goal. I was determined to 'properly' race as I had previously. But what motivation was I going to use to keep my legs pushing the pedals, uphill, in the dark, across murderous terrain, sometimes covering the ground at less than walking pace as I hauled my bike and kit through the deep snow?

I had to remind myself that the race wasn't the goal. This wasn't about winning, it was about proving to myself that the real me was still there and could be trusted on every single level. Not just practical day-to-day and week-to-week planning but more than that. I wanted to know I could still be the husband and father I was before.

Rather than focus on winning, I'd promised to enjoy the experience and use the solitude to think about how I was going to repair the damaged relationship I had with Bev and Croyde. But I clearly hadn't worked hard enough, because rather than utilising the stunning vista in front of me as proof that life wasn't bad, or in fact so different, rather than appreciating that I was incredibly lucky to still be around to be able to enjoy a life with Bev and the kids, rather than enjoying the prospect of helping Croyde and Kiki grow up, I was struggling to see the point of why I was here.

I didn't hide what I was feeling from the cameras. I didn't want to hide it. I remember muttering a miserable line on film which summed up how deeply negative I was feeling. 'I was a day away from never seeing my kids again, so why did I choose pushing my bike through the fucking snow in this place rather than being with them?'

The person I was before the accident wouldn't have thought like that. Even if I had been able to switch off from the competitiveness for a second, Bev and the kids would have been a reason to pick up the pace and get home as quickly as possible. Instead I was feeling sorry for myself, just wanting to sit down and throw my toys out of the pram. I also wasn't being honest. Bev and Croyde didn't want to spend time with me at home because I wasn't me – and the reason for coming here was to see I was still me deep down and take confidence from that. I needed to feel genuinely lucky, happy to be alive and come back as a more positive person that Bev and the kids would want to be near.

If I wasn't in a bad enough place already, I bit on a cashew nut (not recommended at minus forty degrees) and a piece of my tooth fell out.

The last leg of the race was approaching, and a foot of fresh snow fell just as I was facing my biggest climb – King Solomon's Dome. Even the ten-centimetre-wide tyres on my specially commissioned bike that had been designed to cope with riding both through snow and on ice weren't going to be of much use against that much fresh snow.

Any external motivation from the race wasn't happening either. The man who needed no sleep ahead of me was *nearing* the finish line, whereas the guys behind me were over twenty-four hours in arrears.

I couldn't ride the bike up the mountain, so I got off and pushed, consoling myself that what goes up must come down and I'd be on a downhill gradient all the way to the finish. As I scrambled, pushed and, well, threw my bike over the summit, I was alone on the mountain. It was minus forty and snowing so severely the organisers were scrambling the rescue teams and considering calling off the race. Worse than that, though, I was discovering that what went up *didn't* come down at all. At least not in the way that I had counted on. The snow was now so deep that even with gravity on my side I couldn't gain enough momentum to get going. It was swallowing me up. I was going to have to get off and push again. Pushing uphill had been mentally hard, pushing downhill was unbearable.

I thought the whole thing was pointless, stupid and I just wanted to go home. I wanted to quit. 'Quit.' Unless my safety was as risk, that thought would never have been allowed anywhere near my head before the accident.

At that point, the medical team came to check on me.

'Keep going,' Fred said. 'Just pace it out and we'll meet you further down.'

'Is showing I can push a bike down a hill in the snow going to prove anything or make things better?' I countered. 'Let's put the bike on top of the skidoo. There's no one around. No one will know,' I urged him.

Even as the words came out of my mouth I knew I would never have uttered them before the accident.

'Don't make a decision on the fly in a low mood,' Fred reasoned.

A low mood I could have coped with but I was in a mood I didn't even recognise and certainly one I'd never found myself in before.

'Let's go and get the fuck out of here. No one will know,' I repeated.

'No, you'll regret it when you get home.'

'I won't regret it. I won't regret it when I get home. My kids are a day away from seeing me. I don't want to spend that fucking day pushing a bike through the snow in the middle of nowhere.'

'OK, OK, just think a bit more about it and we'll meet you further on.'

He drove off and that was it. He never let me fucking catch up. And he was right. I would have massively regretted it. It was cheating – something I've never condoned in my life. But in my mind, I was so far behind the bloke that had already won and so far in front of the rest of the field – at least the ones left – that I was cheating nobody just cutting out the needless tedium of showing I could push a bike through snow for hours.

No way would the old James have even contemplated, let alone uttered out loud, such despicable thoughts. It was at that point I realised I was different. The accident had changed me. I had never struggled to motivate myself before, especially in a situation like that. Admittedly, I had completed the race and come second – legitimately. I'd hauled my frozen ass across the Yukon and was one of the handful who ended up making it all the way. But rather than celebrate with the crew, Fred and Kent when I crossed the line, I took myself off and cried.

I wasn't proud of myself but I was definitely more aware that people weren't just making it up when they said I was different. Did I think that people's belief in me might be raised now, whether that was Bev at home or the experts who seemed to be continually telling me what I wouldn't be able to do?

More than ever I knew that I didn't want a ceiling to be imposed from the outside upon my capabilities. I wanted to push the limits but I was now coming from the position of admitting that my life and my personality had changed.

I had to accept that my previous baseline where I thought I was behaving normally and everyone else was behaving and treating me differently was wrong. The reality was that everyone else was normal and I was now slightly strange. Bev didn't want me back in the house straightaway when I came back from Alaska, which was hurtful but I understood. I would be tired and frustrated, and therefore at risk of upsetting Croyde. Instead I spent two nights at her sister's, and then I was allowed home.

But once the blisters on my sore bum had healed and my knee recovered from the pounding I had given it, I realised that the Yukon trip had given me the confidence boost I needed which it wouldn't have if I'd bailed out onto a skidoo. I'd wanted to know if it was possible for me to continue my career, not solely for selfish reasons, but to look after my family as well.

I had cycled through hellish conditions and – despite a significant wobble – come out the other side. I was eight months closer to getting my driving licence back. I had less reason to be frustrated with life, my family and myself. I believed that it was possible I could defy all those who wanted to tell me I couldn't do stuff any more.

I could. I would. I believed that.

[Bev]

James returns from the Yukon, thin and hairy. My heart sinks. I had hoped he'd return with more of the 'normal' James. Instead, he looks wild and eccentric. But I'm dying to know about the trip. I desperately want to hear that it was an edifying, rewarding experience. 'Did you enjoy it?' I beam in the arrival lounge.

'I'd say endured rather than enjoyed,' he replied.

'Oh.'

I learn precious little else of the trip from James. He can't articulate what it felt like. All he can say is 'Frustrating.' Only David Harrison helps me to understand how hard it was. I am astonished by the idea that James cried on camera. He normally left that to Ben Fogle. To fully understand what James had 'endured' I would have to wait to see the finished programme.

Our baby is due the first week of April. Throughout March James is busy doing press and publicity for the Discovery Channel who will be showing a 'James Cracknell Trilogy' – *The Toughest Race on Earth* (the MDS); *The Race Across America* (the 'accident' story) and *The World's Coldest Race* (the Yukon). His PR woman, Lou Plank, does a brilliantly discreet and tactful job of scheduling his interviews so that he doesn't get too mentally fatigued. A good team work closely on deciding what he can and can't do.

James and I both write pieces for the *Daily Telegraph* but James's verbosity has transferred to the written word and he is about to submit nearly 4,000 words instead of 1,500 when I intervene. It's bizarre – previously, he would accurately hit his word count; now, it's like his brain runs away with itself and the brakes have come off. He's a good writer and we always worked as a team: I'd criticise his terrible punctuation and he'd pad out my fluffiness with some brilliant facts or analogies. Suddenly, as I trim back his unrecognisably waffling prose, it feels like I've lost my teammate.

As the baby's due date nears I must switch gears mentally to prepare for the birth but I'm finding it incredibly hard. When James returns from the Yukon, we spend hours every week seeing neurologists, psychologists and therapists. James can't relax and – in my opinion – is still not prioritising rest.

When I wake one morning feeling contractions, I assume that as with Kiki's birth we'll have a baby by lunchtime. But as soon as I get up and start talking to James everything stops. My mum takes the kids to my sister's and I focus on staying calm and allowing my body to take over. This time, I've managed a little preparation using natal hypnotherapy, an evolution of good old-fashioned hypnobirthing that I used with the first two. It might sound a bit whacko, but it's basically a form of deep relaxation. Only this time, I've barely listened to the CDs. Twenty-four hours later, I wake up again feeling that proper labour is about to kick in. Then I talk to James and everything stops.

After lunch, I lie down and listen to the Birth Rehearsal CD on my own. It's the most intense, dream-like sensory experience imaginable and I 'come round' knowing exactly what I need to do. I write down ten pointers for James and finish the list as he emerges from the gym.

'I've not been fair with you,' I say. 'I'm assuming that everything will be OK but you probably want clearer instructions.' I hand him the piece of paper as he sits down.

1. If Pam (the midwife) and I need silence, don't be offended.
2. If I ask you to be quiet, please don't argue.
3. Don't ask me if I want a drink. If I need one, I'll ask.
4. Don't ask me if you can do anything – it makes me feel I must make a decision. I know you will help me if I need it.
5. Be kind to me. That's all I'll need.
6. Don't question anything that I say in labour.
7. Remind me to keep my shoulders down and jaw relaxed.
8. Please don't need anything from me for the duration of the birth.
9. If you have any questions – ask Pam.
10. I love you. You'll be great.

He looks at the list, concedes, 'I keep doing that, don't I?' I nod. 'And that.'

'You do.'

'And that one.'

He walks out of the room and I literally feel a shift: as though a mental block has lifted. I'm ready. I reach for my phone to call midwife Pam and as she answers my waters break. Two and a half hours later we have a baby girl.

During the second stage, as I'm in the birthing pool, James and I make eye contact and he smiles, says, 'You're doing brilliantly.'

I take a long drag on the gas and air. 'So are you.'

He chokes a little, wipes a tear from his eye.

Even though we are blessed with another healthy girl, I don't really feel the elation of my previous births. Such a momentous occasion always follows with a 'new start' but somehow I can't separate the event from the present day. I still miss James.

I must protect him from the sleeplessness that a new baby brings into a house so Trixie and I exist in the spare attic room and I breastfeed through the night. On far too many mornings, we are awoken by Croyde banging up the stairs in tears after an altercation with James at breakfast. James follows close behind, furious with Croyde and angry that we've been woken up. The moment my eyes open I must start refereeing, intervening and protecting.

Watching *The World's Coldest Race* a few weeks later is a darkly moving experience. Nothing in it surprises me: his unwillingness to cooperate with director David Harrison when tired and angry; the way that he appears to be unmotivated and curls up in the tent during the race. But I can't help but shed a tear when he is overcome with frustration. 'I've never used the injury as an excuse . . .' And I realise that's true. He could be spending his days in bed, lamenting his loss; marinating in self-pity and deciding that his life is over.

For some reason, I hadn't really considered that his determination to push himself on and on – refusing to sleep; setting new goals; rejecting my attempts to 'put the brakes on' – may be infuriating to live with, but is exactly what he needs to recover. Watching him push a bike through the snow (he was right – it is snow, not ice), I realise that I shouldn't be afraid of that stubborn grit. We will need it if he has any chance of a good recovery.

10

'I used to be James Cracknell. I'm not any more.'

[James]
They call it a PTC – a 'piece to camera'. Essentially they're just a short address via a camera to people in their living rooms. I first did one for *Gold Fever*, a 2000 BBC documentary that followed the lives of the crew (Steve, Matt, Tim and I) from its inception in 1997 to delivery in the Sydney Olympics. These pieces to camera were unscripted, uncensored and honest (well, they were if you're a press-naive rower like I was) and took in how you were feeling about training and each other, nerves, your other halves, personal problems, racing and coping with the frustrations and pressures as the Olympics approached.

The problem was that the cameras became (as I imagine the BBC had planned) like a psychiatrist's couch and I'd rant away about teammates and life in general. What made that worse was the timing. The three hour-long episodes would be aired just before the Olympics, so resurrecting issues that, as a crew, we'd put behind us years earlier.

Since then the PTCs I've done have been a mixture of what I'm going through (often on endurance trips with Ben), where I am (historical or geographical pieces) as well as coverage of sporting events. Most of mine had involved telling the world what part of my body was now breaking down in the face of snow, hot sand and/or sea. The thing is: I'd always got better. A boil on the arse is an absolute bastard especially when you've got to row another thousand miles sitting on it, but all things must pass and it goes away.

This time it was different. My PTC was for the brain injury association, Headway, and for anyone who had suffered a brain injury or loved and cared for someone who had a brain injury. This PTC was intensely personal.

'Last year when I was cycling across America, a truck's wing mirror *smashed* into the back of my head at seventy miles an hour, knocking me off my bike and on to the road. My brain swung against the front of my skull, causing severe damage to the frontal lobes of my brain.

'When I came out of intensive care, I wasn't me any more. All my friends and family told me that my entire personality had changed. My short-term memory was gone. I couldn't make a decision. Had no motivation.

'But I was lucky. I was wearing a helmet. If I hadn't been, I'd be dead. Doctors say in time I should make a good recovery. I'm already back on my bike. Some cyclists will never ride again. I make the choice to wear a helmet.

'I'm nearly James Cracknell. Use your head. Use a helmet.'

I hoped it was a powerful message. I wanted to do everything I could to support such a worthwhile charity. It was designed to educate people into protecting their heads or influence others to persuade their friends and family to cycle with a helmet. I also wanted to do something positive to mark the anniversary of the accident.

I suppose that PTC also summed up my problem. The doctors had told me I would make a good recovery, but there were always caveats. For instance, what did 'good' mean? There were all these '-ists' – psychologists, neurologists, neuropsychologists, occupational therapists – who don't really know you and didn't know you before your injury, imposing limits on your future. But what was all that based on? Statistical analysis of people who've had a similar injury and what their capacity proved to be. I didn't want to bow to their predictions. Everyone's drive, determination, lifestyle and support network of people around them is totally different.

I could not contemplate submitting to any ceiling that was being imposed on me, I would not contemplate it.

I would never get back to where I was if I listened to the experts telling me I wouldn't. It was like seeing a good-looking girl and all your mates telling you that she's out of your league (which, funnily enough, happened quite a lot to me). So if you listen to your mates, you don't dare talk to her and you'll never know what might have happened. If only I could turn back time then perhaps my twenties wouldn't have been such a barren wilderness on the female front.

OK, I had to accept that there were some things that would never get better. My senses of taste and smell have gone for ever, apart from a few extremes – sweet and sour, salt and sugar. That's it. I don't have a favourite meal any more. I chomp through loads of tomatoes and cucumber – which I used to hate – because of the more interesting texture. Lunch these days consists of something that definitely won't make it into a Jamie Oliver cookbook. Although it takes much less than thirty minutes to whip up. In fact, it takes less than three minutes, plus seven to chow down. Surely there's a market for the busy taste-deprived working man out there? Perhaps I could become their culinary guru.

So for those guys: take one chilli (add extra powder) and lentil soup with chopped tomatoes, chicken (for protein) and peppers, topped with liberal amounts of barbeque and Reggae Reggae Sauce (for an attempt at a glimmer of taste). Mushrooms are an optional extra if you're going for the sophisticated approach and trying to impress a lovely lady. But a) I'm married and b) if you imagine what eating the sole of a Hush Puppy is like, that's the pleasure I derive from a mushroom. In fact, perhaps I should try munching on the former to see if my analogy truly works.

Either way, it's shit.

I can live with my new diet. I always had a slightly weird relationship with food anyway. Being an athlete who had to eat 6,000 calories a day, I regarded mealtime as a fuel stop rather than a fine dining experience. I'd vaguely normalised my portion sizes since I'm no longer training six hours a day. I was on the verge of being repatriated into food society when the accident happened. On top of everything she has to endure, it's criminally unfair on Bev, who always loved going out to a good restaurant for a wonderful meal and talking about the food. She used to host a cookery show on TV and knows her stuff, but there's no point for me. For all I can taste, it might as well be a motorway service station takeaway – or the previously mentioned Hush Puppy.

But there has been progress. The Yukon, as disconcerting as I found it struggling for motivation and even wanting to bail out when things got really hard, restored some of my confidence. Because I hadn't bailed out.

If I was in any doubt about how much Bev and the kids meant to me, the Yukon reaffirmed this every hour of every day. It made me ache being away from them but made me appreciate being alive, knowing that I would be able to make the most of their lives – and mine – in future. At my low points, I wanted Bev and the kids to be there. At my happiest, I wanted to share it with them. Just as I want to share my life with them.

I'd had to get back to a fairly decent level of physical fitness to complete the Yukon, but more importantly had discovered that my mind, and not my body, would be the determining factor of my level of ability, competence and mental capability. We were pleased with and proud of the three Discovery films we'd made on the Marathon des Sables, the Race Across America, where I had my accident, and the Yukon. We were now talking about a series that really excited me, following in the footsteps of pioneering explorers like David Livingstone in Africa, Percy Fawcett in the Brazilian Amazon, the '49ers who crossed Death Valley during the California gold rush and the survivors of the *Dundonald* shipwreck in New Zealand.

I wouldn't be reliving their entire expeditions – they would be too much for me now. And I could hardly take four years to reach Victoria Falls as did Livingstone, but I could still investigate key moments of their respective journeys. The only real potential problem, as the Yukon had demonstrated, is that I wasn't the same person as before the accident. For that reason David Harrison was my director once again, as he had been for the MDS and the Yukon. He knew me well enough to know when I was struggling. We spent time with my neuro-psychologist to develop strategies to cope with the times when I wasn't 'me' any more.

Bev was starting to be released from her life post-accident as a single parent looking after four kids to that of a couple with three kids. Unfortunately my transition from a parasite to a pillar of support, both practically and emotionally, was far from complete but at least there was light at the end of the tunnel for both of us.

The DVLA, after assessing my medical records and discussions with my neurologist, had decided that I was ready to have a driving assessment, and if that went well, I'd get my licence back.

The reaction and flashing light sensitivity tests went well, as did my driving for the assessment. So I had my licence back and could fully contribute to family life in a practical way, taking some of the weight that Bev had been bearing alone for over a year. I was also working more closely with my neuro-psychologist and occupational therapist on issues like empathy, affection, anger-management and the ability to plan. These things would have improved faster if I'd bought into them earlier and I deeply regret, for Bev's sake especially, that I didn't fully commit sooner.

One of my biggest problems was missing a goal that I could control one hundred per cent from start to finish. In sport, if you plan, train and race well you'll get the result you deserve. In the media world, where much of my work resides, the results are much more subjective. So I began to get an idea . . . or rather an idea got in touch with me.

In 2009, together with Rebecca Romero, the Olympic silver medallist in rowing and gold medallist in cycling (clever choice of partner, I thought), I had attempted to break the tandem cycling record from Land's End to John O'Groats. After twenty-eight hours we were ahead of record pace and well into Scotland when Becks' knee (which had been causing her pain since Bristol) was really hurting and visibly swollen. Typically of a globally renowned athlete, she wanted to carry on. After wrestling her off her bike I managed to persuade her that London 2012 was more important than the tandem record and that it wasn't worth risking long-term damage.

I hate not completing my goals, so I had unfinished business with riding the length of our country. Becks was busy preparing for London and so when a semi-pro cyclist, Jerone Walters, got in touch and asked if I was interested in giving the men's record a go, with the added incentive of raising money for Headway, I had little hesitation in registering my interest. That was an improvement on my previous form. I didn't just say 'Yes'.

The record of fifty hours fourteen minutes and twenty-five seconds was set in 1966, and countless attempts to break it over the years have all failed. The average speed isn't daunting but it's the remorseless, exhausting, painful and repetitive nature of the ride which makes covering the 842 miles within that time so difficult. But it was just the kind of challenge that really appealed to my masochistic nature.

I knew I was going to have to talk it through with Bev but the Roads Records Association insist on a vehicle with flashing lights and observers being behind the riders at all times so there was no chance of a truck doing the damage it had done in Arizona. I knew I had to be careful with extended periods of no sleep but I thought that forty-eight hours of very limited or no rest was possible if I had extra sleep in the week before the ride. I also made sure there were doctors in the support crew to assess not only my physical but mental state and whether they thought it was necessary pull me from the bike and abort the record attempt.

Jerone understood and agreed. So at 3 a.m. on 1 October 2011 we set off from the start point, the south door of the Land's End Hotel.

For the first thirty hours we were behind record pace but somehow dragged ourselves ahead of schedule. This was something that gave me huge satisfaction as I had rediscovered the self-motivation that had gone so disastrously missing in the Yukon. With only seventy miles to go and well ahead of record pace, the doctors felt that for the first time both of us were quiet, down and knackered. Although it hadn't been a barrel of laughs for the almost 800 miles, one of us had always been 'up' and been able to keep the other going and believing, but with both of us seemingly depressed and exhausted, the time had come to stop the attempt.

At the time the medics pulled the plug, we had been riding for forty hours and the longest break we'd had was for forty-five minutes. Apart from that, we'd stop for between five and ten minutes every three hours. It did mean that the ride was relentless, especially as a tandem isn't that comfy to ride for a long time, with every move you make affecting the other person. So stretching your back, freewheeling, standing up to take the weight off a sore ass couldn't be done impulsively so we'd have to communicate the impending action to the other. This results in you remaining in one position for too long. As the miles ticked by ever slower and the time ever faster, comfort rather than fatigue became the problem. Both Jerone and I wanted to get off the bike more and more often, not through muscular fatigue but discomfort from being in the same position for basically two solid days. Let's face it, just sitting on a sofa for two days straight would be horrendously uncomfortable and spending too much time lying down results in bed sores, but neither a sofa nor a bed is shaped like a bike.

We'd reached Inverness and the people following our progress on Twitter and our website were sending us messages which had changed from 'keep going' and 'tough it out' to 'Congratulations you've got the record' and 'It's in the bag!' But it wasn't. We still had 70 miles left to go, which is a tiny percentage of the total, but long enough, especially having already ridden nearly 800 miles.

I had insisted that the medics be the ones to decide whether or not I was fit enough to go on. I wasn't about to go back on my word or take any undue risks. It wasn't fair on Bev, the kids or anyone who'd given me unconditional love and support to get me back to where I was. Up until the point where the medics pulled us off the road, I'd been mentally very strong, alert and motivated even when after twenty-four hours it looked like we were chasing a lost cause, something I wouldn't have been able to do in the Yukon a few months earlier. When it looked like we were flagging, the medics – understandably – didn't want to take any chances. But I stuck to the agreement. I didn't resist their decision, I didn't put on the 'concrete shoes' I'd developed a habit of wearing since the accident and insist we just grab twenty minutes' kip by the roadside, recover, then carry on to the finish. The decision (as I'd promised Bev) was taken out of our hands.

I travelled back from Scotland with the team the next day

after a night in a hotel. Actually, it was an old train carriage converted into a hotel but as I could have slept on a bed of nails it felt like a five-star hotel, apart from waking up in the same stinking cycling kit that I'd been too tired (OK – lazy) to take off. I would like to blame the brain injury for that unhygienic decision but I fear I may always have had a tendency to think: 'I'm asleep. What does it matter?'

That night I was back at home, or specifically round the corner as Bev and I felt that I'd be really tired and would therefore lack self-control, overreact and behave unpredictably with her and the kids.

So I went and stayed with Bev's sister Cal and her husband Rick for a couple of days to rest up, which was hurtful but also sensible. It was a real reminder of how my life had changed and the constraints under which I now had to operate.

The ride had 'finished' in the early hours of Monday morning and I was back in London that night. On the Friday I had to do a presentation to both my occupational therapist and speech and language therapist about performing at an Olympic Games plus the different skills I'd learned from the adventure challenges I'd done. They committed the presentation to video so that we could go through it at my next session, to see where I struggled to recall pieces of information or failed to get key points across succinctly.

That night there was the Olympic Gold Ball, a fundraiser for the BOA to help them prepare Team GB for the 2012 Games and beyond. I caught up with Justin King (the CEO of Sainsbury's who are a sponsor of the Paralympics) during the evening. It was great to see him especially as I felt I owed him an apology and explanation for not recognising him when we last met. I'd just come out of hospital and was having a bite to eat with Bev after unborn little Trixie's three-month scan when we bumped into Justin. But I simply had not recognised him. I attempted to explain why my facial recognition wasn't too good these days without giving the impression that I wasn't different or limited in terms of the man I used to be. We had a short chat and he invited Bev and me to stay for a weekend at his place in Leicestershire. An incredibly kind offer, all things considered.

The next evening I was sitting at the table in our kitchen with Bev and Croyde. The little man was preparing to be avidly glued to and mimicking the contestants on *X Factor*. I'd be lying if I said I was exhibiting the same level of enthusiasm. Kiki and Trixie were spared those ninety minutes of Saturday night torture by being in bed – lucky things. I was probably thinking about how much Reggae Reggae Sauce I could sneak onto my next meal without offending the chef – Bev. As you can see, Saturday nights round our place are rock 'n' roll.

. . . then it goes blank.

[Bev]

Strangely, it had been a good day. And there hadn't been many. This is the very thought that crosses my mind at the exact moment that James, perched on the edge of the kitchen table with a notepad in his hand, starts to make a weird sound.

I'm cutting up avocados, mixing lemon and vats of chilli flakes so that James might taste something. The girls are asleep upstairs and Croyde is watching the opening credits of *X Factor* in the living-room next door, already chomping his way through a bag of Doritos.

It's October 2011 – fourteen months after the accident – and I'm determined that we're going to have a *normal* Saturday evening. Even though James hates those shows, we will sit down as a family. I will drink a glass of wine. James will drink gallons of tea and we will pick our favourite X Factor contestants while I annoy Croyde by joining in with the songs that I know.

But then James starts making that noise. At first I think he's thinking aloud. 'Err . . .' I expect him to turn to me and say. 'Have you seen my desert boots?' or some other obscure piece of kit that he'll need for his upcoming trip to America in seventy-two hours' time. But instead, his head tips backwards, his hands turn in on themselves, the notepad falls to the floor as his whole body stiffens, contracting in a way that is unmistakably some sort of seizure.

And still the noise continues. 'Errahhhhhh . . .' The knife I had been holding clatters to the floor and I manage to reach James before he slides off the edge of the table. I'm saying his name, over and over, as though that might snap him out of it. I have never seen anyone have an epileptic fit before and it is scary; I feel utterly helpless.

I wrap my arms around him and try to hook a leg beneath his hip which is banging against the edge of the table. He is too heavy for me to lift onto the floor so I concentrate on minimising any further damage that he might do to himself. I need a telephone. But I'm torn: if I yell for Croyde, he will have to witness his daddy having a fit. He's been through so much already that my heart sinks at another shitty episode for him to endure. But he is resilient and I'm confident that we'll just have to manage that like every other bizarre and difficult situation. 'Croyde! Croyde! I need you. Quickly!'

He appears at the wide doorway, all clean and angelic in his pyjamas, a little boy who just wanted to eat all the Doritos before Mummy and Daddy made it to the sofa. I raise my eyebrows and try to muster an 'everything-is-just-fine' smile. 'Sweetheart, grab Mummy's phone.' James's eyes are closed, he's shaking violently in my arms and a dribble of blood has appeared at the corner of his mouth. 'It's OK, baby, it's OK, Daddy's just a bit . . . tired.'

Unsurprisingly, Croyde doesn't buy my explanation and runs back to the sofa. I'll never forget the fear in his voice. 'No! No! Daddy's going to die!'

'Sweetheart, really, it's OK. Be a good boy. Go and get Mummy's phone. *Now.*'

Somehow, he finds my mobile and passes it to me at arm's length. He is scared to come close. 'Good boy, good boy . . . now . . .' I need to give him another job, just to get him out of the room and make him feel that he's helping. If James died right there and then on the kitchen floor as *X Factor* started in the lounge, Croyde had to feel that he was in no way at fault. Whatever happened, I would be thanking him later that night for helping Mummy and being such a grown-up boy. These – I've realised – are the kind of thoughts that pass through a mother's mind in the very moments when life is intent on chewing you up and spitting you out.

Croyde disappears upstairs to get the landline phone as James's shaking starts to subside. I whisper that it's OK; that everything will be OK. His skin is grey. And I really don't know if everything *is* going to be OK. Saliva and blood seep from the corners of his mouth. I reach for a pillow from a nearby chair as I lie him down and a woman answers the 999 call.

The rigmarole of addresses, names and phone numbers seems to take a ridiculous amount of time in these circumstances. 'My husband has had a fit. He had a head injury last year. This is his first seizure.' Croyde appears with the black handset and with the mobile crooked under my chin I manage to ring my sister while the woman on the end of the 999 call seems to turn into one of those infuriating voices that read out 'terms and conditions'.

'Cal!' I'm indescribably relieved that she picks up. 'James has had a fit. Help me.'

That's all I need to say. My sister continues to be my ally, my friend, my confidant; my surrogate husband in times of loneliness; an extra parent with the kids. Yet again, a level of stress was removed by simply knowing she would be on her way.

The woman in the 999 centre has me counting James's breaths. They are slow and heavy and with each exhalation, a little shower of pink bubbles sprays from his mouth. Laid down with the lower half of his body beneath the kitchen table, his head on a flowery cushion, he is actually snoring. I kiss his clammy forehead, then sit back on my knees and look at him. I shake my head at the irony: this is exactly the type of nap I've been nagging him to take.

Croyde has disappeared and I'm relieved that he isn't there to see his daddy taking what looks like the deepest sleep of his life under the kitchen table while surrounded by bits of broccoli from the girls' tea.

A minute later Cal bursts barefoot through the front door. She has had her own key for a while now. Her eyes are ringed with black mascara. You might think that she had been crying or panicking. But we're past the crying stage. And Cal never panics. She'd actually been in the gym changing room after a swim. She hadn't even stopped to put her shoes on. I'm pacing. The ambulance is taking a ridiculously long time and I don't know if James is going to have another fit. Cal just looks at me and says, 'OK?' but goes straight to James and I love her for that. There will be time to make me feel better. He is our priority.

Cal's husband Rick arrives close behind. He's a policeman, calm and kind, and it's impossible to overstate how important he has been in keeping Croyde happy since the accident. He checks James and goes straight to Croyde who is cowering, curled up on the sofa. 'All right buddy?' Rick throws a Dorito into his mouth. 'Who's your favourite judge – Gary Barlow?' I adore him for keeping everything as normal and non-dramatic as possible.

A few minutes later my parents, James's parents and James's brother-in-law burst through the door. My family is always a bit like that – there are always at least two of us knocking around together at any time. But I honestly don't know how we could have coped with everything post-accident without them.

The ambulance arrives almost twenty minutes after the call. James wakes up, blinking, somewhat surprised. The last thing he knew he was writing a packing list for his trip in three days' time and now he's on the kitchen floor as two paramedics and seven family members stare down at him. Rick has thoughtfully taken Croyde, the crisps and the homemade guacamole upstairs to watch TV on our bed.

The presence of the paramedics makes the atmosphere less and yet more stressful. As the weight of responsibility falls from my shoulders, the reality of having two people in fluorescent jackets knelt over James hits home. We are going to *another* hospital.

I run upstairs to throw on some warmer clothes, splash water on my face, muttering 'Fuck, fuck, fuck.' This will change *everything*. It had felt as though we were just emerging from the hideous darkness of the past 446 days. James finally had a proper contract with the Discovery Channel: it was the culmination of fifteen months of relentless work and determination to get him close to being able to do the things he formerly took in his stride.

He could no longer attempt the sort of endurance events at which he was one of the best in the world, but in the Discovery

Channel's *World's Toughest Expeditions* he would be presenting four trips tracing the paths of some inspirational historical pioneers. They would be physically tough, but that would be nothing compared to the psychological and cognitive challenges James was experiencing on a daily basis and of which the audience would know nothing. There was no way he'd be going now – was there?

I kiss Croyde goodbye, make him promise to tell me everything about *X Factor* when I get back and go downstairs, running over the list of people I have to call: James's neurologist; his psychologist; David Harrison – who had worked so hard to get him on that plane on Tuesday; his agent who would have to call the Discovery Channel and break the bad news. And even though I knew how much I'd been nagging James to slow down, to take more naps and prioritise rest, I felt desperately, deeply sorry for him. He wasn't being reckless. He was just trying to live the life he had *before*.

They wheel him into the ambulance with a rug over his knee. It's a cold October night and I drape a sweatshirt over his shoulders. Cal and Jennie will follow in their car.

James is still dazed and confused. It's horrible – reminiscent of his appearance in the American hospital when although he was physically present, so little of his personality remained. But he also looks embarrassed, as though he's caused a fuss. I take his hand. 'Jesus, James, if you really didn't want to watch the *X Factor* you only had to say.'

[James]

When I woke up I knew I was somewhere medical, but I didn't realise it was an ambulance parked outside my house. I had no memory of what happened nor of anything prior to the blankness so I couldn't place it in context. If anything, I was more confused than coming round in America. Or rather than my first post-accident memory in America, which I guess amounts to the same thing. I can't remember coming round in the States but something in my subconscious or my long-term pre-accident memory knew that I wasn't in the UK so strangely I didn't feel as freaked out as I was in an ambulance parked outside my house.

It wasn't just being disorientated and confused: it was that there were loads of people, a lot of worried faces looking at me. I couldn't work out what they were doing here, wherever 'here' might be. I don't remember any of them being around before. That was the problem. I couldn't remember where or what I was doing before I recognised Bev and Croyde, Mum and Dad, Bev's mum and dad, Bev's sister Cal, my sister, Louise, and none of it made any sense to me. What had happened? Why had it happened to me again?

I remember being instantly embarrassed by all the fuss I was causing and when they told me I was in an ambulance, I wanted everyone to go home; I wanted to go home, back inside the house I was outside of and not to another hospital.

Physically, I felt a little slow. Nothing moved at the speed I wanted it to and I didn't feel like talking. Which was probably a relief for Bev as one of the by-products of the accident is that her strong, silent husband who had a grunt for every occasion had suddenly become this verbose talkaholic who would never use one word where a hundred could do. Think of Spud from *Trainspotting* when he's forced to attend job interviews and takes some speed to 'calm' his nerves beforehand, calming everything apart from his tongue. If you've got that attractive image in your head then that's what Bev had pretty much lived with for eighteen months. It's just now the connection between my brain and tongue seemed even further apart than normal.

I had no concept of the time. Charing Cross Hospital is only a couple of miles away but the journey in the ambulance seemed to take ages, or perhaps I was just willing it to take ages. I'd like to suggest that my reluctance to be in the ambulance to get to hospital was because I didn't want to deprive somebody in genuine medical distress. Or perhaps it was because I was frightened that I was going to be forced to endure another long – and in my mind unnecessary – stay.

Once in A&E, I had the same feeling, that I was cluttering the place up and wasting everyone's time. Somehow I avoided being part of the blood-soaked boozer Saturday night brigade that night because I was whisked straight off for a couple of scans, a blood pressure test (which I still hated after the US experience), and an ECG. All seemed OK. Mum gave me a lift home a few hours later and it upset me to see how upset in turn she was. She'd worked in the NHS all her life, and I suppose I assumed she'd be fairly immune to the workings of hospitals, but this was her boy again. No parent should have to see their child in an ambulance on the way to A&E or will ever be able to cope with that experience.

But it was Croyde I felt terrible for. He had been a witness of the seizure – as I now knew it had been – and the effect on him was visible. I'd been spared this in the States. By the time I had come through my amnesia in Phoenix, the rest of the family had become more accustomed to my state. The initial reactions of fear, grief and sadness had dissolved into daily routines, boredom and wishing it wasn't so bloody hot. By the time I came round, my new situation was normalised in his mind.

This time I could see first-hand the effect on Croyde. It must have been traumatic and deeply distressing for him to see me having the seizure, and he was wary. His daddy wasn't better after all. In the States, he knew I wasn't the same and didn't react to things in the same way but at least he figured I was healthy. Now this was an affirmation that aside from being more shouty and angry I wasn't healthy, and I hated myself for putting him through that.

I'd also added a couple of extra fears for Bev. Now I noticed, if I dropped something in the kitchen, her head would whip round to check on me. I'd be thinking: 'Bollocks, I've dropped a glass!' and she would be thinking: 'James has collapsed and is having another seizure!'

Soon afterwards I was told that I wouldn't be able to drive again until I'd been seizure-free for a year, so once again Bev was the sole driver – not for three kids but for four if you included the six foot four 'special' one, as I liked to call myself. Let's face it: no one else was going to. It was yet another example of how the accident had eroded not just my freedom but, more importantly, my family's. Bev's career was stalled yet again because of me.

As for me, a letter that genuinely worried me was for an appointment for the 'Fit Clinic'. It's something they must automatically send out to people who have had seizures. It was bad enough to have a seizure without the accompanying medical assumption that I had lost my fitness too. When I attended the Fit Clinic, there was a further blow to absorb. It was the first time I heard the words 'for the rest of your life' when I asked about how long I'd be taking the medication for.

In fact, my physical fitness wasn't an issue. Aside from biting my tongue, I hadn't sustained any other injuries and hadn't been in hospital for more than a few hours. The after-effects were much more psychological. My faith in my body's ability to cope with whatever stress it faced had taken another significant hit. I'd already noticed the difference in the Yukon, but now it was failing me in leafy Chiswick.

I was devastated that my family had been put through something like that again. There was no escaping the fact that the voluntary sleep deprivation on the tandem ride with Jerone could have been a trigger to the seizure, but neither the neurologists or the DVLA are convinced it was. It was a double devastation: my parents, Bev and the kids had been forced to see me in an ambulance and hospital once again.

In terms of family dynamics, so much had changed for the worse. Since Phoenix, I had steadily been earning back Bev's trust in my decision-making, but I felt that was all gone now. I knew it had affected Croyde and it hurt me that he knew that his daddy wasn't the same person any more. It hurt me looking in the mirror knowing I wasn't the same person any more. My parents and parents-in-law didn't have the same trust in me either and must have been wondering whether I could be trusted with their daughter's and grandchildren's emotions.

When Bev and I went to stay with Justin King, he casually said over dinner that the reason he'd asked us to come and stay for the weekend was because I'd looked so exhausted, drained and run down at the Olympic Gold Ball. Aside from showing what a nice guy he is, I was disappointed that it wasn't my witty conversation and anecdotes that he wanted to revel in over dinner. I was disgusted with myself, that someone I didn't know well could instantly see I was knackered and not myself. Worse still, I was not listening to the person who knows me best when she says that I look really tired. It was only when I saw the videos that the occupational therapy team had made twenty-four hours before the seizure that I saw in me what others had been seeing. I looked grey, knackered, and dead behind the eyes. As the saying goes, the lights were on but no one was home.

At least I had been shown – albeit slightly dramatically – that the only route I could take to move forwards was to get enough sleep. This had been a crucial element in the planning of further programmes for the Discovery Channel. Obviously the type of adventure/endurance films which took a huge toll on the body and necessitated an element of sleep deprivation were no longer a possibility.

I had the seizure just a few days before I was due to fly to the States to start filming the new series, *The World's Toughest Expeditions*, where I would be travelling to Africa, the Amazon, Death Valley and New Zealand, following in the footsteps of adventuring pioneers or brave survivors.

The shoot was inevitably delayed while I was monitored and my levels of anti-seizure medication were set. A strategy was developed to ensure I had enough rest. This cost the production company money and more work for the guys on the crew. Not for the first time I felt terrible and aware of how just many people I kept letting down both at work and at home.

The Yukon had highlighted my lack of self-belief and motivation following the brain injury but it had also boosted confidence in other areas: a confidence that was starting to dwindle. I was anxious about work and my ability to continue providing for my family. Dave had gone through a considerable amount of time and trouble and taken a personal career risk to persuade Discovery that I would be OK and it turned out I wasn't as OK as we thought. Knowing the effort and lengths he had gone to, not to mention the faith and support he'd shown in me personally, I felt terrible. Yet again.

But I did fly to America, in a business class seat so I could get some decent rest (the only upside of having a brain injury), and we did shoot the series. I am proud of it, as were the crew and Discovery. But I struggled in areas where I wouldn't have before. I've mentioned the faith which I had in Dave and yet I constantly felt like a scene was designed to make me look a fool. This was something that wouldn't have previously entered my head. This must have made working with me incredibly difficult, especially as my behaviour was unpredict-able, as were the things that would wind me up.

But I had some amazing moments. Seeing elephants and hippopotamuses up close in Africa, standing on the edge of Victoria Falls, canoeing through crocodiles, having iodine poured on to my blistered hands from wood-chopping for the leader of an Amazon tribe (which was excruciatingly painful). There were plenty of unforgettable experiences – good and bad. Like Livingstone, there were times I was blissfully unaware of the danger I was in and I think that prior to the accident I would have thought about the consequences of my actions in a different way. Fortunately a bull elephant isn't the sharpest tool in the box so it all worked out OK.

For all the limitations, I did try to experience life as the locals knew it. Even chucking off my clothes in the Amazon and tolerating (with winces and much manly screaming) the scraping of my skin with a dogfish tooth comb (particularly pleasant over insect bites and nipples) by a rather heavy-handed village chief. It was a traditional ceremony to give the man who was heading on the journey 'strength and courage'. I hoped the elder of the neighbouring tribe appreciated the effort I'd gone to! It's not yet a 'bon voyage' tradition we have adopted over here and I don't think Croyde will appreciate it before he heads off to school in the morning. Although I still have the offending comb just in case!

Frustratingly for the production company, the channel and me, our show was up against one of the greatest television hits of 2012 in the schedule, the drama *Homeland* on Channel 4.

So this is where we are and I'm learning all the time how I get on with and subtly adapt to the guy who is 'nearly James Cracknell'. People treat me differently; there is no doubt about that. There is an assumption that I'm capable of fewer things in life because I have a brain injury. I did a talk six months after the accident about the London 2012 Olympics. At the end someone came over to thank me. They said: 'Thank you, that focused on and hit every area we wanted to highlight. It was exactly what we were looking for and was really good . . . especially for someone with a brain injury.'

I want to be judged as a person, not someone with a disability. I don't want to be seen as someone with an asterisk. 'Really good . . . for someone with a brain injury.'

With my family, life is different. There is no getting away from it. Bev is brutally honest with me. It's really annoying but it helps. She doesn't hold back. She tells me how I'm behaving with the kids and that I get angry at things that didn't used to bother me. That I'm different with the children, that my tolerance levels have changed. That I keep talking for ages and never listen. (Previously I may have done the latter but never the former.) That I'm liable to get stubborn and put on my infuriating concrete shoes. That's difficult to hear but nothing compared to hearing the words 'You're not the man I married.' I feel she's constantly assessing me, which I find very hard. But the last thing I need or want is for people to gloss over things or not say it as it is.

At times she's said she feels really harsh and unsympathetic, but there's no way I'd have got back to where I am without her. I know there's love and truly unconditional and often undeserved support there and I am well aware how hard it has been for her. She was either pregnant or breast-feeding for eighteen months after the accident. I'm not going down the 'hormones' route but her body was changing on a monthly basis, never mind having to cope with a member of the family who had suddenly become a different person. I think she's been phenomenal.

But if you asked me whether we had the same relationship we used to then, no, we don't. Will we? I hope so but I genuinely don't know. The last thing a neuropsychologist said to Bev and me before I left hospital was that the majority of people with brain injuries get divorced. Not a positive message or the best time to deliver it, but when is a good time to deliver a statement like that?

On top of which we have all sorts of stresses and strains from becoming a family with three kids rather than two, which is an enormous change.

I think Bev will always look at me in a slightly different way. I don't know how she can't. She's seen me have a seizure, she's been summoned to a hospital in America to say goodbye because they didn't think I'd live. Then she was told, OK he will live but he won't know who you are at first and he won't be the same man you married. I don't know how you would or could look at someone the same way after all she's been through.

We'd been married eight years when the accident happened, so we hadn't had exactly the same relationship as we'd had after a week, a month, a year. But we had made that pact (ironically) just before I flew to the States that we would spend more time with each other, make an effort to see our friends rather than get bogged down with work – especially my work. We decided we wanted to try for a third baby.

And along came Trixie. Bev gets really knackered with the kids waking up in the night and due to the anti-seizure medication I sleep incredibly deeply so don't hear them and thus can't help out. Plus there are my nocturnal ramblings to the loo which have also increased due to medication. So it's best sometimes if she has a break by one of us sleeping in another room.

We split shifts when it comes to the children. All those early morning starts on the river mean that I don't mind getting up early with the kids. She worries less about me doing things in the morning than in the evening when I start yawning by 6 p.m. Luckily, not being a morning person herself, her fatigue overrides any anxiety pre-7 a.m. so I get to spend some amazing time with the kids. I love the mornings with them.

If I am honest, it can be hard to feel like we're a married unit any more. We're more of a team but in a weird way like a sporting unit rather than a loving one. We can have some really honest conversations and we both know that we'll be there for one another regardless of how angry or frustrated we are with each other. Ironically probably in a way that Matt and I never did when we were in the pair, which felt more like a business relationship. I appreciate that having a marriage that feels like a good sporting partnership is not ideal but at least it's a firm base to build from and hopefully we'll get back to where we were. On a positive note, we work well together at overcoming problems, but in terms of a relationship, it's not the best thing.

The brain injury has affected my emotional responses and I'm high on the depression scale. The neurologist offered me anti-depressants, but Bev recoiled at the suggestion and I committed to a course of cognitive behavioural therapy (CBT) to rebuild my confidence and combat any issues I haven't addressed myself. I feel the same way about anti-depressants as I did about painkillers when I was rowing. I'd rather feel what's wrong than mask it, carry on pushing through and make it worse. How can you be addressing a problem if you disguise it? Luckily not taking them was something we agreed on. Bev said, 'No, I don't like the idea of you being medicated. Let's get you some proper counselling support and go from there.'

The other practicality remains work.

I was really pleased to be asked to work with BBC Radio 5 and was working covering the last World Cup rowing event of the season in Munich before the 2012 Games. Also there was Crossy, Mark Cross, who was also there at the start of the Redgrave era, winning a gold medal at the 1984 Olympics with Steve in the coxed four. We watched the men's four lose in the semis to Australia and had a laugh on air when one of the presenters, Ian Payne, and I discussed the loneliness of scullers.

Who did they celebrate with, he wanted to know, when they won. I said they're a strange bunch. 'It's like going to the cinema on your own. You've got no one to talk to about the film afterwards. So they talk to each other, even though they're rivals on the lake.' He said he went to the cinema on his own sometimes and just collared strangers to discuss the film with. 'What would you think if I asked you about a film if we were at the urinal?' he asked. 'I'd think you were trying to pick me up,' I said. Well, I would. It may not be the sort of discussion Radio 5 has every day, but they didn't seem to mind.

A few of us watched a Euro 2012 football match afterwards over a bite of dinner – in my case a bite of texture with sauce on it. And that is the last I remember.

The next thing I knew, I was lying in a room and I could tell it was a hospital or at least a strange bed with medical stuff around me. Ann Redgrave was there and I can't remember who else. They told me I'd had a seizure and asked me what day it was. I had no idea. They told me I was in Germany and that seemed to make sense, although I wasn't immediately sure why. The seizure had apparently gone on for a long time. Crossy reckoned five minutes, but it is easy to lose track of time. I felt guilty that I'd put the guys through it, knowing how horrible it is to watch. At the same time, I was glad that Bev and Croyde hadn't been the witnesses this time. Poor Crossy had to witness it twice though as I'd had a second one at the hospital.

Gary Herbert came later and told me how the rowing had gone in the finals (the coxless four had lost to the Australians again) and the doctors told me I could go home the next day. I still had no memory of the seizure itself but somehow I must have sensed what was coming because apparently I said: 'Oh shit!' as I fell on the floor.

Fortunately, the arrival of the Olympic Games in our country gave me the opportunity to work for a broadcasting outlet – the BBC – as well as writing for the *Telegraph*, which

I've done since 1998. I was proud that Britain was trusted as a host nation for the Games, which may or may not have been abetted by my various appearances in Lycra. I was better clothed – well, there was more of it and it was ironed – when I went on BBC2's *Newsnight* programme to discuss with a cardiologist and a marketing guru whether Coke and McDonald's should be allowed to sponsor the Olympics.

I enjoyed it and stuck pretty solidly to my position that obesity and eating habits are something society has to address; people must be educated about the right sort of foods to eat. Citing sponsors of the Olympics as the cause of the nation's obesity levels purely because they sponsor the Olympics is missing the point. Without them it would be a minority sports event with no media coverage, so wouldn't inspire anyone to pick up a pair of spikes, oar, bike, swimming hat, or javelin. I pointed out: 'Show me a health food shop that can pay $500million to the Olympics.' End of argument.

Being at the Olympics was strange for me, as my perspective has changed so much since my last experience of the world stage when only winning mattered. Now my perspective is that I can't win, I can't *defeat* brain injury, but I can succeed, despite it.

[Bev]

After filming the Discovery series James returns to the normality of home life, but losing his licence due to the seizure hits him hard. We can cope with the long journeys: I have to drive while he manages the kids' snacks, DVD players and fights (I think I have it easiest). But it's the short trips that bother me more, taking Croyde to swimming club or Kiki to nursery in the rain. It's popping out to buy a pint of milk – those are the times we look at each other ruefully before I stop what I'm doing to grab the car keys.

But, of course, James is a born problem-solver. Put an obstacle in front of him and he'll work out a way around it. He shows me a picture of a tricycle with a massive box on the front. 'I could get the kids in there!' he beams.

'Over my dead body.'

He buys it anyway, arguing that he can at least contribute to family life by doing a supermarket shop. It's such a sweet gesture that I realise just how much he wants to help. The bike arrives and of course the children literally squeal with delight. James grins from ear to ear as he idles up and down the pavement; four arms waving excitedly above two little helmeted heads. The trike comes into its own on Christmas Day 2011 when he ferries me, my mum, several presents and all three kids round the corner to my sister's. Not driving, I thus spend the day in a happy bucks-fizz-fuelled bubble.

Ever practical, he also insists on riding it to his agent's Christmas party. Romantically, he offers me a blanket – 'Climb aboard, m'lady' – and so, in short dress and high heels, I attempt a graceful entrance and exit (I fail). Coming home, I'm doing the same as TV presenter Phillip Schofield and his lovely wife are climbing into their luxury chauffeur-driven car. Sympathetically, they offer to help. 'Do you want a lift back to Henley?' I yell thanks but as we no longer live in Henley, we only have a short journey home. But it makes me laugh: it says something about James's reputation that they assumed we were heading forty miles down the M4 in a tricycle at midnight.

Mealtimes are still stressful. I watch his face fall with the first bite – as though he hoped that maybe, just maybe, his sense of taste had returned. The doctors say it never will. I hold my nose when

I'm cooking to see if I can elicit any taste from even rich foods and it is so depressing – try it, and imagine that for the rest of your life.

Texture has taken on a greater importance so I watch bemused as he piles up mountains of raw vegetables – mushrooms, carrots, peppers and cucumbers – and cover them with layers of Reggae Reggae Sauce, sweet chilli or ketchup. It makes me feel so helpless – watching him try to elicit some sort of taste from his food. New, uninhibited James rides up to the High Road on his tricycle to visit his new best friend, the vegetable stall man, returning with a bargain lot of bananas, several bags of mushrooms, mountains of carrots and a whole watermelon, explaining in detail how the seller can charge more for a cut-up slice than a whole one. They clearly have a good chat. My main complaint is that the combination of a high-fibre diet and a man with no sense of smell can be deadly for us innocent bystanders.

We don't know what the long-term effect will be upon Croyde. So far, he continues to be a resilient, emotionally intelligent, kind kid who drives us mad when he winds his sisters up; but on the football pitch he's always the first to stop if a player falls over to see if they're OK. He went to another school for two years before moving to the one he attends now. The two met for a football match recently and on the way to school I asked who he wanted to win. 'Kew College, of course,' he said. Kew was his former school.

'Really? Why?'

It was so obvious to him. 'Because they're my friends.' I suspect the competitive gene may have skipped a generation. Hurrah for that.

Recently, James returned from a weekend away, rested and unusually calm. I had noticed, but didn't know that Croyde had also. 'Daddy seems better,' he remarked at bedtime.

'I think so too. What do you see?'

'Well . . . when he came in I was hanging off the bunk bed and he just said, "Get down Croyde", not "*GET DOWN CROYDE*".'

'You're so clever for noticing that, mate. It's good news isn't it?'

He nodded, still hanging off the bunk bed.

But that's not to say that that issue is resolved. Croyde is still James's Achilles heel: the most likely entity to trigger brain injury behaviours. There is a chasm between them that I fear will never be bridged. When other male figures come into the house, Croyde leaps up and asks them to play football with him. He doesn't do that with James. Somehow, James rarely looks able to throw himself into such 'fun' activities. He can appear to literally carry the weight of the accident and everything it means on his shoulders.

A huge motivator for me to write this book was the idea that Croyde, Kiki and Trixie might one day read it to understand their daddy better (and also their harassed grey and wrinkled mother with a gin habit). I hope they will forgive us for the mistakes we must have both made over the last two years. But if they ever dare use the history told in this book as an excuse for their own bad behaviour I will hit them over the head with it – *the hardback version.*

Before the accident, James would live magnificently on four to five hours' sleep a night (like a sporty, male Margaret Thatcher). He'd rise at six, go to the gym before the kids were up, cycle into town, have one or two meetings, make a public appearance or deliver a speech, come home in time for the kids' bath and bed before sitting down to write a piece for the *Telegraph* or do his emails, planning his next adventure. And, without wanting to make any male readers feel inferior, he still had the energy to create three kids! Those days are gone.

In my opinion, he still packs too much into his days but I've accepted that he will never be the kind of guy who can kick off his shoes and watch a movie on a rainy afternoon. He could easily have languished on the sofa and felt sorry for himself. But he didn't. He's still driven to provide; to define himself by his exploits and to show everyone that he is (in the language of sport psychology) a 'highly functioning' individual.

When we met in 2000, *Heat* ran a photo of us under the regular feature, 'We give it two weeks.' Sometimes, I think we only stayed together to prove those buggers wrong. Now, when we hear the statistic about the high number of divorces amongst the brain-injured, I suspect we both have a similar reaction: we'll do everything not to become part of that number. We're still toughing it out.

Some days I think, 'Hey! Who wants to be married to the same man for more than ten years anyway?' And on the bad days, when James is overtired, overworked, unable to get the gist of something or hooked onto an idea; insecure; forgetful but blaming others; running late and getting angry at himself; snappy, irritable, miserable and worried about his future, life can feel very short indeed.

He always possessed a benign selfishness (sports people often do) but now he can be bizarrely narcissistic, too often failing to notice the needs of others.

I wish that I could flick a switch to make him 'happy' – that's all I ever wanted for James anyway. I vividly remember the 'safe, stable and secure' man who took that definition as an insult. But to me, those words encapsulated the strength that made him my rock. I've always been pretty independent and perhaps I didn't need an awful lot from the bloke I would marry. But James's gentleness, warmth, loyalty, kindness and humour fitted the bill just perfectly. He must hate the ways in which he has had to depend on me over the last two years – I don't blame him. The biggest change for couples who endure a brain injury is seeing that dynamic shift. I dearly hope that in time it will swing back towards the centre.

In the bleakest moments, of course I ask myself if I will always be able to live with the long-term fall-out of such a serious head injury. But James has no choice – he has to live with it – and for as long as I possibly can, I will help to carry that burden. On our wedding day, my dad said, 'James will never have to fight his battles alone again.' I think it was a compliment! Nothing brings out my fiercely protective instinct more strongly than the times that I feel James is being unfairly treated or misunderstood.

In 2011, I was asked to present the awards at the Headway Annual Awards Luncheon (James was away – I was the booby prize) and once again, I met remarkable people with devastating stories. I was approached by a pretty woman of about my age who said my story reminded her so much of her own experience that she had to say hello.. Sadly, three years after her husband's accident, they divorced. 'What was the final straw?' I asked.

'His lack of confidence. It killed me. I couldn't live with it.'

I knew what she meant.

Like most elite sportspeople, James has always defined himself by what he does, rather than who he is. Achieving incredible physical goals was the oxygen that kept him afloat – it really didn't matter if nobody was watching. Now, his epilepsy seriously limits the extent of his future 'adventures'. He can no longer endure sleep deprivation (due to the increased risk of seizures), be alone at, or in, the sea; high altitudes could increase his risk of brain haemorrhage; he can't drive. Sometimes, when TV programme proposals land on his desk, the type of gruelling desert-crossing, ocean-spanning, mountain-crossing feats that he would love to do, I see his heart sink a little. He despises the notion of endurance 'lite'. It's hardly surprising: he was just beginning to prove himself to be one of the world's greatest ever endurance champions.

But even on the days in which he seems cast adrift there is a new, eager-to-please sweetness that still surprises me. He asks almost hourly if I need anything. I only have to mention a novel I'd like to read or a movie I'd like to see and it will arrive in the post. He was never the most affectionate man in the world and now whole weeks go by without him offering a hug or a goodbye kiss. But I persist. I know that he doesn't have the necessary confidence to put his arms around me. If you're not careful, brain injury is contagious – James's emotional responses may have been 'blunted' but I won't allow mine to be also. If I fancy a hug while waiting for the pasta to cook, I sidle up and steal one. Sometimes, I think James doesn't even notice. But the kids do. Croyde will groan, 'Mummy, stop kissing Daddy!' but he shakes his head at me, smiling from ear to ear.

Please forgive James the worst moments of this book. He remembers nothing of grabbing me by the neck or the times he closed Croyde's bedroom door so that he could shout at him without me hearing. And – despite his witty one-liner – he doesn't remember my telling him that we were expecting a third baby. The brain is a fascinating and mysterious beast.

A lot of brain injury books talk about the 'grieving' process that families undertake – although their loved one may still be living and breathing. Like a bereavement, it seems to me that you move through stages: the busy-ness of the aftermath; the feelings of anger at the injury; sadness and depression at your loss, and finally – hopefully – moving to a place of acceptance. We aren't quite there yet. I can still feel the dust around me, waiting to settle.

It's ironic that, for me, the London Olympics were a greater test of James's strengths and weaknesses than those he had actually rowed in. I knew his schedule would be relentless so for days beforehand his agents had to suffer my constant assessment of his diary. Following his fits in Germany, we were also trying out a new level of anti-seizure medication. I knew that with so many commitments he could easily run himself ragged, culminating in a general deterioration of his ability to communicate well on live radio or a dramatic on-air seizure.

Despite being a lucrative way for ex-athletes to earn money over the Olympics, we took the decision to turn down any 'extra' corporate appearances. Unlike Beijing, he couldn't commit to late-night news broadcasts as well as early starts. For the first time in two years he would be writing articles 'to deadline'. I had images of it all going horribly wrong.

I was insistent that he stay away for the duration of the Games so that he could sleep uninterrupted by three kids. But I drove him to his hotel at Eton Dorney for the first week a complete nervous wreck. Thankfully, his management team was outstanding, making sure, as arranged, that his daily schedule arrived beneath his bedroom door. It's a shame that rowing championships aren't a daily occurrence because his (newly verbose) commentary was enthusiastic, entertaining, enlightening (and only occasionally border-line 'inappropriate'). Able to focus entirely on one task at a time, he gave it his all and quite rightly came away with a new sense of confidence.

Now he is back to deciding what to do next. The first thing planned is a long-overdue two-week holiday. I'm very much looking forward to it but with a little trepidation: it will be the first time away for the five of us since the accident. Let's be honest, holidays are always stressful for families with small kids. But travel can increase the likelihood of seizures and people with a brain injury normally find new settings difficult to get used to, which can lead to tricky mood swings. We chose a resort with a gym so that James can have time alone and burn off any frustrations. I'm not expecting perfection: just a little space and time for us all to regroup as a family.

The word 'bravery' is often used to describe James crossing ice fields or rowing oceans. That isn't brave. Brave is allowing his story to be told so fully and so openly so that he may help other people in his situation. Brave is refusing to be defeated by the brain injury. That's the man I love – it's an honour to share such a life.

[James]

What would make me happy? Bev has always said I never celebrated my wins or achievements. Instead, I'd always moved on. Now I have different priorities and I worry much more about fulfilling my responsibilities, especially to those closest to me, Bev and the kids. I'm genuinely anxious about whether I can do that. So what would make me happy would be to have the ability to forget for a while. Make those two words come true: 'no worries'. I haven't had that for a long time. Being able to go out and have a skinful of beers with Bev or my mates isn't possible any more. I can't drink in the way I used to as alcohol increases the risk of seizures. One unit of drink would have three times the effect on me now, I'm told. At least I'm a cheap date.

I find it hard to accept there are always limits to what I do now: having a drink, staying up late to watch a film, working into the small hours. Being able to be carefree, not being anxious about work, would, I think, make me happy. But Bev says if I won the lottery, I'd still want to work.

There's not a day goes by when I don't wish the accident hadn't happened. I might say that it has made me try to think about other people more. The man I was at the South Pole did not always consider the thoughts and feelings of others. It was a real weakness at that time, I can see that. I created an atmosphere where the others with me didn't have confidence to be themselves. And yet I was convinced I was enabling them to dig deep and get the best out of themselves. But sadly not everyone thinks like I used to. Now I consciously try to be more supportive and less quick to judge.

I've also discovered the meaning of something which we didn't say at our wedding but which was implied by tradition anyway. The bit about 'in sickness and in health'. Bev's endured that way more than me.

Brain injury is something you don't see. It's invisible to the eye. To most people I'm sure I look and sound pretty much the same. I suppose I'm lucky the changes are subtle. But if to Bev and the kids my personality has changed just by one per cent it might be just the one per cent that really mattered to them. I don't know. We haven't talked about it.

Sometimes I feel isolated by it all and then out of the blue I'll get an email from someone who understands because they have been through it themselves. Not long ago a guy I'd never met took the trouble to write after seeing me on a television show.

'Hi, I'd just like to say how seeing you on TV this morning was like sitting in front of a mirror . . . Seeing that interview has moved me to send you this message so that I could say that you are not alone with the frustrations and barriers you have faced and still do every day and you were right when you said to aim *high with your targets as that's exactly what I did starting three years and three months ago! I have achieved far more than the specialists expected and I just wanted you to know that anyone with this hindrance who was watching you will have been inspired and grateful for you sharing your experience! Thank you very much as, like you, I felt as if nobody would ever feel as I do or understand it!*

PS This was written on Sunday but not unusually I forgot to send it . . . Keep smiling and stay positive.'

It seems pretty good advice for the guy who used to be James Cracknell.

Epilogue

[James]

So eight years after my second gold medal in Athens, I was again at an Olympic lakeside, just not weighed down by oars and expectation this time. I'd swapped my Lycra for an old T-shirt as I was in the privileged position of co-commentating the races at Eton Dorney, the Olympic rowing venue, for BBC Radio 5 Live. But the adrenalin was still there. As were quite a few of my old rowing mates: Steve Redgrave and Matt Pinsent were working for BBC TV; Alex Partridge, who but for a rib injury would have been in the four at Athens, was racing, as was Matt Langridge, who I'd have rowed with if I'd carried on. Kath Grainger was on her mission to trade in her three silvers for a gold and Greg Searle, who I'd won the under-18 World Championships with twenty-two years earlier, had come out of retirement.

I was glad I was there, along with tens of thousands of others, to witness so many moments that will go down in rowing history, but for me, the Olympics was a time of light and shade.

It was fine in the commentary box, working with Alan

Green, with that accented voice that everyone recognises from his football commentary. It's brilliant that the voice of the nation's number one sport chooses to work on rowing at the Games. It was great work, if you can even call it that. All I had to do was keep passing him the tissues as the guys and girls did the business on the water and Alan got emotional.

It was fantastic that the women's pair won the first gold medal of Team GB's haul. It gave our sport great profile; leading the giant swag bag the Brits lifted from the Games. And there was also something very satisfying about army captain Heather Stanning (who was bound for Afghanistan) and new girl Helen Glover (who hadn't even been in a boat four years earlier and got into rowing through the Sporting Giants Talent ID scheme) not only blowing away the field but the common misconception about all rowers being born with a silver spoon in their mouth and a place at public school.

I think you can hear my triumphant 'Ha-haaaah!' in the background of Greeny's commentary, followed by what Chris Evans says is his favourite piece of commentary at the Games. In response to the media starting to get twitchy about a lack of gold medals for Team GB, as Heather and Helen crossed the line, I may have said: 'Don't panic, here come the rowers!'

With 750 metres to go it looked like the men's eight, with Alex Partridge on board, were going to get a courageous gold against a German crew that had been unbeaten for three years. A gold that I believe Alex above anyone deserved because he went into this race prepared to risk silver to win gold. I said on commentary that if they wanted to win they were going to have to sacrifice themselves and force the Germans to ask questions they hadn't yet faced. And in all honesty, the Olympic final is not a place where people often come up with a brilliant answer. I started to shout: 'He's done it!', meaning Alex, and I was so pleased for him until the Germans cranked it up, the Canadians came through and we had to settle for bronze.

At least our guys had given everything. There were no 'if only's surrounding the men's eight's performance. They went for it and didn't settle for silver. That won't have been any consolation during the second week of the Olympics but in time they'll know they couldn't have done any more. I was gutted for them but didn't cry, especially as there were only so many tissues lying around and Alan Green had all of them.

I did find it hard three days later when the men's four raced. The boat I won my medals in. It wasn't that I wished I was still racing or in any way begrudged them a fantastic win. They raced incredibly well in both the semi and final under enormous pressure, both historical and because they'd only been formed during the Olympic season due to the dominance of the New Zealand pair, so had to hit the ground running.

The reason I struggled was more subtle than any feeling of jealousy or regret. An Olympic athlete, whether active or retired, lives their life in four-year chunks so each Games acts as a watershed. More than ever it was a realisation that I've got to move on in my life and I am no longer able to have the future I'd imagined when I won in Athens that lifetime ago. I had celebrated with a shiny new gold medal and accompanying 24-carat self-belief that I could do anything I wanted in or out of sport. But sadly that is no longer the case after Arizona.

I was on BBC's *Newsnight* again, but found it a real challenge to get my point across clearly and concisely. I found myself answering the questions better in the taxi heading home. However, I am not going to hide away from testing myself in that environment and I'll do everything I can to get as much of my 'high-level executive cognitive function' back. I'm even starting to remember the phrase.

It was great to receive positive feedback and people seemed to appreciate my analogies. But there were moments when the ones that popped into my mind were hardly appropriate. A Cuban Greco-Roman wrestler in the over-120kg event looked like a blown-up version of the late-1980s Mike Tyson: athletic, muscular, ridiculously strong and vast. I was trying to explain the all-fours grappling position they assume halfway through the three-minute round without mentioning either 'doggie-style' or 'taking it up the ass'. Hard on radio when that's what it looks like and there are no images allowing you to duck the issue. The presenter said he could see the words in my eyes and was inexpressibly grateful that they did not come out of my mouth as well: a rarity in my unfiltered world.

But I did struggle when forced to describe two unathletic Middle Eastern gentlemen (again in the over-120kg category), in the end resorting to the commentator's cliché book by describing the contest as a 'fierce local derby' before I looked to see where they came from. In hindsight my comment might have been on the insensitive side as they were from Iran and Iraq. At least I didn't mention their hairy shoulders!

Off-piste events included entertaining Prince Harry at the Olympic stadium in my role as a British Olympic Association (BOA) ambassador. I pointed out to the BOA that the entertaining was going to be up to Usain Bolt in the 200 metres. Personally my highlight was travelling to the stadium. I discovered that the best thing about being a member of the royal family is that you never have to walk anywhere, open a door or call a lift everything just flows, as does the traffic, which admittedly is always likely to happen if guys on motorbikes are stopping other traffic and you're allowed to drive the wrong way down the road. Harry was great company and very easy-going.

I thought the Olympics were brilliant. The exploits of Bradley Wiggins following up his victory in the Tour de France, the Brownlee brothers and Anthony Joshua stand out among all the great stories of the Games. I was interviewing Alistair Brownlee while his brother, Jonny, was throwing up. 'Oh, he'll be all right, it's a tough sport,' said Alistair, as only a brother can.

I stayed away from home due to logistics and early call times, so I only saw Bev and the kids for a few hours here and there. I remember thinking that this must be what it's like for people who are divorced. A few hours with the children and then back to a room on your own. Perhaps that and a fair bit of time on my own to reflect contributed to my feeling a bit down as the Olympics wore on.

Summer 2012 feels like a watershed. The medal winners in London will look back on the Olympics as a sporting event that was the time of their lives. I want to look back and think they also marked a turning point for me. I hope I make the right decisions. I hope I make my family happy. I hope I keep improving. Since stubbornness remains one of my character traits, I'll channel that properly and accept that I'm not and never will be the same James Cracknell of two years ago. But I'm doing everything I can to ensure that there's a better version coming.

Further Reading

[Bev]

While writing this book, I decided to track down Cathy Crimmins, the author who wrote *Where is the Mango Princess?*, and tell her how much her writing inspired me as a fellow 'TBI wife'. I was gutted that the first mention I found online was her obituary. After battling for years to get the best possible care for her husband, they had sadly (perhaps, inevitably) divorced. Her daughter Kelly has grown up and is now a college student. Tragically, Cathy, who was fifty-four, broke her ankle and contracted an infection during surgery to re-set it. Kelly lost her mother after (almost) losing her father. I hope *Where is the Mango Princess?* now sells thousands of copies so that Kelly continues to benefit from her mother's hard work. Close this book and go buy it.

Acknowledgements

[James]

To the paramedics and the chopper pilots who flew me to Phoenix, I'm gonna track you all down and take you out for a pint.

Croyde – more than anyone you've suffered with me being different since the accident. I'll keep trying to make sure the shouty man is replaced by the man that tells funny jokes and dances like John Travolta.

Kiki, for being the most brilliant, happy little girl, not judging me and giving me a reason to smile for so much of the last two years. Just don't get a boyfriend!

Trixie, for being the miracle child. Catching you in the birthing pool was the most amazing moment of my life.

Mum and Dad for all my life never failing to be there and asking the tough questions. Over the last two years thank you for asking them of other people on my behalf.

I guess it's true: 'Small kids, small problems. Big kids, big problems.'

Joyce, for not only managing to have the energy of a Tasmanian devil but as many limbs as an octopus. I don't know how you manage to support all of us so unconditionally.

Roger, I'll forgive you for supporting Man Utd. If their players had the same loyalty, commitment and compassion as you and your kids, the rest of the Premier League would really be in trouble.

Louise Cracknell (sorry, can't write Furniss) and Jon Furniss (OK, I can write that). Lou for having my back when I've needed it all my life and especially in the last two years. And Jon for coping with the phenomenon that is my sis. The Aussies don't know what's heading their way! Will miss Jossie and Reuben. And thanks to Eva for teaching us all about what's important in life.

Adi & Abi, Cal & Rick. For not only being the most amazing family to marry into but also the best friends as well. Your attention may be off with Lana and Taylor now, but they're only new, and babies are surprisingly resilient . . . don't think we've let you off the hook yet!

Mark Perkins for being amazing in the States before and after the accident. Bev would have gone mad without you there, Croyde would have torn the place down and who else would have let me drag them round the hospital for twenty hours a day. (Mind you, still not sure we made the right choice in trusting you to be Trixie's moral guardian!)

Fred Wadsworth, at least Trixie's going to know which one of her moral guardians will be guaranteed to ask her a tough question. My personal favourite: 'Is that an excuse or a reason?' Still working on the answer to that. Thanks buddy.

Bernie S, for having my back.

For my mates for being there despite dropping in and out of your lives. I blame too much time mucking around in boats! I can't list you all here plus I know that you lot will never read the acknowledgements anyway. Especially Luka, Nick Moody, Russ, Daws, Dunny – hang on, you lot have only ended up getting me into trouble . . .

Shep for putting in the hours (even after school) teaching and coaching the most talented, hard-working, intelligent, funny and humble pupil you've ever had . . .

I'm so grateful that the Berlin Wall collapsed; releasing the most honourable, challenging, fair, single-minded and fun man anyone could want as a friend and coach. Thanks Jurgen Grobler.

Steve Redgrave, Matt Pinsent and Tim Foster. Thanks for being the other three blokes in that boat at Sydney. Without you I couldn't have . . . hang on, I ain't writing that. You fellas know the truth. As do you, Ed Coode and Steve Williams from four years later in Athens.

Thanks to everyone I ever shared a boat with. I learned from each of you. Bobby Thatcher, sorry for not making the start line in Atlanta 1996 – we'll never know. Alex Partridge – gutted we couldn't race together in 2004. Nick Clarry, thanks for making me challenge myself and not be content with being a big fish in a small pond.

Headway, especially Peter McCabe, for supporting me and my family and the chance to meet and learn from other people with a brain injury. I hope your decision to make me VP will work out for you!

All at the *Daily Telegraph*, especially Murdoch MacLennan, Mark Skipworth and Keith Perry. It's been an honour to work with you and the paper. Here's to another fifteen years. (Do you give contracts for that long now?)

Thanks to all the companies, inspiring people and great relationships I've built over the years, including: Karrimor, BMW, QinetiQ, MITIE, Rio Tinto, Red Bull, Merida, Nokia, Lucozade Sport, SIS, Camelot, EDF Energy, Adidas, Oakley, Samuel Windsor.

And to Alpina helmets for literally saving my life.

[Bev]
We'll probably never know the men who scraped James off the Arizona tarmac in Winslow and put him in a helicopter, but thank you for his life. Similarly, to the doctors and rehab team at the Banner Good Samaritan Hospital in the US – especially Dr R. Odgers, Jennifer Sanchez, Nathan Elwell and Jaclyn Knoll. We

remember James's 'sitters' Denise and Charles with great affection – 'Good job y'all.' Thanks also to his medical team in the UK. OT Lara Hartley and Speech & Language Portia Lloyd – you made a huge difference. God bless Heart of Hounslow and the NHS.

Thank you John and Jennie for being strong and supportive, but also sharing a few dark laughs throughout this whole ordeal (did we make the right decision about the Paralympics John?!).

Mum & Dad – any strengths I have, I learnt from you. (We can put my faults down to dodgy ancient genes.) If ever in doubt, I think, 'What would Mum or Dad do?' The answer is always there – no greater gift to give your children. I love you to the moon and back.

Cal & Rick, Adi & Abi – my best friends who just happen to be my siblings and their partners. 'Thank you' doesn't cover it. I have a lifetime to pay you back. Quite simply I would have crumpled without you.

Louise Furniss and Jon (Jossie & Reuben too!) – thanks for all your support. Hope Oz is awesome. We are going to miss you all so much.

Mark Perkins & Fred Wadsworth – thanks for your time and persistence with James. Baby mentors extraordinaire.

The Barnes singers – Chrissie Marty, Lorna and Cam Blackwood, Rachel Welch, Lara Giusti, Marie, Josephine and Nicola. Ninety minutes of laughter per week. The best medicine. You saved my soul.

The Moodys – Lisa, Nick & Jasmin. For rescuing me and the kids when I was sobbing in my dressing gown. True friends.

Ben & Marina Fogle – thanks for good food, good fun and always being there.

Louisa Joyner, Vanessa Jeffery, Russ & Danni Kingdon Dawkins, Ruth & Tim Wood, Chiara Evetts, Olivia Hunt, Sue Heyes, Richard Lee, Emma, Kirsty and apologies to the countless other friends who I have missed but who keep me smiling.

Thanks to the *Daily Telegraph* for all your continued support, especially Fiona Hardcastle and Maureen O'Donnell.

[Both]
Thanks to Sue Mott for being the journalist who always got more out of James than he wanted to give. This book benefits from your annoying persistence, experience and talent.

David Harrison – ridiculously good film maker & friend. (The only man about whom Bev can say, 'I am happy to put James's life in your hands.')

Monika – Bev's surrogate husband; marriage-saver; sanity-preserving nanny. So sorry you have to live amongst this 'crazy family' and share our difficult journey. Thanks for keeping the ship afloat with organisation and love. If it wasn't for you . . .

Pam Wild – thank you for catching our babies (but letting James catch Trixie) & always being there. Our Fairy Godmother.

Emma Wade – we will never forget your selfless, unconditional support, advice & hard graft. You are truly one in a million.

Sadie Stoneham – thank you for stepping into Emma's shoes. Whether it's organising, liaising or hanging out James's washing (!) you continue to fill them beautifully.

To everyone at James Grant – especially Nicola Ibison – for just 'getting it' and then sticking with us. Without your vision, faith and backing, so much of the recent 'good stuff' (including this book) just wouldn't have happened.

Lou Plank – the coolest, calmest PR woman in London. You and Sally Kent somehow take all the pressure out of the press.

Thanks to Luigi Bonomi for moving fast and efficiently. Your guidance and expert advice is immensely appreciated.

All at Random House, especially Ben Dunn, for giving Bev and me the opportunity to write the book in this way and being constantly available to reassure, cajole and make us laugh. Francesca Pathak for against-the-clock editing; Natalie Higgins for buying into our vision and making it work. All the sales team – without your vital work, it would still be sat in a warehouse. James would like to say, 'I know I've been a pain in the ass but you should try living with me!'

Picture Acknowledgements

©Cracknell Family Collection ©Ben Fogle ©Turner Family Collection © John Cracknell ©Getty Images ©Shaun Botterill/ Getty Images ©Mike Hewitt/ Getty Images ©Robert Laberge/ Getty Images ©Clive Brunskill/ Getty Images ©Jon Furniss/ Getty Images ©Stuart Dunn ©Mark Gillett ©Richard Wearne ©BoBridges.com ©Ed Coats

The author and publisher have made all reasonable efforts to contact copyright holders for permission and apologise for any omissions or errors in the form of credits given. Corrections may be made to future printings.

Index

(the initials BT refer to Beverley Turner; JC to James Cracknell)

and occupational therapy 34–5, 63,
191, 201, 202, 223–4, 261, 264,
268, 279
'old dad' fear of 102
and parents' Triumph Herald 7
penknife collection of 15
physical attributes of 22
Pinsent stamps on 43
PM writes to 229–30
poses naked for charity 95
and positive parenting 6, 11
post-accident 29, 34–5, 62–3, 129–
31, 173–203, 227–54, 259–69,
274–86, 294–6, 297–301
and press 76, 117, 202, 215, 221,
243, 290
Princess Anne lunches with 54
rebellious nature of 24–6, 36–8
Redgrave trains 40
Richmond Park training sessions of
152
rows English Channel 168
school detentions given to 23
schooling of 4, 7–8, 15, 16, 64
shy nature of 10–11
sister bullied by 13–15, 16, 27
snacking technique of 150
South Pole Race (2008–9) of 29
sports science MSC studied by 56
stag do of 78–9
Sun-In love affair of 24–5
Sydney Olympic gold won by 5, 8
and tandem-cycling record 265–8
taste and smell senses lost by 261–
2
tattoo acquired by 25
teeth incident of 57–8
third child of 2
32nd birthday of 118
tonsillitis suffered by 52, 55
'trouble-maker' branding of 44–5
truth-telling obsession of 30
TV appearances of 130–1, 161, 164,
168, 182, 188–9, 216, 222, 230,
238, 239, 255, 257, 259, 273–4,
279–80, 286, 291–2, 295–6, 299

TV/radio appearances of 67, 71,
118–19
at university 32, 45
weight loss of 143–7
at World Junior Rowing
Championships 26
and world politics 72
'Yorkie effect' of 86
'zero' IQ of 11
Cracknell, Jennie (JC's mother) 54,
59, 76, 77, 79–80, 125, 303, 307
character traits of 3–4, 5–6, 23–4,
30–1
as childsitter 119, 139
at Christmas 144
competitive streak of 24
JC inspired by 7–8
and JC's 'developmental' check 10–
11
and JC's first day at primary school
7
and JC's 'legendary' Victoria
sponges 235
and JC's TV appearances 73
John meets 5
as 'the law' 25–6
leopard-print clothing of 10
physiotherapy training of 3, 8
post-accident 178–82, 185, 189,
200, 236, 274–6, 278
Trivial Pursuit prowess of 23
Cracknell, John (JC's father) 19, 21,
23, 59, 242, 303, 307
cars owned by 7, 9, 13
character traits of 4
at Christmas 225, 245
cigar-smoking of 9
early life of 5–6
and JC's 'developmental' check 11
and JC's educational/career choices
30–1, 133
and JC's oak-tree incident 13
Jennie meets 5
post-accident 29, 178, 178–81, 185,
189, 197, 209, 231, 234, 236, 245,
275

Headway

the brain injury association

Headway – the brain injury association is the UK-wide charity that works to improve life after brain injury.

Through its network of more than 100 groups and branches across the UK, it provides support, services and information to brain injury survivors, their families and carers, as well as to professionals in the health and legal fields.

The charity has supported James and Beverley since James's accident in July 2010. Since then, the couple have worked tirelessly to help raise the profile of the charity and increase awareness of the devastating effects of brain injury.

In April 2012, James was appointed Vice President of Headway in recognition of his outstanding contribution to the charity and his determination to continue to help others affected by brain injury.

The support available from Headway to people affected by brain injury includes:

- a freephone helpline (0808 800 2244, helpline@headway.org.uk);

- a comprehensive website containing information and factsheets on all aspects of brain injury (www.headway.org.uk);

- an award-winning range of booklets and publications designed to help people understand and cope with the effects of brain injury;

- an emergency fund to assist people dealing with the financial implications of brain injury immediately post-injury;

- Headway Acute Trauma Support (HATS) nurses to support families whose loved ones are in the acute stage of care following brain injury;

- a network of more than 100 groups and branches that provide physical, cognitive and social rehabilitation and support to individuals and families.

For more information about brain injury or to find out how Headway can help, visit www.headway.org.uk or call the helpline on 0808 800 2244.

KARRIMOR & CRACKNELL
BUILT DIFFERENT

The Alpiniste three-layer jacket from Karrimor is built using eVent technology.
eVent is the only waterproof fabric that lets the sweat out.

It breathes better so it keeps you dry, inside and out, even in extreme weather. Genius.
Add that to intelligent, ergonomic design for further protection and specialist features
like a height adjustable hood to accommodate a helmet. It's not just built different. It's

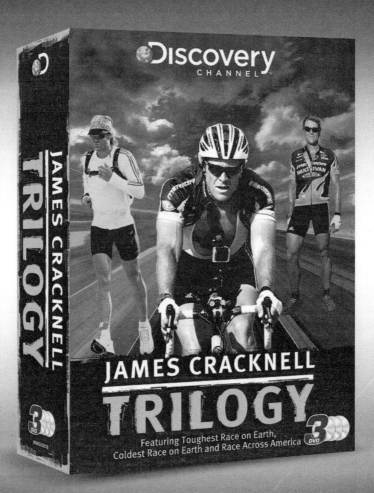